The Working Drummer

Compiled And Updated From The Best Of Modern Drummer Magazine's *Club Scene*

Written and Edited by Rick Van Horn

Design and Layout
Javier Jimenez

Published by:
Modern Drummer Publications, Inc.
12 Old Bridge Road
Cedar Grove, New Jersey 07009 U.S.A.

Contents

Acknowledgements

First and foremost, I want to thank *Modern Drummer*'s editor and publisher, Ron Spagnardi, for seeing some potential in an unknown drummer/writer over seventeen years ago. Were it not for his ongoing faith and support, there would never have been a *Club Scene* column in *Modern Drummer* magazine, and there certainly would never have been this book.

I also want to acknowledge the dedicated efforts of the current *MD* editorial and art departments, who were faced with the daunting task of helping me wade through twelve years worth of material—and then putting it into a contemporary, reader-friendly format. Thanks, folks!

And finally, I wish to extend my thanks to all of the *MD* readers, past and present, who have called or written to me to say that they found my columns informative, entertaining, or in some other way valuable. The encouragement I received from those readers was the inspiration for this book, and it is my earnest hope that the work will in some way return that favor.

Dedication

To my mother, Lucille Pauley, who—because "nice young ladies" growing up in Iowa were not permitted to play drums—was thrilled when her four-year-old started banging on pots and pans...

To my father, D. W. Van Horn, from whom I inherited my gift of expression...

To my wife, Crystal, who's always known that she comes before my drumming (but just barely)...

To my daughter, Jennifer Robin, who danced to drum solos before she was born...

And to my son, Colin, who is my staunchest fan and my favorite roadie.

Foreword

A New Club Scene

To some drummers, performing in anything smaller than an arena is "playing clubs."

As managing editor of *Modern Drummer*, I have a number of duties, including writing equipment features and product reviews, editing the work of other *MD* writers, coordinating *MD's* Festival Weekends, and a slew of other chores that keep me pretty occupied. As a result, a while ago I had to give up the thing that got me connected to *MD* in the first place: my monthly *Club Scene* column. But the spirit recently moved me to dust off the ol' word processor and get back in the literary saddle again.

There are a couple of reasons why I decided to compile and update my *Club Scene* material into a book at this point in time. To begin with, the first column I wrote ran in the April 1980 issue of *MD*. That's over sixteen years ago! Youngsters who were barely able to *read* then are entering the professional drumming market now. And though I continued with my column for the next twelve years (the final installment appeared in July of 1992), many of the subjects I covered have come up again in the form of inquiries sent to *MD's It's Questionable* department and phone calls that I get almost every day. It's obvious that a whole new generation of drummers are ready to start their playing careers, and they might be able to benefit from the type of information I offered in *Club Scene*.

The other reason for a new beginning is that the "club scene" itself has undergone some dramatic changes over the past few years. When I began my column, I was writing about a job market that was pretty much comprised of Top-40 bands playing steady, long-term gigs in nightclubs and lounges. Some traveled, while others were local, but the essential format of their performances was the same.

Recently, however, a different type of club scene has become more prevalent in many areas. While Top-40 groups and lounge acts still exist, they are declining in number, due to a similar decline in the number of places that employ such bands. Instead, the "rock club" has gained in popularity. These can be anything from hole-in-the-wall, storefront-sized rooms where local hopefuls can play their first gigs, to dance clubs or theaters of significant size where B-level recording groups can gain some experience and notoriety prior to jumping on the coattails of a more prestigious band as an "opening act." In fact, to some of the drummers interviewed in *MD*, performing in anything smaller than an arena is "playing clubs."

One of the most significant differences between Top-40 clubs and rock clubs comes in the area of engagement length. While Top-40 clubs tend to keep their groups for long-term engagements, many of the rock clubs book groups for one, or possibly two nights only, and often present several groups per night. Some are designated as "showcase clubs," but most are simply trying to offer the largest possible number of bands to their clientele. This difference in engagement length presents a different set of challenges and advantages.

The challenge of playing a Top-40 club is to be able to play in one place for *several weeks* at a time, keeping the act fresh and exciting by staying abreast of all popular styles and updating the material often. The advantage of such a gig is that the band has the opportunity to establish a personality of its own in the club, attract "regulars," and generally build a reputation in the area.

A group that only plays one-nighters has the advantage of not needing to worry so much about keeping the act up-to-date. In fact, they can keep the same act for months, as long as they change venues every night! On the other hand, it's extremely challenging to make any sort of lasting impact on an audience when they only get to see and hear the band once.

Many of today's rock clubs tout the fact that they hire only "originals" bands—which means that the groups are performing their own material, as opposed to covering the popular tunes on the radio. The challenge here is to be *truly* original, but still marketable. It's a somewhat sad fact of the music business that while people *claim* to value originality, most actually seek familiarity. As a result, many "original" groups tend to be carbon-copies of a very limited number of "big name" acts (and hence carbon-copies of each other). This "cloning" could be an advantage *or* a disadvantage, depending on the musical tastes of the people who frequent a given club.

On the other hand, performing other people's tunes with professionalism and style—retaining their original character yet offering something individual as well—is a challenge that requires talent and hard work. I've often wondered why so many people—including musicians who should know better—tend to look down on Top-40 bands who cover other people's tunes, but thrill to hear Bruce Springsteen or U2 doing it.

Before it sounds as if I'm saying that *my* kind of club scene is better than *your* kind of club scene, let me say that my point is simply that many of the challenges faced by today's club players are different than those I was faced with when I played full-time. (For example, although I did some traveling and I certainly had to move from club to club, I was never faced with the rigors of one-nighters for months on end.) But many remain the same. (For instance: The need to perform in a fresh, exciting, and entertaining manner remains paramount under any and all circumstances.)

And before you wonder what this old fogey is doing preaching to those who are really *out there* in the trenches, I'd like to let you know that I'm out there, too. In fact, I'm drumming regularly in a "club scene" that falls somewhere between the full-time Top-40 gigs I used to play for a living and what many of you are doing now. I'm playing local clubs, generally for two-night stands (Fridays and Saturdays). It's a cover band, but we play everything with an original slant; we don't take a "purist" approach to our material. Our primary object is to have fun ourselves while entertaining our audience.

Since joining this band, I've learned a lot about what works and doesn't work for today's club audience. I've also picked up some new playing, loading, traveling, and other logistical experience. Most importantly, I've been able to look back at some of the information I put forth in twelve years of *Club Scene* columns, to see what still applies and what has been superseded by new technology or techniques. With all that in mind, I hope this book will offer something of value to all the new "club drummers" out there—and perhaps to you veterans, as well.

Introduction

The Art Of Entertainment

At times a club band is faced with an audience coldly staring, as if to challenge: "Okay, here I am, now entertain me!"

The columns and interviews presented in *Modern Drummer* magazine generally feature tips by drummers performing in specialty areas: rock, studio, jazz, etc. But a large number of professional drummers are not fortunate enough to perform music of their own personal preference. Instead they make a living playing in the most grueling and demanding of all musical occupations, the club scene. No studio musician, no recording artist, not even a drummer on the toughest concert tour is expected to play high-quality music in a multitude of styles for five hours a night, five or six nights a week.

Let's start by defining terms. When I talk about the "club scene," I'm talking about the typical local venue (hotel lounge, neighborhood pub, etc.) that features live music (and often dancing) as an attraction to drinking customers. The band's job in this situation is to fill the room with people, keep them entertained, and most important, keep them buying drinks. A manager will judge a band's success by the bar total at the end of each night.

In the club, the band does not have the psychological advantage that a show group or concert act enjoys. Generally people have not paid admission to see them. They have not listened to their music at home on records. They are not predisposed to enjoy the show. In fact, quite often the opposite is true. At times a club band is faced with an audience coldly staring, as if to challenge: "Okay, here I am, now entertain me!" Often the clientele is largely local—"regulars" who get to know a band's material almost as well as they do. The fact that a band may be booked in one club for several weeks adds to the difficulty of sustaining audience interest. And no other type of musical act, be it recording, concert, or show, is faced with the responsibility of holding an audience that has only to walk to the next club down the street if they are dissatisfied with the music.

Even on busy nights, with a lively crowd, it's likely that most of that crowd came to dance, not to watch or listen to the band. It's a sad side-effect of today's "dance clubs" (read: discos) that audiences have been conditioned against responding to the music with applause. Live bands are often treated as nothing more than human jukeboxes.

Musically, the demands made on club drummers are extensive. They must play well in all popular styles. They must be solid and steady in order to give support to the dancers. They must be delicate with a ballad, and dynamic with a hard-rock tune. They must be ready to field requests from a wide variety of areas. (You may get a polka-crazy party one night.) More often than not, club bands are small, and the drummer is required to add to the vocals. This can be a major problem in itself, since many drummers find it difficult to keep steady time while concentrating on song lyrics and melodies.

The club group has to remember that they are asking people to stay and watch them for several hours. They must therefore be visually interesting, or showy, and the drummer must do his or her part.

With all these things in mind, the club drummer's responsibilities include the following:

1. Be totally versatile. You must be competent in all musical styles, from disco to C&W, hard rock to tasty ballads. You never know what the next request will be.

2. Be professional. This means being able to play the same repertoire night after night and make it fresh and exciting each time, for yourself as well as the audience.

3. Be dedicated. You've got to be able to survive slow nights and apathetic audiences and still want to come back and play the next night.

4. Be entertaining. You have to make your audience want to stay, watch, and listen. They haven't invested more than the price of a drink in you, and unless you catch their interest, they'll go bar-hopping down the street.

In the following chapters, I'll focus on these and other special problems faced by the club drummer, and give some suggestions and ideas that I've found helpful in over twenty-five years in the club scene.

Part 1: Playing The Gig

The Drummer As Entertainer

Always look as if you enjoy what you're doing. There are nights when you don't, but the audience must never know it.

One of the most difficult problems facing the club band is to keep an audience entertained over several hours, thus keeping them in the club. Drummers need to do their part to add to the performance of their group visually as well as musically.

Let's start with the assumption that your playing is good. You fit all of the musical requirements of your group, and the audience enjoys listening to you. What more can you do to increase your entertainment potential so they'll enjoy watching you as well? Here are some suggestions:

1. Be visible! The drums carry a built-in fascination for most people in the audience. Almost everyone has had contact with a keyboard at some point in their lives, and in recent years a large percentage of the population has plucked a guitar. But the average audience member has never come into close personal contact with a set of drums. The drums seem to be the most visually complicated. Look at all that crazy hardware! Disks of metal flying above colorful, multi-sized cylinders! Pedals, stands, booms—a forest of chrome! What an eye-catcher!

So what happens to all this visual excitement? Nine times out of ten the drumset gets buried in the back corner of the stage, often partially obscured by amplifiers and nearly always behind the members of the band standing out front.

I'm the first one to admit that club stages are small. But the drummer is a member of the band, and it's to the band's advantage that he or she be seen by the audience. You should try to compromise with the other members of your band on how much space you can use. If it is necessary to be in the rear of the stage, get your drumset up on a riser. After all, since you are seated, you're only half as tall as the standing members anyway. The best method is to set up your kit, figure how much floor space you need in square feet, and build a riser that size. The height of the riser should be determined by the types of places you play most often. Many stages are low-ceilinged alcoves, so you can't make it *too* high. Twelve to eighteen inches is a standard height.

If you play long-term engagements in one place, you can often get the management to supply or at least finance the construction of the riser. In that case, of course, it becomes house equipment. If you wish to carry your own riser with you, you must build it yourself. There are commercially manufactured risers available, but they tend to be expensive and not tailored to your specific needs.

2. Catch the light/catch their eyes. The drumset—whether a small jazz kit or a monster rock assembly—is covered with reflective surfaces. The chrome lugs, the shiny surfaces of the shells, the hardware, and the cymbals all catch the stage lights and sparkle back at the audience. With this in mind it becomes important that the set is not buried in the shadows of equipment, other band members, or ceiling overhangs. Most clubs have some sort of stage lighting, if only a few colored floodlights. Be sure that some of that light catches your set. And if you have a say in the color of that light, make sure it is a flattering color—something that enhances your set's appearance. If you are able to be in a spotlight for feature numbers, so much the better.

If you are familiar with the lighting provided by your club, perhaps you can add a light or two of your own to their system. An effective and inexpensive floodlight can be made from a porcelain socket base screwed to the bottom of a coffee can painted black, and holding a 75- or 150-watt floodlamp. These come in a few colors, or you can use white lamps and place plastic color media (gels) in front of them.

3. Keep it clean. The best lighting system in the world won't flatter your set if it's dusty or dingy looking. The atmosphere of a club is full of smoke, sweat, grease, and other elements that combine to coat a drumset with a film that catches and holds dust. Long weeks of playing will coat cymbals with this film, and hold dirty stick marks. A dull surface does not reflect light well. Dust your set each night before you start the performance. It just takes a second, and the benefits are enormous. You should thoroughly clean the shells and hardware before each new set-up.

Cymbals are another story. I know many drummers do not like to clean their cymbals, because they feel it removes the mellow quality they favor. I won't argue the issue from a musical standpoint. If you feel that the dirt in the grooves of the cymbals gives you that quality, then by all means don't ruin your sound. But be aware that your cymbals are the only reflective surface on your kit that also *move*. They can flash and sparkle under the lights with each crash, so dust them each night, at least. And if you *can* be happy with the sound of a clean, shiny cymbal, you're way ahead in the visual department.

4. Be a showman. I would like to say here and now that there is nothing negative about the word "flashy." You are in the entertainment business, and anything you can do to make your playing more entertaining is to your advantage. While stick twirls won't make anybody a better drummer, they will make you a better showman. Carmine Appice has a modified grip that allows him to twirl his sticks like a dervish. Lionel Hampton used to bounce his sticks off his drums and catch them in mid-air, never missing a beat. These effects are visual dynamite, and if you can learn to twirl your sticks you've got a great eye-catcher going for you.

Even if you're not a stick juggler, you can develop your showmanship, and if you play with physical dynamics you can make the audience *want* to watch you. By "physical dynamics" I mean: Play with enthusiasm; play sharply on your cymbals, with a flourish. And even if it is, don't make it *look* too easy. A fellow drummer might appreciate "effortless" playing, but the average audience member is impressed by the intensity with which the drummer is performing. And I don't mean volume. You can play a ballad with brushes and still look sharp about it.

Always look as if you enjoy what you're doing. There are nights when you don't, but the audience must never know it.

Practice in front of a mirror, ask your friends what you look like while playing, or—better yet—get a friend to videotape you on a gig. It's important for you to be aware of the look on your face, your physical attitude, etc., because if you don't appear to enjoy your playing, nobody in the audience will. On the other hand, if you really do enjoy playing, that joy is transmitted to your audience.

Over twenty years ago I saw John Barbata when he was playing with the Turtles. Aside from his fine musical ability, he impressed me as the *happiest* drummer I had ever seen. He took a positive delight in what he was doing, adding flourishes and twirls, and he was thoroughly entertaining. The late Keith Moon also had this quality.

Enthusiasm radiates to your audience. It can also inspire the other members of your group. Showmanship is the key word in the club scene. Without it, you're behind before you start. With it, you're miles ahead of the game.

Analyzing Style

> **The trick is to *play with understanding* as well as with technique.**

Question: What do Kenny Aronoff, Chad Smith, Carter Beauford, Vinnie Colaiuta, Jim Sonefeld, Eddie Bayers, Dennis Chambers, and Charlie Watts all have in common?
Answer: You. . . if you're playing in a Top-40 club band. And if you take your job seriously, you can face a tremendous amount of frustration trying to meet the musical standards set by those gentlemen, and the dozens of others whose work you are expected to present to your audience. After all, you might be an exceptional player in your own right, but you're faced with an impossible situation. Carter wouldn't be expected to sit in with the Stones and lay it down like Charlie, Jim might feel uncomfortable playing Vinnie's intricate syncopations, and I doubt that Eddie and Chad would enjoy changing places. But night after night, your group is performing music by each of these great players. How do you handle it?

Let's examine the problem. You are paid to do a job, which is to play competently and entertainingly in a variety of popular styles. Besides the Top-40 music featuring the drummers I've mentioned, you might pull a couple of country tunes out of the bag, and maybe some dance-club style R&B. Throw your own personal musical tastes and influences into this melting pot, along with the original licks you cherish, and it's hard to figure out what to play, what not to play, and how to go about deciding who you are as a musician.

As I've talked with players in other club bands about this situation, I've come across two recurring approaches to solving the problem:

1. The total duplication approach. This calls for a virtually transcripted version of each part of each individual song. I don't like this approach, for two reasons: First, you can't honestly hope to achieve total duplication, since you're not the original artist, nor are you performing under the same conditions as the recording. Even the recording artists themselves don't duplicate their original parts note for note when performing live.

Second, when you try to re-create someone else's work, you're not doing any creating yourself, and music is a creative art (even in a Top-40 format). If all you do is try to play other people's parts, then you're using other people's imaginations, and denying your own. You are using skills you've probably worked hard to develop, but using them only to copy, not to originate. Picasso didn't spend his life making "paint-by-numbers" pictures. Why should you perform "play-by-numbers" musical parts?

2. The "To-Hell-with-the-original, we're-going-to-do-it-our-way!" approach. I don't wholly subscribe to this theory either. We have to realize that club bands are hired to play songs that are familiar to the audience due to repeated radio airplay. If you're going to play Top-40 (and this goes for popular country, R&B, or any other style), it's self-defeating to make the songs too different from the original versions. All you'll do is alienate your audience. You owe it to them to keep the tunes recognizable so they'll be comfortable with them, and thus with you. If you can't live without being totally "off the wall" with each tune, then restrict yourself to original material, or go into a show format where fresh arrangements are what make the show appealing.

I think there's a way to reconcile these two different approaches through what I call the character analysis of any given tune, or any particular drummer. Rather than transcribing the song note for note, concentrate on the unique character of the playing; how the music is structured and where the emphasis is placed. If you're studying with a teacher, work together on this. Listen to a song you wish to perform and compare your impressions of the song's key elements. A trained, objective ear can often hear qualities or nuances you might overlook. In some cases, it's easy to get a basic concept for a style of music, which can then be applied to several songs, even if they are by different artists. "Disco-esque" dance-music is a classic example. A very heavy, four-beat bass drum pattern, a solid backbeat on 2 and 4, and either a doubled 16th-note hi-hat pattern or an open/close pattern on the "&" of each beat, and you pretty much sum up the character of the standard dance beat. From there on, any variations or fills are up to the individual player. With contemporary rock, you might want to note how the hi-hat is often played half-open and ringy, usually with just straight quarter or 8th notes against a heavy backbeat. This heavy ride might carry over to the bell of a cymbal or a cowbell. Power fills tend to be triplets or 16th-note patterns across a wide range of toms.

These are, of course, oversimplifications. But if you approach a song or a style in this way, it gives you the means to establish a recognizable structure to keep the audience happy, while giving you that structure as a foundation upon which to build.

You can apply that same sort of analysis to the playing of individual drummers. What differentiated Steve Smith from other rock drummers when he played with Journey included the way he used his toms and ride cymbals to keep a steady rhythm while still creating varied melodic patterns. (Listen to "Don't Stop Believing" for an excellent example.) Carter Beauford's use of syncopation between bass drum and snare is a fundamental feature of his style. You don't have to duplicate his patterns, but you should be aware of *what those patterns are made up of,* so you can create your own in a tastefully similar (if not identical) manner. With Stewart Copeland's still-influential playing, a strong reggae feel is present in his basic grooves, but the liveliness of his fills reflects his jazz influences. His tuning and dynamic snare attack are also key elements that make his playing recognizable. You can incorporate such elements into your performance without sublimating your creativity. When it comes to Charlie Watts, the great key is his simplicity. If you can capture the way Charlie uses space to allow the rest of the music the room it needs, then you have the character of the Stones' playing.

The trick is to *play with understanding,* as well as with technique. And the most important things to remember are *when* and *how* to apply the analysis you've made. In music, as in any art form, it's true that contrast and shock value can work as a special effect. It *is* possible to put a Buddy Rich fill into a Bruce Springsteen tune for such an effect—but you wouldn't deem it appropriate to play like Buddy throughout the tune. If you're a fan of one particular style of music, or of one drummer's playing, you run the risk of over-incorporating that style into any and all music you perform. This is the most difficult piece of musical discipline to master, because you are working against your own enthusiasm, your own tastes, and your own personal enjoyment. But remember, you might otherwise be working against your source of income because you won't be a desirable commodity to your band if you can't sublimate your desire to shine personally in favor of your ability to support the entire band's performance. Be aware that if you're playing Carter Beauford funk beats in a Hootie & The Blowfish tune, the audience isn't going to care whether you've got them down perfectly. All they know is, it *doesn't* fit the tune, and it *doesn't* move them to dance.

Take comfort in the fact that you actually enjoy an advantage that most recording artists don't—you get to perform with variety. I've interviewed several major drummers who have expressed a certain boredom with the music they've been playing in concerts over the past few years. They aren't really allowed to stretch out, because their audiences expect to hear their hits over and over. You, at least, are playing the hits of many different groups, so you *do* get to stretch out. Take advantage of that, and work to achieve a thorough understanding of each style of playing, as well as the highest possible degree of creativity within each one. In this way, you can keep your audiences thrilled, keep your band happy with your work, and keep yourself sane and satisfied.

Soloing With A Purpose

> **People have an instinctive reaction to the sound of drum rhythms, and this reaction gives you a power possessed by no other instrumentalist.**

When contemplating a solo, club drummers are faced with a unique problem due to the nature of their audiences. They're not really in a concert situation, where people have paid to sit, watch, listen, and appreciate their playing. The music is more accurately a *part* of the total entertainment environment provided by the club, along with dancing, drinking, and general socializing. One would hope that the musical performance is the focus of attention, but in reality, a club band rarely monopolizes that focus. So the problem becomes how to incorporate a drum solo in the musical performance to entertain the listeners, keep the dancers moving, be musically supportive to the band's performance, and still enjoy the solo yourself, from the standpoint of your own musical integrity.

The solution to that problem is to approach the solo with a sense of *purpose*. That purpose must be based on many considerations, not all of which are up to you. For instance, the point in the evening where you do a solo will likely be up to the bandleader, so you and that person need to have a clear agreement on what the solo is intended to achieve. In one club where I worked, the first set was often what we called a "listeners" set. The room might have been relatively crowded, but most of that crowd were people waiting to be seated in the dining room, and often few approached the dance floor. In this case, we were in more of a concert format, and we'd use a drum solo at the end of the set as a "theater piece"—something both visually and musically entertaining. It also helped to build excitement and anticipation for the opening of the next set. This type of solo is what I call a *visual* or *show solo*, and I'll detail its form a little later.

On the other hand, when our audience was lively and active, we'd save the solo for later on in the evening—generally at the end of our third or fourth set. The solo served as a climax for the set, and the purpose was to put a "capper" on the excitement generated by the music up to that point. This is what I call a *dance-rhythmic solo*, and I'll expand on that one in just a bit too.

Once it's time to play your solo, the concept of *purpose* becomes even more important. Along with all the musical considerations that go into a good drum solo, there are also several psychological considerations you should be aware of. A drum solo, more than any other form of musical improvisation, has the *potential to motivate an audience.* People have an instinctive reaction to the sound of drum rhythms, and this reaction gives you a power possessed by no other instrumentalist. So it becomes extremely important that along with your musical direction, you have a definite plan in mind (your *purpose*) as to how you wish to affect your audience through your solo. Do you want to entertain them? Do you want to impress them? Do you want to move them physically? Do you want to liven them up? All these things and many more can be achieved if *you* are aware of your purpose.

The Visual/Show Solo

This type of solo is used when you can count on your audience to be *watching* you, rather than up on the floor dancing. In this solo you'll want to emphasize technique and employ as many visual effects as possible. If you can play cross-overs, here's the place to use them. Stick twirls during a solo are impressive, too. You are here to entertain, and *any* device that adds to your entertainment potential is a valid and desirable tool.

In a show solo you also have the opportunity to use a wide range of dynamics. You can drop the volume, switch to brushes or mallets, play on rims, use delicate cymbal work, and employ a whole variety of subtleties that would not work well in the dance/rhythmic solo. This is your chance to honestly show off—remaining, of course, within the limits of musicality.

There are some cautions that should be observed in a show solo. Because the audience is not dancing, they are not "locked in" to the rhythmic patterns you're playing. While this gives you the freedom to vary the solo, it also puts on you the responsibility of keeping the solo interesting, fresh, and directed. You *must not* get so involved in what you're playing that you lose contact with your audience. You must be aware of the level of their interest in what you're doing, so that you can gauge how long to play. *You're not up there to entertain yourself,* or to demonstrate every lick you've learned in the last fifteen years. Your *purpose* is to be musically and visually entertaining, and hopefully exciting. So keep in control of your playing, and keep a mental radar trained on your audience so that you can combine the two to bring the solo to a climax at the most effective point.

There are some purely mechanical things to remember when it comes to any type of solo. However, since they might be even more important in the context of a show solo, I'll mention them here.

1. Be visible. I've mentioned before the necessity for being seen clearly by your audience. There's no real point in doing a lot of visual things if your audience can't see them. If you're in the rear of the stage, you should be on a riser. If your fellow bandmembers normally stand in front of you while playing, ask them (courteously) to stand to one side during your solo. This should seem obvious, and yet I recently watched a lead vocalist enthusiastically clapping and cheering on a soloing drummer—while standing directly in front of the drumset looking back at him. Not only could we not see the drummer, but we were treated to the backside of the vocalist all through the solo! On the other hand, I've seen some situations where the rest of the band leaves the stage entirely. I like that idea, as long as they don't have to cross in front of you coming and going, and as long as there is a clearly understood cue to bring them back. I don't like to see a drummer obviously gasping for rescue. If lighting is available, and you know that you're going to be doing solos, you should arrange for a spotlight.

2. Avoid sounds that are physically aggravating. This is a hard concept for some drummers to accept. There are some purely physical/audio principles involved. You must remember that the earlier in the evening the solo is placed, the less time everyone's ears have had to accustom themselves to the volume level. It's a fact that most bands get louder as the evening progresses. And since the audience is a part of the gradual process, they can handle it. But if your solo is placed early in the evening, the ears of the audience are still fairly sensitive. I would caution against much cymbal crash work, except as brief punctuations. Machine-gun rim shots are also dangerous. You can rely more on technique and less on power in the earlier sets, so use that to your advantage.

3. Don't overplay. This is the cardinal rule expounded by every major drummer who has ever given advice about soloing. But I mean it here in a slightly different sense. What I mean is, in any solo—but especially in a show solo where (hopefully) all eyes are on you—you should be at your best. This is not the time to be experimenting, or reaching for that "not-quite-yet-perfect" pattern. There's nothing that will burst the bubble of excitement you've created as fast as a missed riff, or a dropped stick. Temper your musical ambition, and keep your *purpose* in mind. You are here to manipulate your audience, and you can't do that unless you have 100% capability to play everything you intend to play.

4. Select a good musical vehicle. It is important for you and your bandleader to select a tune with a tempo and feel in which you work well, and can be creative. For a visual/show solo, a fast, funky tune usually works best for me. Sometimes a jazz-waltz or Latin tune is good for show solos. The key is for you to be comfortable and fluid in whatever style is chosen. For the dance/rhythmic solo, obviously a good dance tempo is important, but the tune should have a good fundamental rhythmic base for you to work from.

Arrangement of the tune is also important. I feel it is most effective (and only fair) if the band returns only briefly to put a musical "finish" on the solo. The song should not extend another chorus, because that diminishes the *feature* status of the solo. After all, a drummer generally gets only one solo a night, versus several for the other instrumentalists. The band should give the drummer his or her due, and should not play on so that the audience has time to forget the solo before the tune is over.

The Dance/Rhythmic Solo

This is the solo played later in the evening, for the benefit of a crowd that's already dancing and into your music. The *purpose* of the solo is to capitalize on the excitement that has already been generated, and often to act as a finale to a particular set, or sometimes the entire evening. Your responsibility here is slightly different, and your approach should reflect that difference. You want to keep them moving and keep them with you. So you should concentrate on rhythmic patterns that they can easily lock into, and not go for a wide variety of technique-oriented riffs. The absolute rule is: *Stay in tempo!* This is *not* the time for a free-form solo. And I suggest that your dynamic range be more limited. Remember, you're at the end of a set. Their ears are accustomed to a fairly high volume level, and you want to keep them motivated. If you drop the volume *too* low, you run the risk of losing intensity—of losing that "drive" that is so critical. I have always believed that when you want to move a crowd, the way to do it is with simple, repetitive tom-tom patterns. We all react instinctively to the "jungle drums" effect, and you need only listen to successful drum-oriented songs to illustrate this: Krupa's "Sing, Sing, Sing," "Wipeout," "In-A-Gadda-Da-Vida," and the Afro/Latin rhythms of Santana's percussion section on "Soul Sacrifice." I don't cite these as monumental examples of drum technique, but as highly successful examples of physical motivation through rhythm.

It is good to achieve a contrast in sound within these patterns, so perhaps you could establish a theme on the toms, then vary it over to the snare, or play on closed hi-hats. In a dance solo, you can sacrifice some of the visual element in favor of the musical motivation. I've found that the use of open stickings, rests, and placement of musical space achieves more in this application than a very busy solo with blazing fills. Once again, there are some cautions I would suggest:

1. Watch the audience like a hawk. This is where your talent really comes into play. You simply cannot allow yourself to be absorbed 100% into what you're playing, and forget to pay attention to your audience. We're assuming that they're up and moving to your solo. You want to keep them that way. You must be aware of whether or not what you're playing is motivating them. If it doesn't seem to be, change it—*fast!* Watch to see if any couples are leaving the floor, shaking their heads. It usually means that they couldn't dance to what you were doing. That often happens because tempo was not maintained; other times it's because the drummer got too busy and left out the fundamental drive. Sometimes this happens en masse—usually because the solo has gone on too long. If any of these should happen to you, learn from it, and approach your next solo accordingly.

2. Take your length cue from the audience. Happily, this usually occurs naturally. There is a sort of energy feedback from an audience that can sustain a soloing drummer. If they're clapping along, and shouting, "Go, Go, Go," then you find yourself charged with adrenaline and able to play enthusiastically for a substantial length of time. On the other hand, if the crowd is simply absorbing the energy you're putting out without returning any of it to you, you'll find yourself tiring very quickly. When this occurs, let it be an indication to you and keep the solo short. Prolonging it will be fruitless, since you won't be playing at your best and the audience will not be receiving it in the most positive manner.

There are, of course, those glorious and rare occasions when a dancing audience will come to a standstill, grouped around the stage and cheering you on. This is where you can really give it your best shot. You know they're with you and paying attention, so now you can switch over and throw in some of the show solo licks, along with the visual elements. I've found that in this situation the energy given back to me by the audience is almost limitless, and the only danger I face is running out of ideas. I just don't seem to ever run out of steam. I repeat, these occasions are rare, but when they do happen, they seem to make it all worthwhile. Remember, the key to a successful solo, at any point in the evening, is keeping your *purpose* in mind. You'll feel better about the solo yourself, and you'll maximize its impact on your audience.

Tips For The Singing Drummer

A singing drummer is more likely to get a job over a non-singing drummer, even if the non-singer is a better player.

It's an economic fact of club work that small groups are more profitable than large ones, both for the members and the management. The club can pay less to the band, and the members split it fewer ways. I think it would be fair to say that the average club group would comprise four people, perhaps five at the most.

But it's a musical fact that the bigger a group's sound, the more popular they are likely to be, and thus the more profitable for the room.

To me, the best answer to this apparent conflict is "doubling," which means playing more than one instrument, or doing more than one thing for the group. For drummers, who rarely have the opportunity to perform on another instrument even if they play one, it most often translates to singing as well as drumming.

Vocals are always a selling point for club bands, and groups in which each member sings enjoy an advantage over groups with less vocal capability. What does this mean to the club drummer economically? It means a singing drummer is more likely to get a job over a non-singing drummer, even if the non-singer is a better player. The additional vocal skill is a definite asset.

Many drummers don't have any difficulty singing and playing. Some have the ability to sing well, but find it difficult to concentrate on the vocal and the drum part at the same time. Others maintain that singing interferes completely with their concentration and they just can't do both.

The whole key to singing and playing comfortably is a sort of split-focus concentration that I call "mental independence." This means being able to concentrate on one thing while doing something else almost automatically.

I sing both lead and background vocals from the drums. I find that with an established tune, I'll play the drum part almost on reflexes, and my entire focus will be on the vocal. After several performances, the vocal also becomes automatic, and I can switch my focus back to the drums. This may sound like *lack* of concentration, but it's not. What it amounts to is an *ease* of concentration based on rehearsal and repetition.

Of course, when learning a new tune, more effort is required to remember both the drum part and the vocal. This is where practice comes in. You have to practice that split-focus technique so that you can employ it as a tool toward learning new material. It's easy to develop, because most people do it all the time, like fixing dinner while watching the six o'clock news, or eating a hamburger while driving. You just need to develop your memory so that a song comes as naturally to your mouth as it does to your hands and feet. Think of it as another facet of independence training.

Sing while you're working, sing in the shower, sing along with the car radio. Program your mind to reproduce a vocal automatically, without 100% of your attention. Then, practice your drumming while singing. Again, work with the radio or recordings. Learn to play a song as automatically as you just learned to sing it. Thus you gain the mental independence to focus your concentration only where you *want* to, not where you're *forced* to.

Let me make one thing clear: By "automatically" I don't mean mechanically, lifelessly, or without expression. I mean comfortably, easily, and without conscious mental *effort*.

Now we're ready to consider another point: concern for showmanship. Once you're comfortable singing and playing, you can turn your attention to what you look like while you're doing it. Remember, you want to express something in a song—but it shouldn't be pain. A lot of drummers who sing seem to close their eyes and go into some sort of trance.

Others seem to be working so hard at singing that they look like they're about to burst at any second. Neither of these conditions is pleasant to watch. By all means, emote (as is appropriate for the song), but be aware of what you're projecting visually as well as vocally. Practice singing in front of a mirror, either along with a recording or (better yet) while practicing your drumming. Pay close attention to your facial expressions. Then, as a test, get someone to photograph or videotape you on the job or at rehearsal. This can be very revealing, and often surprising.

You'll also find that mental independence will make you more aware of things on stage—like the parts the other musicians are playing. This enhances ensemble playing, and makes your group a tighter musical unit. It also means being on top of the situation in case of emergencies, like a broken guitar string or a voice problem, which might necessitate a quick arrangement change.

The bottom line is that by developing your mental independence you make yourself:

1. *A singing drummer:* more marketable and more profitable.

2. *A more comfortable performer:* Less effort accomplishes more for you.

3. *A more valuable member of your group:* more flexible and more aware.

Establishing Tempo

> **When any individual counts off a tune, he or she is pulling a tempo out of thin air.**

Even though drummers from different styles of music might express widely different philosophies or advocate various techniques of playing, they all seem to agree on one thing: the importance of keeping good time. Bandleaders and bass players are often quoted as saying that good timekeeping is their number-one requirement in a drummer.

I define "good time" as the ability to control the consistency of the tempo within a song. That might mean keeping the tempo rock-solid (against the tendency of a soloist to rush or drag, for example), or engineering deliberate shifts in the tempo in order to achieve an intentional effect.

Unfortunately, having the best time in the world won't help a group if they have difficulty establishing the correct initial tempo for a song. This is a common and very understandable problem among club bands. When any individual counts off a tune, he or she is pulling a tempo out of thin air, and that tempo is going to be based on his or her particular concept of how fast that song should be. On any given performance, that concept is going to be influenced by a number of what I call "controlling factors." These include:

1. Basic metabolism. Different people live at different speeds. This is why we call some people "hyper" and others "laid back" or "low key." These people will actually perceive the "correct" tempo for a song at widely differing rates of speed, based on what is comfortable for them relative to their own inner clock.

2. Physical fatigue. A tired player will generally feel tempos slower than one who is fresh. If you come to the gig after a long day of yard work, and the other players have spent the day on the couch watching the ball game, you're likely to feel the tempos at a slower rate than they will.

3. Emotional state. If you're depressed about something, your perception of tempo is likely to be slower than normal. On the other hand, if you've had an extremely "up" day, and you come to the gig excited and happy, you could have a tendency to feel the tempos a good deal faster than usual.

Conflicts over initial tempos arise when some members of the group fall into one of the above-listed categories, while the rest fall into another. Thus, the perception of "correct" tempo differs from player to player, and nobody feels comfortable. The importance of "correct" tempo to a cover band is based on a simple fact: Your audience is already familiar with this music. They have heard the songs on their car radio or on their stereo at home, and they are used to the tempos they have heard. The feel, and especially the danceability of the song, are affected if your tempos are too different from what they are used to. Many customers will criticize a band with something like the following statement: "They sound fine—they're good players. But they seem to rush (or drag) everything; they just aren't danceable. The complaint isn't that the tempos shift within the song (that the time isn't consistent), but rather that the initial tempos aren't comfortable.

Of course, audiences are subject to the same "controlling factors" that I listed for players. On a crowded, busy night, the general enthusiasm level tends to build. As people's adrenaline level rises, their perception of tempos usually accelerates. This is why concert acts usually play their songs faster than the recorded version. But you have to keep in mind that *your* audience members are also including physical movement—dancing—in their reactions to your songs. So while their emotional level might accommodate a different tempo, their bodies may still not be comfortable with anything other than the original one. You can't let the charge you get from a happy audience allow you to run away with tempos. That happy audience can become alienated very quickly without ever realizing why.

Standard procedure with most bands is to have one individual determine the tempos. Most often this is the bandleader, who counts off all the tunes. But he is not impervious to the "controlling factors," and although he may be very conscious of them, there's no guarantee he can overcome them. He's only human. Recognizing this situation, one band I was in took the responsibility off the shoulders of the leader (or any of us, for that matter) and gave it to an individual who was not subject to the "controlling factors": a metronome. And before you decry my cop-out to a mechanical device instead of relying on training and musical ability, let me tell you how we used the metronome, what it achieved, and what our attitude was toward its use.

How We Used It

The idea was simple. Since most people feel that the correct tempo for any given dance song is the one they've heard on the original recording, we played the recording for each of our tunes and clocked it against the metronome to establish the beats-per-minute tempo setting. (It was interesting to note that very few tunes were rock-steady against the metronome. Even recorded versions tend to accelerate and decelerate within each song.) Once we had the tempo settings, we listed them alongside each title on our song list.

We used an AC-powered metronome, so it would not be subject to battery slowdown or require re-winding as a clockwork unit does. We could rely on it to remain accurate at all times. The unit had a blinking light on top, as well as a switchable click sound, which we left in the "off" position. I simply mounted the unit in an inconspicuous place on stage where I could reach it, and masked it from the audience with a little gaffer's tape. The bass player and I could see the blinking light; our audience could not. When our bandleader called a tune, I checked the tempo setting on the list we had made, and set the metronome to that reading. I took a few beats from the blinking light and then counted off the tune for the band accordingly. It didn't take long for me to begin to memorize the settings for our most frequently-played songs, so there was very little time taken up for this operation. Since many of the songs were at the same basic tempo, I was not required to make setting changes for each and every one. Also, we tended to play our slow songs without the metronome at all.

What It Achieved

We achieved very dramatic results using the metronome, and they weren't all musical. Since we now had an objective, reliable source of tempo information, we no longer had conflicts between bandmembers over what was the right tempo for a given song. This had become a serious source of discord, caused only by the difference in personality-related tempo perception I have already mentioned. The metronome was not subject to either physical or emotional highs or lows, and could give us the same tempo, night after night, for each song.

This released us from a tremendous psychological pressure. We became free to concentrate on playing well, rather than on how fast we were playing, whether the audience was comfortable with it, or whether *we* were comfortable. Our complete attention could be turned to the expressiveness of the performance, rather than to the technical elements of playing. We discovered that the metronome could even be used to adjust to the ups and downs of audiences. If it was a busy night, and the audience was excited and energetic, then the overall pace of the evening could go up. To achieve this, we merely increased each listed tempo setting by a few beats per minute. In this way, we and the audience felt more comfortable, and the songs maintained the same general impression of tempo variety relative to each other.

Our Attitude Towards It

At first we were skeptical about using the metronome. None of us liked the idea of relying on a machine to control a major element of our performance. But as we started working with it and we realized how far afield some of our tempos had gone from the original recorded versions, we saw the need for some kind of reliable guide. We also had the sense to realize that this was a tool, and *we* were to use *it*, not the other way around. As might be expected, after a few weeks of using the unit, we improved our own sense of tempo, and did not rely on the metronome for each song. But when critical songs came up, we had it there as the final arbiter of "correct" tempo. We could turn to it to be sure we were giving our audience the "danceability" they sought.

Every drum teacher I've ever known has advocated the use of a metronome to improve a student's ability to play comfortably and well at various tempos. We simply took the same approach as a band. We used the metronome to help us establish the best tempos to work with in order to make our performance as enjoyable as possible—for our audience and for ourselves.

Evaluating Room Acoustics

It's the drummer's responsibility to familiarize himself with the acoustic properties of the room and adjust his tuning to achieve sound and projection.

In a later chapter I'm going to discuss tuning a drumset specifically for club work. But before we tune the set, let's talk about what we're tuning it *for*: the acoustics of the club itself. To do this, a club drummer should have an understanding of the factors that combine to create a room's acoustic properties, and how those factors relate to tuning the drums.

A concert drummer tunes for the sound board. The sound engineer has the responsibility of making the drums fill the hall and sound good at the same time. The studio drummer also tunes for the board, and there is no necessity for projection from the drums over any great distance. In both cases, equalization and other electronic effects can be applied to enhance the sound of the drums.

But the club drummer's set has to project into a reasonably large area, through amplified music, *and sound good doing it*. In this case, the drums are tuned for the human ear, not for an electronic board. What the drums project is what is heard, with no electronic assistance. I think it's safe to say that in most local clubs the drummer is not miked (although bass drum and snare/hi-hat mic's are fairly common) and most club bands do not have a sound engineer out front. It becomes the drummer's responsibility to familiarize himself with the acoustic properties of the room and adjust his tuning to achieve sound and projection. To help you with that familiarization process, I'm going to list eight factors you should consider when analyzing acoustics:

1. Room size: Obviously, the larger the room, the more projection required to fill it. But small rooms can be deceiving, because other factors can combine to reduce projection. You should have someone play your set while you listen from the most distant point possible, then from a middle point, and then from a close one. The drums should project adequately to the rear of the room without being too boomy or explosive at the closer point.

2. Room shape: It would be nice if all nightclubs were built like concert halls, with clear paths from stage to audience, but this is rarely the case. Seldom is entertainment a major design consideration. Often a room is very long and narrow with the stage at one end. Also common is the wide room, with a stage placed in the middle, creating deep "wings" to the right and left, but only a shallow area directly in front. The worst situation is an L-shaped room, or one with niches or compartmented areas. These are extremely difficult to deal with since sound is directional and doesn't turn corners well.

3. Stage placement: If the stage is at one end of the room you have the problem of a *long throw* to reach the other end. The drums need to be punchy, directional, and slightly flat to carry with power. If the stage is in the middle of a wide room, you have to fill the areas at either side, and in this case the drums need to have more radiance to project in a 360° pattern. Sometimes the stage is in a corner of the room, facing out diagonally, and then you don't have a straight shot at *anybody*. In this case, a compromise tuning is generally best.

4. Stage configuration: The actual architecture of the immediate stage area can sometimes assist you in achieving projection. If the stage is in a corner, or recessed into a sort of alcove, the walls act as a funnel to concentrate and direct the sound. A low ceiling can also help in this way. However, if the stage is wide open on three sides, and the ceiling is high, much of your sound dissipates into the expanse of open air around and above you before it ever gets to the audience. It's extremely important to have a feeling for *how much* help or hindrance you're getting so you can tune accordingly.

5. Overall room architecture: In addition to general

shape, other architectural factors of the room affect your sound. Once again, high ceilings can allow the sound to get lost, while low ceilings will help contain it. The type of ceiling material makes a difference, since it reflects the sound back down to your audience. The typical spray-on acoustic ceiling represents a middle-ground between reflective and absorbent types. The drop ceiling, of the type with heavy cardboard-like panels hung on tracks, is a little more reflective. Solid wood-beam or wood-panel ceilings are even more reflective, unless the wood is very soft.

There are, of course, extremes when it comes to ceilings. I worked in one club that was a converted quonset hut, with a huge, umbrella-like domed ceiling of solid corrugated steel. The echo was tremendous. I worked in another where the entire ceiling was crisscrossed with rugs and tapestries, and the sound seemed to stop dead an inch off the drums.

If the room is more or less an open bay, you've got a good chance of achieving an even projection. If the floor plan includes lots of individual booth areas, small side-areas off the main hall, or even several different levels, then you have a problem. Objects such as stand-up bars, high tables, room divider panels, and hanging decorations all interfere with projection as well.

6. Upholstery and wall coverings: Room decor may be important to the visual design, but it can be a nightmare acoustically. The typical "steak house" look calls for lots of rough-hewn wood, plush tweed-like fabric, and soft cushions—all in all, a very large amount of absorbent material. This deadens the overall sound response and reduces projection. On the other hand, a lot of clubs are into the chrome, vinyl, and plastic look in their decor. These materials provide a much harder, more reflective surface, and keep the sound more *alive*. But they also contribute to a *bounce* characteristic that you'll need to be aware of.

Wall covering is also an important factor. A polished hardwood wall, brick, stone, or similar dense material will reflect sound, as will metal panels or mirrors. Drywall (sheetrock) covered with paint or wallpaper is slightly less reflective. Walls covered with fabric or plush wallcoverings—or heavily hung with rugs, macramés, and the like—are much more absorbent.

The amount of reflective items in the room, such as mirrors, metal lampshades, table surfaces, and non-carpeted flooring areas, contribute to the *bounce* of sound, keeping it live and in the room. Heavy carpets, rough wood beams, and even fabric-type lampshades all act as absorbent baffles to actually remove the sound from the air.

I worked for several years as the house drummer in a room with the typical "steak house" decor, but that also featured a stainless-steel dance floor, surrounded by mirrors and topped with a low, mirrored ceiling. The rest of the room had a very high ceiling. Consequently, sound on the dance floor area was very live, while sound in the seating area was very dead. I couldn't tune precisely for each area, but it was important that I be aware of the difference. On a slow night, when the audience was dancing less and watching from their seats, I adjusted my tuning for a little more projection into the seating area. On nights when the dance floor was packed, I made sure my drums were strong on the dance floor in order to give the music the support it needed for the dancers.

7. Atmosphere: This is a subtle factor, but very important. If you've ever wondered why your drums are very live and clear one night and muddy or flat the next, with no change in tuning or amp settings, pay attention to the air temperature and humidity in the room. Cool dry air carries sound well and makes it more *brittle*, letting highs through unimpeded. Warm dry air is similar, but tends to mellow the highs. Cool damp air carries sound, but tends to lack clarity; the sound seems *diffused*. Warm damp air will muddy up the sound, muffling the bass and swallowing the highs. Temperature changes also affect the resonance of drum shells and the response of heads, plastic or not. And remember what else is out there in the air besides your music: Smoke, dust, and the warm breath of your audience all act as barriers to the clear transmission of sound.

8. Size of audience: Bodies act as sponges to soak up sound. The more bodies in the room, the lower the projection. Additionally, the more people in the room, the greater the volume of voices, clinking glasses, and other noises competing with your music.

All of the above are factors you need to be aware of when deciding how to tune your set in a given environment. I'm often discouraged by drummers who have an attitude of "I've got my drums just the way I want them, so I don't ever change the tuning." *The way you want them may not be the way their sound is reaching your audience.* The same set can sound radically different in two different rooms. Your thinking and your musical ear must extend beyond the stage and into the space where your sound is being heard. Once you've learned to evaluate the acoustic qualities of a room, you'll be able to maximize your sound everywhere you perform.

The Fine Art Of Listening

It's simple physics; you can't relate your playing to that of the rest of the band if you can't *hear* the rest of the band.

I don't think there's any question that a musician's talent is primarily judged by how well he or she *plays*. But I also firmly believe that a large portion of that same musician's abilities depends on how well he or she *listens*. How many times have you heard a well-known player complimented for having "big ears"? We're not referring to hat supports here, but rather to that player's ability to listen to everything going on in his or her musical environment, to assimilate it, and to translate it into "just the right thing to play"—or not to play, as the case may be.

I once had an opportunity to see and hear several drummers performing in a competition. It was like a scientifically controlled experiment: the same band, the same tunes, the same sound system and acoustic environment, the same audience; only the drummers were different. Each drummer played on his own kit, and each played in both solo and ensemble spots. And although each was an excellent player in his own right, there was a clearly displayed difference in musical awareness. That difference was mainly how each drummer *listened* to what was going on around him.

The greatest danger facing a club musician is complacency. When you play in the same rooms frequently, and when you play the same basic repertoire for extended periods of time, a sense of creative apathy can set in very easily. It's not so much boredom as simply "settling into a routine." That routine may become very comfortable and easy—but not particularly exciting or interesting. And that lack of excitement or interest on the part of the band is readily perceived by the band's audience.

I've always felt that a parallel can be drawn between a long-term club engagement or circuit tour and a long-running Broadway show. How do the members of the cast of *Cats* keep their performance fresh and vital in a show that's been running for over ten years? The answer is a concept that's called in theater "The Illusion Of The First Time." Simply put, it means that you approach each performance as if it were the first time you were doing it. All aspects—creative, emotional, and technical—are freshly dealt with every time. I believe that this concept should be applied most directly to listening. You should be listening to every element of your performance as if it were the first time you were hearing it.

Before The Band Starts

The place to start applying "The Illusion Of The First Time" is on your drums, before the band ever starts. If, for example, you're playing a long-term gig where you leave your kit set up, you should listen to the tuning of your drums each night as if you had just set it up in a new room. Remember, an extremely gradual decline in tuning quality, head condition, and other factors can take place over a period of time. This can happen *so* gradually that you may not notice it from night to night. At the start of each gig, the drums will sound pretty much like they did at the end of the night before. The problem is that they may not sound the way you'd like them to in the ideal sense; it's just what you've gotten used to over the course of the engagement. On the other hand, if you come in each evening and *listen* to the kit as if it were the first time you'd heard it, you'll keep the tuning at its optimum and thereby produce your best sound. Listen for heads that are unevenly tensioned or going dead, listen for rattles or squeaks in lugs or pedals, listen for cymbals that are mellowing due to accumulating dirt. Taking whatever steps are necessary to keep your sound fresh will go a long way toward keeping your playing fresh as well.

Playing With The Band

Once you start playing with the band, "The Illusion Of The First Time" really applies. Think of all the factors that combine to create a musical performance: each player's individual part, the arrangement of all the parts combined, the balance of individual volume levels, the "feel" and sense of time, the inspirational nature of solos, the "lock" in the ensemble work (especially from the rhythm section)—the list goes on and on. And while it is possible to fall into that apathy I mentioned earlier (and thus to let each of these elements simply run its "normal course"), it is also possible to approach everything freshly each night—thereby creating an exciting, original performance that overcomes your own complacency and also projects your best efforts to your audience.

The way to make sure that everything is working together in your band is to listen to everything else *first*, and yourself *second*. It's simple physics; you can't relate your playing to that of the rest of the band if you can't *hear* the rest of the band. Listen to the ensemble balance, and adjust your own level so that you provide either the support or the leadership that is called for at that moment. If it's your turn to shine, then shine brightly, but be prepared to sit back and groove quietly when it's someone else's turn. You'll also find that there are often subtle nuances in the playing of others that you can "latch onto" in your own playing, thus creating a musical interplay that is always enjoyable (and can be another way of overcoming complacency in often-played arrangements). But you have to be *listening* for those nuances in order to catch them.

You'll find that there is a political benefit to listening, too. You'll get along much better with the vocalists and soloists in your band if they realize that you are actively listening to their playing and trying to support them, rather than blazing your way through every tune, oblivious to what anyone else is doing. If you make a point of playing behind the vocalists and soloists when it's time to do so, they'll be much more willing to give you some room to stretch out yourself.

Listening also has its practical advantages, which include flexibility and the ability to respond quickly to "emergencies." If you can hear that the vocalist is having throat problems, you can adjust your volume level—which, in turn, will likely bring the band's overall volume down. If the guitar player breaks a string or loses power during a solo, you might be able to cue in someone else to cover (or even do so yourself). "On the spot" arrangement changes can be made if everyone is listening to everyone else and communicating on stage. And let's not forget that listening is the only known method of overcoming the "snowball effect"—that legendary situation that every band experiences. (Someone can't hear himself or herself adequately, so that person turns up, causing someone else to turn up in response, and so on until everybody is playing at a megadecibel level, and nobody—including the audience—can clearly hear anything.) I'm not suggesting that every style of music should be played softly. Appropriate volume levels are all relative to the style of music, the size of the room, and many other factors. My point is that if *everyone* in a group is listening to *everyone else first,* it's easier to maintain a proper balance. It may also go a long way toward preventing hearing loss.

Listening *is* an art. And as is the case with any other art form, you must practice it constantly in order to achieve a high level of proficiency at it. But especially to the club drummer, the benefits of developing listening skills are enormous. Without those skills, even the most proficient technician is merely that—a technician. With them, a musician truly becomes an artist.

Attention To Detail

It never ceases to amaze me that drummers can be such fanatics about certain elements of their drum sound, and almost totally oblivious to others.

Every so often, I get the chance to go out and see other club bands perform. I like to take those opportunities to evaluate—from the point of view of an audience member—what differentiates a good band from an *excellent* one, and what separates a talented drummer from an *outstanding performer* on the drums. I believe that the difference can be summed up in one phrase: attention to detail. While the vast majority of club groups meet the basic requirements necessary to keep them working, a few exhibit an attention to detail that makes them that little bit better, that little bit more entertaining, and most likely, that little bit more marketable.

Conversely, drummers and groups who *fail* to pay attention to details tend to leave a poor impression on their customers—even when the greatest portion of their performance is fine. In fact, the better the overall performance level, the more the small omissions stand out. In other words, the better you are, the better you have to be, because more is expected of you.

I'm going to give you a few examples of what I mean, based on what I've seen and heard from groups I've encountered in the past. This will by no means be a comprehensive list of dos and don'ts. It will, however, give you an idea of the kinds of things that have the potential to greatly increase the quality of your performance (or greatly diminish that quality by their absence).

Drum Sound

It never ceases to amaze me that drummers can be such fanatics about certain elements of their drum sound, and almost totally oblivious to others. It's my opinion that a "middle-of-the-road" tuning is best when you have to play a wide variety of styles. But whether you use that sort of tuning, a flat and funky studio tuning, or a big and boomy rock tuning, the important thing is to pay attention to the overall effect. Is the sound consistent from drum to drum? Do the drums complement each other; do they produce an ensemble sound? In other words, do you play a *drumset,* or just an assortment of drums? I once heard a drummer who had a large kit, including timbales, rack and floor toms, and quite a bit of percussion. I looked forward to hearing some interesting drumming, and I was not disappointed in that respect. But I *was* disappointed in the sound he produced. The timbales sounded tight and ringy, as one would expect. The rack toms were flat and very dull—the cardboard sound—while the floor toms had tremendous depth and resonance. The bass drum was single-headed and miked up, so it had a very tight, high-pitched attack sound, with very little depth or punch.

Had this drummer been the type of player who selectively and deliberately used different portions of this widely varied set for different songs, I would have understood such a nonhomogeneous tuning. But he was playing pretty standard fills, using all of the drums on a pretty much equal basis, as one would on any drumset. The result was a very uneven sound from his kit, which, in turn, made his performance sound unpolished and unprofessional. When I spoke to this drummer later, he told me, verbatim: "I don't pay much attention to my tuning; the crowd here is so dead, they wouldn't know the difference." There's a good chance that the crowd sensed this drummer's attitude through the sounds he produced, and it didn't surprise me that they were "dead" in terms of their reaction to his playing. An attempt to improve his sonic output might have resulted in an improvement in their reaction to it.

In another club I visited, the band specialized in hard rock. The drummer's kit featured deep-shelled toms and a tremendously powerful bass drum. The drummer worked the toms frequently with impressive fills, and it was apparent that he was tom-oriented. It was made more apparent, unfortunately, by the fact that his snare sound was totally inconsistent with the rest of the kit. It was a deep snare, yet it was tuned very tightly, and heavily muffled. I asked the drummer if this was because of some miking problem, or even done at the request of the rest of the band. He told me that the snare had been tuned that way when he bought it from a friend—who had played jazz/funk in a horn band—and he hadn't gotten around to changing the tuning yet. I didn't ask how long ago he had purchased the snare, because it didn't really matter. He hadn't considered the importance of immediately adjusting his snare to fit his own set and his own playing; consequently, he was performing on a piece of equipment that demonstrated his inattention to detail with every backbeat.

It seems to me that all the really fine drummers I've heard performing in clubs had certain similar elements in their drum sound—no matter what the basic tuning might be. Their drums were consistent, they were well-maintained (no hanging snare wires to buzz, no pitted heads, no cracked cymbals, no squeaking pedals) and the tuning suited the type of music being played. Details like this should be taken into consideration—and attended to—by every drummer who hopes to maximize the impact of his or her performance.

Band Mix

This is not always an area that is under the drummer's control, but every drummer should be aware of the potential for disaster represented by an unbalanced sound mix. I once saw a very talented show band whose act featured a wide variety of styles, excellent vocals, exciting stage presence—all the elements of an outstanding performance. Unfortunately, their sound mix had two drastic flaws. One was that the vocals were too far down—a problem common to many club groups. A second (much more aggravating) problem was that the bass drum was mixed up so high that it was the loudest element of the band's sound. I'm the first person to enjoy a good solid bass drum, and I recognize that the foundational beat is very important to a dance band. But this level far exceeded the need, resulting in a very unpleasant "pile driving" effect behind the dance tunes and a totally inappropriate plodding behind otherwise gentle, moving ballads. The fact that this group employed a sound technician made such a situation inexcusable. Of course, a large part of the problem was the fact that the sound tech spent most of the evening seated at the board, just off stage, *behind* the sound cabinets.

A sound technician should listen to the mix from out in the room, where the audience hears it. If the sound board can't be out there, the technician should walk out front frequently to listen, and then return to the board to make any necessary adjustments. If the band is handling the mix from on stage—admittedly a more difficult situation in which to achieve a good balance—it is the drummer's responsibility to make sure that the drums are mixed properly. They must be balanced among themselves, as well as balanced in the overall band sound. You need to have someone whose judgment you can trust listen from out in the room and give you an indication of your balance *while you play!* Nobody in your band can play the way you do, so it does you little good to have someone else bang on the snare or kick the bass drum while you go out front yourself.

The point of my example is that an otherwise top-notch band's performance was dramatically impaired by this inattention to one small detail that could have been corrected merely by adjusting a dial. On the other hand, we've all heard bands whose playing was only adequate, but whose sound was so well balanced that their performance was tremendously enjoyable.

Arrangements

There's an unwritten principle in club music that basically states that the older or more obscure a song, the more liberties you can take with it. Conversely, the newer and more popular a song is, the more you need to stick to the recorded arrangement. Even if your band decides to make certain changes in a popular tune, it is critical to retain those characteristics that gave the tune its popularity in the first place. The bigger the hit, the more important it becomes to "play it straight." When you lose sight of this detail, you run the risk of alienating your audience by appearing to show a poor regard for what might be their favorite music. At the very least, you can affect them, subconsciously, so that they don't react favorably to the music, even though they think—and you wish—they would.

A case in point occurred with the same show band I mentioned previously. At the conclusion of one of their sets, they launched into their "finale," which was Michael Jackson's "Beat It." As soon as they started the introductory phrases, the audience recognized the tune, an anticipatory "Ahh" went up, and the floor became packed. But when the band moved into the body of the tune, the drummer was playing an inappropriate bass drum pattern! It wasn't a variation on the original; it wasn't just different; it was *wrong*! Everything else in the tune was fine, but the basic beat was not what the audience was familiar with. So they danced...for a while. But no one was smiling, and in twos and threes they left the floor. I actually heard one young woman say as she passed me on the way to her seat, "I don't understand it; it's my favorite song, and I couldn't dance to it."

Of course, not every inattention to detail that a band might exhibit relates to the drummer. But I think a drummer has more details to be concerned with than any other musician in a club group. Each little detail offers a potential boost or a potential pitfall in regard to the band's performance. Take a moment to evaluate all the small things that are often taken for granted—or overlooked entirely—in the repetition and (sometimes) apathy that club performing can involve. If you spend a little effort on those details, you'll not only improve your act, you'll also keep your concentration level high and become more creative in an overall performance sense.

Studying Yourself

There's nothing egotistical in listening to your own playing, when the purpose is to evaluate, critique, and hopefully improve.

If you were to ask a group of club drummers who they listened to for drumming influences and education, they'd probably name many different artists from all areas of music. And there is much to be gained from studying the playing of as many other drummers as possible. But, there may be even more to be gained from studying one's own playing with the same intensity, and I don't think nearly enough club drummers do that. The tendency (especially on long-term engagements) is to let the present status of the drumming take care of itself, and to seek improvement in areas that aren't really being put to use on the job. In other words, the philosophy tends to be, "I can already cut this gig; I need to develop my chops for bigger and better things to come."

If this attitude smacks of complacency, that's exactly what it is, and it's a situation that far too many club musicians fall prey to. It's true that there is a certain tedium—a sameness—to club performing that takes a conscious effort to overcome. One of the methods I recommend to overcome that tedium is to periodically record your playing with the band, and to critically evaluate that recording—both alone and with the other members of your group. There are several advantages that are gained by this procedure, all of which combine to keep your performance sharp, your skills up to date, and your ego healthily deflated.

Here are some of the things to listen for when evaluating your own drumming with your group:

1. The quality of your performance with the band. You should listen to the total sound of the band and how well the drums contribute to it. Is your playing solid and foundational? Do you support soloists and vocalists well without being obtrusive, or are you overly busy? Do you put fills in appropriate places, or are you sounding as though you're soloing throughout the tunes? Do you have a tendency to rush fills, even though your time is solid during the balance of the song? Do your dynamics correspond with the rest of the band's playing, or do you tend to stand out? How do your drums sound, in terms of tuning and projection, within the overall context of the band's sound? (Do you have a jazzy-sounding kit in a hard rock band, or a deep, fat kit trying to play techno-pop music?)

The above considerations can be discussed and evaluated among all of the members of the group (along with similar aspects of *their* playing). Suggestions can be made for improvements in individual performances, or in some aspect of the band's playing as a whole that can be improved (such as arrangements, time taken between songs, or dynamics).

Another aspect of the band's performance that can sometimes be surprisingly revealed on a tape is the fact that things aren't being performed as they were originally rehearsed. This can occur so gradually over a period of time that it isn't really noticed during the performance. But if this week's tape is compared to the tape made six weeks ago when a tune was first introduced, the difference can often be startling. That's not to say it's necessarily *bad*, but it's important that the band be *aware* of the evolution rather than having it happen unconsciously. This same point applies to your drumming, and will also be readily apparent on the tape.

2. The current state of your personal playing. You should listen to your drumming with an ear to your time (particularly whether it varies from the beginning to the end of a given song). If you are responsible for counting off the tunes, it's important to note whether or not you actually begin to play the song at the tempo you counted off for the band. This has been a particular bugaboo of mine in the past. I have a tendency to gain excitement over the short space of time it takes to count off the song, which sometimes causes me to pick up the tempo in the very first few beats. At other times, a fatigue factor has caused a situation in which I was able to *count off* a tune at the correct tempo, but I was unable to *play* the tune at the same speed. These flaws might be virtually unnoticeable at the time they occur (at least to you) but they can drive the other members of your band crazy if you are consistently prone to them. The tape will incontrovertibly show you where any deficiencies lie in this area.

You should also evaluate the quality of your fills in a different light than has already been mentioned. This time, listen to the fills from the standpoint of taste and originality. If you are in a cover band and you seek to copy original fills deliberately, see if your fills are accurate reproductions. If you seek to play in an original manner, then evaluate the fills to see if they are appropriate to the style of the tune, yet fresh and interesting. If a fill only takes up space, and offers no real musical contribution, perhaps it's unnecessary.

You should listen to the *sound* of your kit, especially during any solo spots you may have. Do the drums complement each other, producing an ensemble sound? Does each drum speak with an equal yet individual voice within the overall kit sound? If you hear something that stands out in a negative sense (like a dead head or an off-pitch sound), you should make the appropriate alteration. If, on the other hand, something on the kit sounds good, you might want to re-tune the rest of the kit to match that particularly good sound. A tape will hear your kit with a slightly more objective ear than yours (during the performance), and often from a different vantage point.

Lastly, you should listen for the purely mechanical, technique-oriented aspects of your own playing. Is your sticking clean and precise, or do you hear rims being struck and sticks clicked together? Is the hi-hat ride work precise, or do you hear a mushy, poorly defined ride pattern due to a hi-hat closed too loosely? Are the dynamics of your playing clearly evident, or do the fills tend to be consistently louder than the time playing? Do certain drums seem to be struck more cleanly or clearly than others? The old adage that "tape doesn't lie" is very true, and although what it reveals isn't always flattering, the objective study of your own playing can't help but improve your drumming (and your contribution to the band).

3. The educational aspect. Transcribing tapes of your own playing is one of the best methods I know of improving your reading and writing ability. You should work both with complete tunes and with drum solos, and transcribe as accurately as you can. You have an advantage in this case over trying to transcribe someone else's playing: Because you are the one who played the part originally, you can most likely remember what you played (or at least be aware of how you usually tend to play such passages). Not only are your reading and writing skills improved in this manner, but the resultant chart gives you a *visual* means of evaluating your playing, in addition to the tape's *aural* one. You can also keep the charts as records to how you played particular tunes for future reference, or in the event you have to miss a gig and employ a substitute on short notice. Very few club drummers are likely to literally read their way through a gig. However, the opportunity to look over the charts you've prepared, in advance of the gig, can give your sub a real head start.

4. The historical aspect. You should definitely keep as many tapes of your playing as possible (or at least a selection of representative ones). These provide a historical review of your playing, and give you an opportunity to listen back for evolutions in your own style, technique, and taste. You can sometimes retrieve useful little tricks and fills that somehow went by the wayside for lack of use.

Mainly, you are able to get a historical perspective on your career and your involvement with music. For example, since I began keeping tapes of my bands, I have recordings of myself playing soul music in the mid-'60s, psychedelic rock in the late '60s, hard rock in the later '60s, jazz-rock and funk in the early '70s, and then a succession of semi-pro and finally full-time pro Top-40 bands up to the present day. During that particular "era," my bands showed evolutions of their own, from pop-rock to disco to hard rock, as musical trends shifted rapidly. Each of these musical stages in my life called for adaptations in style and performance technique, and represented major shifts in my musical growth. It seems important to me to have that growth documented in tape form so that I can listen back and understand the reasons why I play the way I do.

Suggested Taping Methods

There are various ways of obtaining a tape recording of your playing with your band. Some are easier than others, and some provide more quality than others.

1. Engineered "remote" recording. A professional-type "live" recording (employing multiple mic's and someone to mix them) will provide the best results. This is generally impractical for most bands, however, because of the expense and the logistical hassles of arranging such a recording within the club environment. On the other hand, if you have access to a decent-quality multitrack recorder (such as one of the several direct-to-cassette "mini studios" on the market) and someone who is willing to play engineer for you as a favor, you might enjoy trying this system.

2. Stereo remote microphone placement. If you have a quality stereo cassette or DAT recorder and you can place two remote mic's in a favorable position in the room, you'll get a very realistic recording of the band's sound in the club. Unfortunately, you'll also get a lot of crowd noise and usually the "boominess" associated with room ambience when mic's are placed at a distance.

3. Microphone placed directly at the PA speaker. If your recorder can attenuate the incoming signal adequately, you can place a mic' directly in front of the PA speaker. This will give you much better isolation of the band's sound than can be achieved with mic's placed out in the room. Make sure, however, that both the mic' and the recorder can take the high-volume input from the speaker, or you'll get nothing but distortion on the tape and you'll risk damaging the equipment.

4. A direct tap from the PA board. This is the method that I favor. It gives you a direct-line connection to the most accurate signal carrying the band's sound, with the least amount of interference or outside noise. If all of the instruments are miked through your system, this method is virtually perfect. Even if they aren't, the vocal mic's will generally pick up enough of them to give a pretty good total sound. (Remember, this is a study tape, not a live album for public release.) The beauty of this system is that there is no mix involved. What you get on the tape (once you've set the initial input level to avoid distortion) is a faithful reproduction of the mix that is going out to your audience. What more could you ask for, considering the purpose of making the tape in the first place?

Some additional suggestions include using a quality cassette or DAT recorder. There's no point trying to evaluate your sound when the reproduction of that sound is inferior and non-revealing. For the same reason, you should use quality cassettes. This is additionally important from the standpoint of durability: If you are going to use this cassette for transcribing purposes, it's going to get a *lot* of play-rewind-play use: It should also be durable in order to last a long time for historical reference purposes.

There's nothing egotistical in listening to your own playing, when the purpose is to evaluate, critique, and hopefully improve. That is simply good musicianship and professional attention to your craft. As a matter of fact, there's nothing wrong with enjoying what you hear, either!

Studying The Competition

It's important to objectively evaluate a drummer's performance musically, so that you can determine what makes that performance good or bad.

In the preceding chapter, I discussed the value of studying your own playing, and it goes without saying that there is also a tremendous amount to be gained from studying the work of all the top drummers in the business. But let's not forget a basic rule of business that applies as much to club performing as it does to selling shoes: You've got to know what the competition is doing!

Let's face it, there are certain aspects of the club scene that apply equally to almost every group. There is a phenomenon that occurs in almost any community where live entertainment is prevalent, and that phenomenon is called a "circuit." This simply refers to a group of clubs, situated in the same general vicinity, that have a tendency to hire bands from the surrounding area. What generally happens is that a group of bands will work such a circuit in rotation, playing at each club in succession. Quite often the people who frequent these clubs will see and hear each band on the circuit several times within a relatively short period of time, offering an excellent (and, in fact, inescapable) opportunity for direct comparison. And since clubs on a given circuit tend to attract a similar clientele, that means that the music played in those clubs is likely to be very similar. This, in turn, means that the bands are very likely to appear similar as well—some might say interchangeable.

The problem faced by the ambitious club band, then, is how to meet the demands of the circuit, in terms of the songs the audience wants to hear, and still retain an individual quality that makes that particular band stand out over the others appearing on the same circuit. In other words, how does a given band maintain an edge over their competition?

If you're playing in a Top-40 circuit, that pretty much means that you're playing the same tunes that every other band on that circuit is playing, give or take a few select oldies. You can't avoid it; there's only one Top-40. If you try to keep current with your material, your selection is dictated by what's on the radio play lists. So the quality of your repertoire is not determined as much by *what* you play as by *how* you play it.

Finding out how other club drummers perform the material that you are also performing is the "studying" I'm referring to in the title of this chapter. It's important to objectively evaluate a drummer's performance musically, so that you can determine what makes that performance good or bad.

I once had occasion to listen to two club bands on the same evening. They were working in neighboring clubs on the same circuit, and they had many similarities. Both were five-piece groups featuring guitar, bass, keyboards, drums, and a stand-up vocalist, both had excellent equipment, both were attractively dressed, and both appeared comfortable in their surroundings. The most striking similarity was in their musical repertoire: In listening to about a set and a half from each band, I heard at least a dozen songs that were performed by both. Yet I found one band extremely entertaining, while the other struck me as much less so. What made the difference, given all the similarities I've outlined?

The outstanding feature of the band I enjoyed—and especially of that band's drummer—was their precise execution of parts, and their tasteful use of dynamics. The drummer did not over-play, yet what he did play was clean, well-executed, and musically interesting. Conversely, the drummer in the band I did not enjoy played in a very monotonous (and I mean that quite literally: mono-tone) manner, keeping good time but showing very little imagination with accents or fills. What fills he did play were done without "snap," and they didn't stand out because his dynamic level never really changed.

Let's discuss a few playing techniques and musical considerations that you should listen for when studying your competition. If you hear them being played by another drummer, note how they contribute to the music's appeal. If you don't hear them, note how their absence is felt.

1. Dynamics. This is the single most important element that separates a musical drummer from a nonmusical one. You should listen to whether the drummer achieves a proper balance behind vocalists and soloists. Does the drummer use volume to get attention—to make a musical statement—or as a way of life? Accents should be clearly defined, and sufficiently louder than the balance of the drumming to differentiate them from the time playing. On the other hand, the standard backbeat should not be an accent; there needs to be "headroom" for slightly louder playing when fills or accents are called for. Listen, too, for the drummer's use of low-volume dynamics. A statement can be made just as effectively by a sudden *drop* in volume as by a sudden increase. See if the drummer can play a dinner set without sounding boring or stifled by the imposed reduction of volume.

2. Arrangements and taste. You should note how well the drummer plays solid time when it's called for, but also how punches and accents are used to spice things up. Does he or she employ fills only to take up space, or do they actually mean something to the music? Listen for dynamic buildups and introductions to instrumental leads or vocal sections. See what the drummer does in a ballad to enhance the dramatic quality. A nice trick that's used often in ballads and blues is a simple roll crescendoing to an abrupt cut, a two- or three-beat silence, and then a return to the time playing. This simple device has all the elements of high drama: a quiet introduction, a dynamic increase of tension leading to an abrupt climax, and then a breathless moment before the release of that tension. It sounds much more complicated when described verbally than it is to perform, yet it's very effective. Does the drummer you're studying use devices like this effectively?

3. Precise execution. Does the drummer play devices such as the one described above cleanly and with precision? (The only drawback to using such a device to enhance your music is when you cannot execute it well. In that case, the musical device becomes a detriment rather than an enhancement.) You should also listen for a clear definition between accents and time playing.

Precision also refers to the sound of the drums, to the extent that clean sticking can be ruined by loose, buzzy snares, and precise timekeeping can be destroyed by hi-hats closed too loosely, creating a "washy" sound with no pinpoint definition of the time.

4. Interaction. Does the drummer work with the other instrumentalists, catching their riffs to create "punches" and "kicks" that make the music interesting? Does the drummer sometimes work in a contrapuntal fashion, playing *against* the riffs of the other musicians to create a syncopation? Both of these approaches provide musical variety, as long as they're done sparingly and with control. They can, of course, be overdone, creating the situation of a too-busy drummer trying to be a virtuoso instrumentalist and forgetting his or her fundamental role as a timekeeper. Too much of a good thing can be just as boring as not enough.

5. Listening. Does the drummer you're studying listen to what the other musicians in the band are doing, and give them space in which to do it? Most poor playing by club musicians is partially the result of musical egocentricity: They listen only to themselves, and only think about their own part. While this may or may not be done consciously, the result is the same: a very noncohesive sound from several musicians on stage, as opposed to a tight, unified sound from a *band.*

Once you've taken the time to study some of the drummers playing the kind of jobs you play and evaluate what they do that's good and what might be bad, it's time to go back and evaluate those same elements in your own playing. Incorporate the good and eliminate the bad, and you'll definitely have the edge over your competition!

On The Clock

> **I've never been able to understand the attitude that leads musicians to "see how much they can get away with" in terms of starting late or stretching breaks.**

I once had a club manager ask me, "Why is it that all club musicians can keep time, most of them can 'make time,' but damn few of them can *tell* time?" He was referring to problems he had experienced in the past with bands that were constantly late in starting their performances and/or took overly long breaks. I found myself at a loss to answer him, because I've never been able to understand such behavior myself (even though, over the years, I've worked in bands that exhibited it to some degree).

Playing music in a nightclub is unlike almost any other job or profession in most respects, but in one respect it is exactly the same: There are "working hours," and you should adhere to them. I've never been able to understand the attitude that does—regrettably—exist among a lot of musicians that leads them to "see how much they can get away with" in terms of starting late or stretching breaks. I believe that if you are going to be a professional, you should act in a professional manner. And the most fundamental demonstration of this is the simple act of sticking to your performance schedule.

Now that I've gotten all this sermonizing out of the way, let me go on to add that I also believe that the scheduling of a club performance can benefit from some flexibility in certain areas. That flexibility needs to be thoroughly discussed, understood, and agreed upon by both the band and management before an engagement begins. The time to bring up your reasons for shifting a schedule is not when the manager is upset with you for having done so. Let's look at some of the aspects of being "on the clock" in a club situation.

Starting On Time

Simply put, there is no reason, short of unforeseeable catastrophe, for not starting a performance on time. We all know that last-minute technical difficulties can and do arise—more often than we would sometimes like to admit. But forewarned should be forearmed. Since such problems arise, you should allow yourself time to deal with them prior to the performance. That time should be included in your total pre-show preparation time. Musicians should be responsible—and sensible—enough to realize that we don't go "on the clock" when the first chord is struck in the club. We actually start work at the point when we begin to get ready to leave home (or the hotel room) for the gig. That includes time to eat dinner, shower, dress, gather up instruments, load the car, travel, arrive at the club, set up mic's and instruments, deal with any technical problems, tune, socialize, etc. When you figure the variables there, you can see that they require a substantial amount of time—and there is simply no way to arrive at the club and start on time without allowing yourself that time. I don't mean to imply that a flat tire on the way isn't possible, or that some other inescapable calamity cannot occur (although you should allot a certain amount of travel time to account for possible mechanical problems, traffic, or whatever). I just mean that you should be aware of how long it *really* takes you to do everything necessary to play your first note on stage—and that you should consider yourself "on the clock" from the time you must begin.

Using myself as an example, for a 9:00 P.M. start in a club where my equipment was already set up, I'll eat dinner around 6:30, shower and dress at 7:30, leave my house by 8:00, and arrive at the club between 8:15 and 8:30. That gives me a full thirty minutes to check everything out on my kit, make all microphone connections, and still stop and visit with the "regulars" before we go on stage. I honestly believe that coming in at the last possible second before your starting time is not only unprofessional, but also affects your performance negatively. You need time to adjust—mentally and spiritually—to the club environment, and to the fact that you are now "on the job."

Breaks

Breaks are probably the biggest point of contention between bands and management in clubs. Even volume level doesn't seem to create as many problems. The simple fact is that many bands do extend their breaks, for a variety of "reasons," most of which are unacceptable to management. Generally, the time and length of breaks are spelled out in a band's contract, and club managers often feel that any deviation from the schedule represents a breach of that contract. If the length of the break is at issue, then I generally side with management: You've agreed to take breaks of a certain length, so that's how long they should be. I've always felt that, since you're in the club anyway, you might just as well be on stage playing as doing anything else. Although table-hopping and socializing with the clientele is an important part of your job, it certainly is of secondary importance to your primary responsibility: providing the musical entertainment.

I've known managers to use a stopwatch to clock the times a band started and ended its sets and breaks. I think this is carrying things to extremes, but I've come to understand the motivation for it. As an audience member, I've felt cheated when a band I was listening to took extended breaks. I was paying an "entertainment price" for my drink, and I expected to be entertained. This attitude is naturally extended to the club in general, so a "lazy" band can be directly responsible for the club losing customers.

It's also important to make clear that returning from a break "on time" doesn't mean getting up on stage at the appointed time, only to spend the next five minutes tuning, noodling, or finishing a drink. This should be taken care of *prior* to your appointed return time. By the time you are supposed to be playing, you should be ready to count off the first tune.

If your problems with management stem from a disagreement on *when* breaks should occur in the evening, then some negotiation is in order. Many contracts stipulate that each set will be a certain length, with a break occurring at a specified point. (In California and Hawaii, forty-five minutes on and fifteen minutes off was the standard; in the East, I've found forty minutes on and twenty off to be more common.) It's not unusual for management to stipulate that the sets must run from the exact hour (or half hour) starting point to the exact forty- or forty-five-minute break point, and then start again exactly on the next hour or half hour. In this way, it's much easier for management to keep track of how long the band's breaks are and to schedule other activities in the club (such as shift changes, which often must correspond to peak periods of business within the club).

Unfortunately, it's not always to a band's advantage to stop playing at a precise time. There are evenings when the momentum is rolling, and the crowd is "into" the entertainment. In such cases, bands often like to extend the set to take advantage of the "good vibes." In order for that to happen however, it is essential for you to have discussed such situations with management beforehand and to have received your approval to extend a set when you deem it appropriate. *How* you adjust the schedule should be discussed as well. You should not take a correspondingly long break after a long set; the length of the break should remain the same as usual. Instead, a later set might be shortened, when the intensity level is not quite so high.

I've played evenings that started with a standard set, featured two sixty-minute sets (due to crowd enthusiasm), and finished with a fifteen-minute "closer" set. As long as management received the total amount of music time that was called for, they didn't really care how we arranged it. They relied on my band's professionalism and on our ability to "work the crowd" (while meeting our contractual obligations at the same time). I think that this is the best arrangement for all concerned, since it is to both the band's and management's advantage to maximize the enthusiasm displayed by the audience. If they dance a little longer, they'll be all the more thirsty when they finally do sit down.

The bottom line on this issue is that it shouldn't be an issue. You should be professional enough to know when you are expected to perform—and to be there when it's time to be. Management may reasonably be requested to respect that professionalism and to give you a bit of latitude when it comes to scheduling (to your mutual benefit). As long as all of the parties involved work together with a common understanding, being "on the clock" should be an enjoyable experience.

The Etiquette Of Sitting In

Part 1: The Good Host

The thing you want to achieve is a smooth, enjoyable, and professional musical experience involving your guest.

One of the nicest things about working in the club scene is the sense of community that exists among club musicians, especially those who work steadily in the same general area. Probably the best expression of that camaraderie is the time-honored tradition of "sitting in" with other groups. Even if the musicians involved don't know each other, their spirit of openness and the benefits gained from the exchange of musical ideas encourage this practice among most groups I've seen or worked with. Naturally, there are a few dos and don'ts that should be observed, whether you're the guest drummer sitting in or the host drummer inviting someone to play with your group. In this chapter, I'd like to discuss some of the finer points of etiquette involved in being a good "host" to drummers sitting in on your gig.

Let's start by assuming that you're the drummer in a club group, and you are approached by a player you don't know who asks to sit in on a tune or two. Here are a few suggestions I would make:

1. Screen the potential guest a little and try to get a feeling for his or her competence on the drums. Ask what group your guest drummer is with, and what kind of music that group performs. Talk a little bit about equipment—anything to get some idea of your guest's credentials. Do this casually, of course, not as an interrogation. But make sure you feel good about letting this person play. Even with a guest drummer, it's still your band's performance at stake, and if a genuinely incompetent drummer gets up there, the entire band is going to look silly.

Remember too that you're working in a bar: It's important to determine whether or not the guest drummer is sober. Many an aspiring—but unqualified—amateur gets delusions of grandeur after a couple of stiff drinks, and the potential for damage to the kit and/or embarrassment to the group from such an individual is very high. Even if the potential guest player is a personal friend or a well-known drummer whose reputation is outstanding, if he or she is not straight, you should politely—but firmly—refuse. It's your gig and your kit, and that must come first.

Other members of your band will sometimes introduce a friend of theirs who plays drums, and ask if that friend might sit in. Generally, there is little problem here, because the band-member will have heard the drummer play and will have an idea about his or her abilities. Just be sure that your colleague knows that you still have final approval or disapproval of anyone using your equipment. This has never caused a problem in any group I've ever worked in, simply because we all respected each other (and each other's equipment) too much. Nobody wants a drunk or an amateur playing *their* axe, so they aren't likely to suggest that such a person play someone else's.

2. Once you've established the credibility of your guest, invite that person up on a break to check out your kit. A lot of drummers have a tendency to say, "Oh, I can play on anything; it's just a couple of tunes." Unfortunately, when they get up on the kit, they discover that they can't get comfortable with the bass drum pedal, or the toms are much too high, or some other factor is preventing them from doing a good job and enjoying themselves. There's nothing more embarrassing than being introduced to the crowd as a guest artist, and then looking and sounding incompetent simply because you aren't comfortable on the kit. Even if the player doesn't think it is necessary, ask him or her up anyway. You can use the pretext of wanting to explain some things about the kit before your guest plays it. In this way, guest drummers can discover that they cannot play at their best on your kit, and can politely withdraw the request to sit in (or decline your invitation, if that was the case), without "losing face."

3. While your guest is examining your kit, it's a good time to

discuss any limitations you'd like observed. You might not want any stands moved, or you may prefer that the drummer not play with the butt ends of the sticks. If you have any such requests, talk them over at this time. Don't wait until the drummer steps up to play with your band; there won't be time then and it would be unfair to your guest.

If you happen to know this player and are familiar with his or her technique, then there's nothing wrong with mentioning differences between your playing styles that might require limitations such as those I've mentioned. When I worked in Hawaii a few years ago, I often invited a local rock drummer to sit in with us. He played very hard, and used thick, heavy cymbals on his kit. I had a couple of thin crashes in the same places on my kit as his much heavier crashes were on his. I had to ask him not to use those particular cymbals when he played, lest he crack them. Since I had other, heavier crashes on the kit that he *could* use, he had no problem playing, and was very understanding and considerate about not damaging my thinner cymbals.

Once again, remember that while it's important to be a good host, it's even more important to protect your investment and your gig. Any truly professional player sitting in will understand that philosophy and respect it.

4. Get together with the rest of the band (or at least the leader) and your guest, so that you can discuss the choice of tunes your guest might perform. This should be done on a break, so that you don't disrupt the momentum of the evening's performance by bringing the guest up, and then standing around trying to determine what you all know. This only serves to make the band look amateurish, and to cheapen the "guest appearance" quality of the person sitting in.

This is also the time to discuss any details of your musical arrangements that might differ from what the guest is familiar with. The stock phrase "We play it just like the record" is rarely valid. Even though many bands play the same Top-40 material, no two bands play a song exactly the same way. It is simply a matter of courtesy to your guest (and insurance for your band's performance) to make sure the arrangements are clear in everyone's mind. If you plan to just "jam" together, it's important that everybody keeps an eye on everybody else so that cues can be exchanged. The thing you want to achieve is a smooth, enjoyable, and professional musical experience involving your guest. You don't want it to look and sound like amateur night at the Bijou.

5. If the drummer is someone you don't know, be sure to get his or her name, and any applicable credits (such as the name of the band he or she plays with), so that you or your bandleader can give your guest a polite and accurate introduction over the microphone. I don't think there's anything as unprofessional—and downright rude to your audience—as having someone appear to just walk out of the crowd and sit down behind the drums, and then to have the bandleader mumble, "We're gonna have John jam on a couple of things with us." The audience feels left out: Is this part of the show? Can anybody just walk up and play with the band? Does the band know this person? Has this turned into a private band party? At the very least, an introduction should be complete and clearly made, in the same way you would introduce a song or deliver any other message from the stage that you would expect your audience to understand: "Ladies and gentlemen, we'd like to bring up John Smith, who plays here in town with the so-and-so band. John's going to play some drums with us." If you're going to have a guest artist, make it a special feature for your audience.

Now let's take the case where either a personal friend or a name drummer happens to be in the audience, and you'd like to invite that person up to sit in. By all means do so, but don't take these individuals by surprise, calling them up over the microphone. Do them the courtesy of asking them privately first. Most players will appreciate the invitation, but in some cases, they'll have some reason why they'd prefer not to play. Putting a person on the spot in front of a roomful of people is inconsiderate and unprofessional. When you invite them personally, you not only exhibit your own courtesy, but you allow them the opportunity to decline your invitation gracefully, if they so desire.

As a general policy, you should be very clear about management's attitude about people sitting in. If you're on a long-term gig, you probably have fairly free rein about what you do on stage. However, if you travel, you may find that house policy differs from place to place with regard to guest artists, and it doesn't do you any good politically to create problems.

A lot of managers operate on the philosophy that if you let one person sit in, you'll have to let anyone else who wants to do so, and naturally that can lead to trouble. Therefore, the management asks the band not to let *anyone* sit in at all. You should respect this policy; after all, it's their club. (By the way, you can sometimes use such a policy—whether it exists or not—as a reason for turning down a request to sit in from someone you'd rather not permit on stage.)

You should never feel *obligated* to let anyone sit in at any time. It may not be a good night for it to happen, and again, the pros will understand that. If the evening's performance isn't going smoothly, it might not be a good idea to throw in any additional kinks. And realistically speaking, guest artists, no matter how talented, present a risk to the host band. There is always the possibility that the playing will not blend, and the performance will be disrupted. On the other hand, once in a while the guest appearance of a given drummer can spark an otherwise dull night for the band, and often boost the enthusiasm of the crowd as well.

The key to being a good "host" to visiting drummers is combining courtesy with common sense. You should show courtesy to your guest, to your band, and to your audience, keeping their best interests in mind when you make your arrangements with the drummer sitting in. You should also show common sense in the way you protect your equipment, your band's performance level, and ultimately, your gig, by the manner in which those arrangements are handled.

The Etiquette Of Sitting In
Part 2: The Considerate Guest

My band once arrived at a gig, only to find a local horn player already on stage and tuning up!

In the preceding chapter we talked about the points of etiquette involved in being the "host" drummer to another drummer sitting in with your group on your equipment. This time, we'll discuss those that apply when *you* are the guest drummer, either requesting an opportunity to sit in with a band or being invited by the band to do so.

There are several reasons why you might want to sit in with a group. The most common one is simply for the fun of it. There's a camaraderie between club musicians, and sitting in is the ultimate expression of that. Players who know each other can have a great time swapping licks and patterns, and players who don't know each other find this musical exchange the very best possible kind of introduction. Lasting friendships and musical associations have begun with an unfamiliar player joining the band just for a tune or two.

Another common reason for a drummer to sit in with a band is that drummer's own reputation. If a name drummer drops into a club, the bandmembers will often invite that person to sit in, in order to enjoy his or her abilities themselves (and perhaps to gain a bit of prestige by having that musician appear on stage with them). It's a sincere form of appreciation offered to the artist (and, at the same time, it's a nifty little bit of PR with the band's regular audience and management). If you have a strong reputation in town, you may very well be invited up by a club band; it doesn't just apply to top-name recording artists. Most cities have a "pecking order" among their club bands, and some bands just enjoy a better reputation than others.

Another reason for sitting in with club bands is to make your availability known when you're looking for a gig. In other words, sitting in can be a combination of public exposure and an audition all rolled into one. The group you sit in with may not need a drummer, but somebody else in the club might. The least that sitting in with various groups will do for you is get your name onto the "grapevine" of club players around town. In some cases, you can actually arrange to sit in with a friend's group on a particular evening and have potential employers come to see you. This is almost a "personal showcase," and it could save you a lot of audition time running around to various groups' rehearsal sites.

Another common reason for people asking to sit in is to show off for friends. There's nothing inherently wrong with this; we all have a certain amount of ego. If we have the talent to back it up, it's nice to be able to display it once in a while. Naturally, a major problem occurs when the skills aren't there to back up the ego.

Whatever your reason for getting up and playing with a band other than your own, there are several things to remember, in order to make the experience enjoyable for all concerned. Let's take a look at some of the conditions under which you might be sitting in, and how you should go about it.

Approaching The Band Yourself

There's nothing wrong with approaching the drummer in a band and asking to sit in on a couple of songs. Naturally, this should be done on a break and privately, so that you don't interfere with the band's performance. You should introduce yourself and briefly establish your credentials as a drummer, so that the host drummer will feel comfortable about allowing you to play. If the host asks you some questions, don't feel put down. Remember, a drumset represents a major investment, and besides that, the drummer has the good of the band to be concerned with. You wouldn't want just anybody off the street banging away on your kit, so be prepared to reassure your host about your competency. Don't be arrogant and assume that, because you play in the same town in such-and-such a band, this drummer will have heard of you and be eager to have you sit in. Always ask to sit in as politely as possible and be prepared to be turned down.

In some cases, you may be approaching a band in which you know some or all the members. In this case, it's generally much easier to ask to sit in, especially if the drummer is already an acquaintance. But don't interpret one or two opportunities to sit in as an open invitation. All too often I've been in bands where either real or self-imagined friends would come in, two or three nights a week, with their instruments under their arms, on the *assumption* that they could come up and play *anytime.* My band once arrived at a gig, only to find a local horn player already on stage and tuning up! Don't strain a friendship with other players by becoming a nuisance. At the very least, ask the drummer or bandleader each and every time, as though it were the first time, and take no for an answer if that is, in fact, the answer.

Before sitting in with any band, I always like to listen for several sets or even for a couple of nights so that I become familiar with the repertoire. Not only will that make your playing sound more polished when you do sit in, but it will allow you to suggest tunes for you to play from the band's own song list. This eliminates a great deal of hassle when you do get your chance to play; you won't be sitting around trying to figure out what tunes you and the band both know. Nothing maximizes the good feelings that can occur when you sit in more than being able to play with the band as if you were a regular member. The band will feel more comfortable, you will play more naturally, and the audience will be more impressed.

Being Invited By The Band

In some cases, you will be invited by a band or a drummer to come up and play. This may be due to your own reputation, or to the fact that you are a friend of one or more of the band's members. I can think of no higher form of flattery than a band's having enough confidence in my playing or respect for my reputation to invite me to join them on their gig. After all, they're taking a pretty big risk. No matter who the guest drummer is, anytime someone sits in on a gig, there is always the potential for disaster, and a group's gig is always on the line. If you've played with the group before, this situation is minimized, but if they are inviting you up "sight unseen" (or in this case "sound unheard") you should definitely feel flattered. Do your very best to see that their faith in you is justified.

On the other hand, you shouldn't feel obligated to play if you would prefer not to. Perhaps you're just out for a quiet night with friends and want to get *away* from playing; perhaps you wouldn't feel confident in an unrehearsed situation; perhaps this group doesn't play a style you care for. For whatever reason, you have every right to decline an invitation to sit in. Just remember to do so politely and graciously in return for the graciousness of their invitation. I would suggest leaving the door open for a future invitation; there may come a day when it will be *you* who wishes to sit in with *them.*

Before You Play

If you are going to sit in with the group, there are definitely some things you should do before you actually come up on stage to play. The first and most important is to come up on a break, along with the host drummer, and examine the drumset. I don't care how talented a player you are, the old saw that "a good drummer can sound good on any kit" is just not true. The drumset is the most personal of all musical instruments, being tailored to the physical attributes of the individual player. Drummers set up in such a wide variety of ways that it is not uncommon for one drummer to be terribly uncomfortable on another drummer's kit, and often unable to play at all. I tend to sit quite high, with my rack toms at a medium height and my hi-hat quite high above my snare. Drummers who normally sit low, with their toms low and their hi-hats just barely above the level of the snare, have found themselves physically incapable of playing on my kit. I would have an equally difficult time playing on theirs. The point is, coming up to sit in with a band and *then* finding out that you can't play well on the kit can make you look and feel very foolish. Finding out ahead of time that the set is impossible for you to play gives you the opportunity to withdraw your request to play (or decline their invitation) privately, with no loss of face or disruption of performance.

There can be some occasions when you know ahead of time that you're likely to be sitting in. In this case, it might not be a bad idea to have your own bass drum pedal in the car, along with a pair or two of your own sticks. But don't walk into the club with them under your arm; ask to sit in *first,* and then go back to the car and get them. Otherwise, it looks as if you're coming in *expecting* to play, which puts the host drummer in an awkward position. It's a rude thing to do to a drummer who is your friend, and extremely arrogant if you don't know the drummer.

Whether you know the drummer or not, once you decide that you can play the kit, always ask permission before you use the host's sticks, and ask if there are any limitations you should be aware of. Sometimes the host will ask you to be careful of a drumhead that's getting worn out or to stay away from a particular cymbal. Be sure to pay strict attention to the host's requests; it's common courtesy and good politics. You may want to be asked back. Also, ask permission before you make any type of adjustments or do any repositioning of stands. Some drummers are fanatics about keeping their kits inviolate; others are more flexible. It often depends on the type of hardware and how easy it will be for the host to find the original positions after you've played. Again, have some professional respect and courtesy, and if the host doesn't want things moved, don't move them. Either play the kit the way it's set up or don't play.

Once you've established the fact that you'll be able to play the kit, it's time to decide what songs you'll play. This should also be done on a break, before you actually come up to perform. Get together with the host drummer and the bandleader, and look over the band's song list. This is where listening to them ahead of time really helps. You can suggest one or two tunes that you know, and save a lot of stumbling around that would otherwise occur when you come up to play. In this way, the momentum of the performance is not interrupted by your appearance.

While You Play

No matter what you play, don't try to show off. If the tune calls for simple drumming, you'll make a better impression by playing simply. Perhaps in the tunes you suggest you can come up with one that lets you shine a little. You might even check out the possibility of a brief solo. Again, this is more likely with a band or drummer who already knows you or your reputation. Don't let your emotions get the better of your musical sense; Neil Peart fills don't belong in a Bruce Springsteen tune, no matter how well you can do them.

Be careful about the host's equipment; don't play too hard and break sticks or heads. If you do break something, be prepared to pay for it or replace it immediately. The resident drummer is most likely working the very next night, so you can't come back next week with a replacement head or pair of sticks from your own stock. Either come up with the cash on the spot, or arrange to provide a replacement item yourself before the next night's gig. That means getting it and delivering it to the host drummer. (And don't forget a sincere apology for causing the host the inconvenience of having to finish the night with broken equipment after your appearance.) This is what I would expect from a drummer who broke my sticks or heads; I would expect to do nothing less for a drummer whose equipment I damaged.

Lastly, whether you've requested to sit in or were invited to do so, be professional in your manner. Don't get half drunk and decide to impress your friends. If you're sitting in just for fun, let it be fun for everybody. If you're trying to make your name known around town by sitting in with various groups, make sure that a good reputation is the result. Treat this sit-in like an audition; it very well may be one. If you keep that attitude first and foremost in your mind, you'll maximize the good time for all concerned and reap all the various benefits—musical, emotional, spiritual, social, and professional—that sitting in can afford.

Hecklers And Hasslers

The "classic heckler" is a person who—for reasons unknown and indeterminable—has decided it's "pick on the band" night.

An unfortunate—and seemingly unavoidable—occupational hazard of performing in public is the occurrence of heckling or interference with your performance by members of the audience. How you handle such interference can often be a strong indication of your professionalism. The longer you're in the business, the better you should become at fielding jibes or comments from the crowd, or at handling more serious interference problems—if for no other reason than repeated experience.

Hecklers

Before we talk about how to deal with hecklers and hasslers, let's define a few terms. I define a "heckler" as someone who verbally interferes with your performance in any way. This could be someone who simply makes a lot of noise—shouting, whistling, singing bits of songs—*in conflict* with what you're doing. Please understand, I've nothing against an audience member "getting into" what my band is doing, and wanting to participate in some way. Singing along, clapping, showing appreciation verbally—all of these things are wonderful, as long as they remain within reasonable limits. But we've all experienced the unwanted "support" of the over-enthusiastic (and generally over-lubricated) patron who continually shouts at the top of his or her lungs, whistles at glass-shattering frequencies and volume, and generally becomes a nuisance. There's nothing malicious in the person's intent, but he or she is aggravating nonetheless.

Then there is the "irrepressible requester." This is the person who constantly shouts out a request for a tune you've already said (politely) that you don't play. Sometimes this person takes the patronizing approach: "Hey man, you guys are good. You can play it. Sure you can! You know, it goes...da da de dumm.... C'mon, you can play it." No amount of calm reasoning can convince this person that you aren't going to be able to fake the tune, and so the request is continually thrown at you.

Other times, the requester becomes insulted and belligerent when you don't perform his or her favorite tune. My pet peeve in this area is the patron who comes up to you on a break and initiates a dialog that goes something like: "Do you play (tune title)?" "No, I'm sorry. We don't." "Well, how about (other tune title)?" "No, I'm afraid not." "Man, you guys don't play s—t!" This dialog usually takes place after the band has been playing three sets of music to which the patron has been energetically dancing.

Finally, there is the "classic heckler." This is the person who—for reasons unknown and indeterminable—has decided it's "pick on the band" night. He or she will sit at a table and verbally berate the band for its choice of material, its wardrobe, the quality of its jokes, or any other element of the performance. The classic heckler may be drunk or sober (although is most often at least partially drunk), male or female, alone or with a party or date. (Most often, it seems, the classic heckler is a member of a small group, trying to "show off" for his or her companions.)

Hasslers

Hasslers are people who *physically* interfere with a band's performance in some way. Due to the potential for damage to equipment or injury to performers, they represent a greater problem than do hecklers. From my own experience, here's a list of hasslers with which you may be at least partially familiar:

1. "The Aspiring Musician/Singer." This is the person who grabs a mic' to "help the band sing," or tries to play one of the instruments uninvited.

2. "The Litterbug." This is the person who decides that an amp, keyboard, floor tom, or (in the case of a friend of mine who was *playing* at the time) the lowest bar of a marimba is just the perfect place to deposit his or her half-empty beer bottle.

3. "The Dynamic Dancer." Invariably, in a small club where there is no stage and the band must share the dance floor with the crowd, someone just *has* to do an imitation of James Brown—and requires more floor space than is available to do it. This person generally winds up bumping into the band, knocking mic' stands into the teeth of vocalists, tipping over guitars on stands, toppling cymbal stands, and the like. (And let me not forget the aspiring "go-go" dancers—male or female—who want to jump up with a band *on* a stage to demonstrate their moves for the benefit of an "adoring crowd"—who usually couldn't care less.)

4. "The Great Communicator." This is a variation of the "irrepressible requester." This person deems it absolutely imperative that he or she communicate a request to the guitar player—on stage and in the middle of that player's solo.

5. "The Commando." This is the worst of all possible hasslers: the individual who invades the stage for the purpose of fighting with one or more members of the band. I've played in clubs for over twenty-five years, and have been fortunate enough to have been in that situation only twice. But both instances were frightening and involved injured people and damaged equipment. In some cases, a fight that has nothing whatever to do with the band can "spill over" onto the stage or performing area, putting the band and the equipment at risk. (Witness the band playing behind chicken wire in *The Blues Brothers.*)

Dealing With Hecklers

When dealing with hecklers, you have several options. Which ones you choose to employ will generally depend on how great a problem the heckling is. As long as the heckling remains verbal—and assuming that it doesn't really disrupt the performance to the point that the rest of your audience is alienated—it's often best to ignore a heckler. There's no point in giving hecklers encouragement by paying attention to them. If a heckler gets no response from you, he or she may get bored and cease the heckling (or may leave, which you might consider even better).

If the verbal abuse is, in fact, disruptive, you may be able to take a "fight fire with fire" approach. This simply means that you engage in a verbal sparring match with the individual in an attempt to "put him (or her) down" and "shut him (or her) up." Quite often, hecklers annoy your crowd as much as they annoy you. If the crowd is on your side and can see you get the best of your heckler, you can actually gain favor in their eyes at the heckler's expense. Sometimes a quick barb over the mic' will do it: "What a carnival we have here tonight folks: music *and a clown!*" Other times, you need to really stop the action and focus in on the offending party so that you draw the audience's attention away from the disruption of *your* performance and onto *your disruption* of the heckler's "performance." It might go something like this: "Ladies and gentlemen, we obviously have someone here tonight who enjoys playing games, so we're going to pause just a moment to play a little game with him." Then, to the heckler, you say, "How 'bout it sir? Want to play a little game? We'll play horse. That's where I play the front end, and you just be yourself!"

Assuming that the heckler is sober enough to realize when he or she is being insulted—and that the rest of the audience is in support—this course of action usually works pretty well. Of course, if the person is too drunk to be aware of that insult, it won't do much good. (In that case, however, it might be time for management to evaluate the customer's condition and consider asking the patron to leave.)

Dealing with the "irrepressible requester" is usually a matter of negotiation. Your simplest solution, of course, would be to try to fake the person's request. If you can succeed—even moderately—you may be able to turn a heckler into a supporter. If you simply cannot play the requested tune (there have only been four or five hundred thousand songs recorded in the last twenty years, after all) then perhaps you could agree on an alternative from your repertoire—or even another "fake." As long as your format permits this (it's tough to do in a tightly rehearsed, segue-oriented show, for instance), it's to your advantage to try. You may gain points with the crowd for your effort, and you will at least stand a good chance of silencing your heckler.

Dealing With Hasslers

When it comes to dealing with hasslers, I firmly believe in the old adage that "an ounce of prevention is worth a pound of cure." The very first thing you should do when playing in a club for the first time is meet with the management and discuss their entertainment policies. This includes breaks, drink prices, sound levels, and all the other things you'll need to know, of course. But be *sure* to include a discussion of the club's policy regarding interference with the band. I've played in some clubs where there *was* no policy—and no sympathy. The management's attitude was, "It goes with the territory." I've also enjoyed the other extreme: In Waikiki, I worked in a club where the band had complete autonomy. If we didn't like how a customer was behaving, we had only to snap our fingers for a bouncer, and the offender would be ejected—no questions asked. In most clubs, the policy lies somewhere in between. Performers are expected to be able to field verbal abuse and to tolerate a certain amount of "over-exuberance" on the part of the crowd. But no one should be expected to suffer physical injury or damage to their equipment.

The Territorial Imperative

A great deal often depends on stage setup. There is what I like to call the "barrier syndrome." When you're on a stage, clearly separated from the audience by a railing or some other architectural feature—or perhaps only by the different floor levels—an audience generally stays in its "territory" and allows the band to enjoy its own. Most physical interference problems occur in smaller clubs that do not have a dedicated entertainment area as part of their layout. In these cases, the band must share floor space with the audience, and there is no clear delineation of "territory."

Surprisingly, it doesn't take much to establish your "territory" in these situations. Creating a "border" is often more a matter of psychology than the use of a physical barrier. I know one band that takes a set of stanchions and a white rope—similar to those used to guide lines of theatergoers to box office windows—to every gig where there is no stage. They set up the stanchions and stretch the rope around their playing area, creating a visible "line of demarcation" between themselves and their audience. The rope certainly would not physically *prevent* anyone from crossing the line, but it does *deter* people psychologically, simply by serving to define whose area is whose.

Personal Action

Assuming that you have the club's support when it comes to physical interference, you have the option to inform the offenders that they risk ejection if they don't stop bothering you. I believe that this warning should be given politely a first time, and very clearly and firmly if a second offense occurs. Three strikes and they're out.

If, however, there isn't time to discuss the matter—if someone is in the process of grabbing your cymbals or banging on your rack toms, for instance—then the appropriate action is up to you. If you know that you have a good relationship with management, and that they will support you, you have every right to defend yourself and your equipment. Just let your actions be guided by reason and cool judgment. For example, I recently played a club where an obviously drunk patron wandered up to the band (there was no stage), stood for a moment "getting into" the music, and then decided to help me play by reaching over to play bongo-style on my rack toms. I knew that the patron meant no harm, and that his fingers could certainly not damage my drums. Consequently, I merely smiled, and then gave him a "no-no" sign with my finger, as you would to a misbehaving infant. He apparently got the message and went away without doing further harm.

However, on another occasion, a patron who was obviously *not* drunk, but was trying to show off for his date, thought it cute to lean over from the dance floor to pinch my crash cymbals while looking at me with a "Do something about it; I dare you!" look on his face. I simply demonstrated what happens when someone's fingers make contact with a cymbal that is being soundly crashed with the butt end of a drumstick. He went away with his hand bones tingling up to the wrist and his date saying, "It serves you right."

Let me make it very clear that I am not advocating physical abuse or violence toward your customers. This could conceivably lead to lawsuits or to the return of that violence directed toward you. However, I do believe that there is a point beyond which no performer should be expected to tolerate rude or disruptive behavior, and certainly not physical interference with his or her person or equipment. Your best defense is clear communication with your bandmembers, with management, and with your audience. Be friendly, be patient, be tolerant—but be prepared to deal with any eventuality.

Regulars And Followers

More often than not, it will be your followers who will be first on the dance floor, and we all know what a joy it is to have someone break *that* barrier.

In the preceding chapter I described the kinds of people who can make a musician's life miserable, and yet who seem to be an unavoidable element of the music business. In this chapter, I'd like to talk about—and offer my gratitude for—the people who represent the opposite of that undesirable element: "regulars" and "followers." It is a fortunate circumstance that these people, too, seem to be an ever-present element of the music business. And in some cases, their presence can be the difference between a successful and enjoyable gig or an unsuccessful and tedious evening's ordeal.

Regulars

I define "regulars" as people who more or less "come with the territory." These are customers who frequent a particular club because they live nearby, or because they enjoy the particular atmosphere of the club, the style of music, the food, the management, the good-looking waitresses—whatever. In some cases, these individuals will patronize the club regardless of what band is performing there; in other cases, the presence of a particular band is an extra incentive to bring them in (or keep them away).

The benefit that "regulars" offer to you is that of a dependable, ready-made audience. When you go into a given room, you know that you can count on at least a certain number of people being there. If you work a group of rooms in rotation, there is also a psychological benefit to seeing familiar faces when you come in to play. Even if the regulars represent only a very small percentage of the entire crowd, they at least give you someone to relate to at the beginning of the evening—someone to make eye contact with right away. Their presence can put you a bit more at ease, and allow you to expand your contact from them out to the rest of your audience.

Very often, regulars spend a great deal of time and money in a single club. This ingratiates them with the management, and can, in some cases, give them a certain amount of influence. With that in mind, it's to your advantage to cultivate their favor as much as is reasonably possible. Remember that they will get to know your repertoire fairly well if you play in "their" room frequently. To avoid comments from them about your "playing the same songs," try to make sure that a few of those songs are their favorites. This doesn't necessarily mean that you should go out of your way to learn new songs. Fortunately, it almost always happens that something in your repertoire *becomes* a particular favorite with the regulars. This may be because something happens the first time you play it that involves them, making the song an "inside" joke between them and you.

We once played a club in which a group of regulars was celebrating the birthday of one of their "gang." His name happened to be Johnny, and his friends were joking about his reputation with the local ladies. When they asked if we could play a song in his honor, we immediately launched into Chuck Berry's "Johnny B. Goode," changing the lyric in the chorus to "Johnny *is* good." From that time forward, that entire group considered "Johnny B. Goode" as "their" song. Another example of this type of association occurred when we played Elvis Presley's "I Can't Help Falling In Love With You" as an anniversary request. The couple who requested it enjoyed it so much that night that they requested it every time they came to hear us.

Why go to the trouble of playing particular songs for regulars? I mentioned before the influence they can have with club management. That influence can be a very real factor in your continued employment in a given club. Fortunately, that factor has always been positive for my bands. On more than one occasion, club managers were persuaded by regulars to re-book bands I've been in because they enjoyed our performances. But I have also known of bands who were *not* rehired for gigs, based on poor reports given to the management by club regulars. You never want to alienate *any* member of your audience, but it is especially dangerous to alienate people whom the club management regards as favored customers.

The nice thing about paying attention to regulars is that you really only need to do so in a musical manner. Since they are regular patrons of the club, rather than of your band specifically, it is the club's job to cater to them as far as the occasional complimentary drink or other goodwill gesture is concerned. It's the club's responsibility to keep them coming in. But it's to your advantage to show them an *especially* good time when your band is performing there. Simply be friendly, acknowledge their presence as friends you're pleased to see again, and *be sure to play their song!*

Followers

"Followers" are those wonderful people who enjoy your band so much that they are willing to travel to different locations in order to see you. In other words, instead of waiting until you come to their club to play for them, they take the time and trouble to go wherever you go.

There is a long list of advantages to having "followers," not the least of which is that they can help make a gig in a new room much more comfortable for you. There is a certain insecurity that every band feels when performing in a club for the first time. Even if you have confidence in your ability and in your material, there are many unknown variables you have to deal with. How will the sound system handle the room's acoustics? Will this audience relate to your material favorably? Are these people "dancers," "watcher/listeners," or "ignorers"? Should you rely on the music and move from song to song as quickly as possible, or should you try to inject a bit of between-song humor to establish a rapport?

The presence of a group of your followers in a first-night audience can relieve a lot of the anxiety that you're likely to feel. For one thing, they can once again give you someone to relate to—at least to begin with—when it comes to establishing communication with your audience. That's not to say that you should restrict your efforts to them entirely. But you can *begin* with them, get a bit of a "vibe" happening, and then expand that vibe to include as much of the total audience as possible. More often than not, it will be your followers who will be first on the dance floor, and we all know what a joy it is to have someone break *that* barrier. Also, it's not uncommon for bands to rely on the input of followers in regards to volume levels and balances. Your followers should have a pretty good idea of what your best sound is like; they can give you at least a layman's opinion regarding any differences they hear in the new venue.

Even on a return engagement it's good to have the followers there, because they reaffirm to management that you are a "draw." If you can demonstrate that employing your band automatically ensures the club an extra ten or twenty guaranteed customers, that might carry significant weight when the management is planning its booking schedule.

How does a band go about acquiring followers? The first thing to do, obviously, is to entertain people at every performance. When people find you entertaining, they will look forward to hearing you again. If they find you entertaining *enough,* they'll be willing to go out of their way to hear you again. They will be willing to become followers. At that point, it's up to you to make it as easy as possible for them to do that.

The best way to promote a following is to establish a mailing list. There are many ways to do that—some more expensive than others. The simplest way is just to let your audience know that they can see any band member on a break and leave their name and address to be placed on the list. Have a notebook, a card file, or some other method of collecting names and addresses handy on the stage. I've known some bands to place table tents on every table in the club, with a form that could be filled out and placed in a special "mailbox" on stage. This can get a bit expensive, but it does look classy.

My bands have employed two different methods. At one point, we had someone associated with the band (in a non-musical capacity) handling a notebook. We simply pointed that person out, and asked our audience to see him in order to be added to the list. In the absence of such an additional person, we used a system involving business cards. We had cards printed up that were twice the size of normal business cards and perforated at their midline. The top half was our business card; the bottom half was a name-and-address form. We asked patrons to fill out the bottom half and return it to us, and to keep the top half. In that way, both the patrons and the band got contact information at the same time.

Once you've established a mailing list, be sure to keep the people on it posted as to your playing schedule. Some bands send a fancy newsletter, others use a simple calendar format. The main thing is not to let your followers lose track of you, or start to think that they are forgotten. Besides your playing schedule, use your mailing list to send holiday greetings and other goodwill correspondence. These people can very often serve as the "core" around which your audience will be built at gig after gig, so it's worth a little extra effort and expense to keep them interested in you.

Besides keeping your followers posted via the mailing list, you should definitely promote their goodwill when they attend your gigs. Naturally, you should play their favorite songs, in the same way as I described earlier for regulars. But you also need to remember that these individuals are *your* customers—not necessarily the club's. It might be a good idea to buy them a round once in a while. It's certainly important to socialize with them on breaks, and thank them personally for supporting you. You want them to feel that they are part of your musical "family," and that their presence is important to you. (This should be easy if you realize that their presence *is* important to you!)

Every band likes to have things go smoothly on a gig—to play comfortably and well for an enthusiastic and appreciative audience. Unfortunately, in the music business—and especially in the club scene—there are no guarantees that this will happen on any given night. But the contributions that regulars and followers can make towards making such gigs a reality cannot be overstated. Let's face it: We all feel better with friends on our side. Make it a policy to win as many friends as possible!

When Things Go Wrong

There are those occasions when some element in the equation isn't right, and the outcome is anything but "normal."

It's been my experience that, more often than not, things go pretty much the way they're planned to go on a gig. If your group is prepared, professional, and experienced, and if your audience is of a reasonable size and at least moderately enthusiastic, the night can be expected to go pretty well.

However, as we all know, there are those occasions when some element in the equation isn't right, and the outcome is anything but "normal." In some cases, the "problem element" may be under your control; in other cases, it may not. In *any* case, it's up to you—individually and/or as a group—to deal with the problem in such a way as to get through the night as successfully as possible.

I don't mean to imply that every single gig you ever play should seem like a sellout at Madison Square Garden. Some gigs are "really hot," while others are simply "another decent night." But there should be a certain standard below which you must not allow your performance to fall, no matter what. Let's take a look at some examples of the kinds of problems I'm talking about, and what you might do to overcome them.

Technical Problems

No band is immune to technical problems, and the more sophisticated your equipment, the greater the potential for such problems to arise. It's important that difficulties with equipment should not be allowed to disrupt the flow of the performance any more than absolutely necessary.

Recurring, seemingly uncontrollable feedback is probably the single most common technical problem that bands experience. Unfortunately, it's also the problem that's most obvious—and most annoying—to your audience. It must be dealt with quickly and thoroughly. If you have equalization on your system, and feedback occurs during a song, *don't* try to fine-tune the EQ at that point. Make your best guess as to which frequency is causing the problem, and kill it entirely. After the song is over, make some brief apology to the audience for the problem, fine-tune the EQ as quickly as possible, and get going again.

With systems that don't incorporate equalization, feedback is an even more common problem—and one that's harder to deal with. Speaker placement vis-à-vis the microphones, overall volume, tone settings, and effects (especially reverb) can individually or collectively cause feedback problems. Generally speaking, the best quick-cure for feedback in a song is to back off from the mic's, reduce the overall volume, and turn the PA speakers away. Again, try to do only what is immediately necessary during a song, and then deal with the problem in greater detail at the first appropriate opportunity.

Equipment failure, such as an amp that goes dead, is always a possibility. I was on one gig where the lead guitar player's amp died, and the guitarist simply refused to play through anything else. Instead of recognizing the fact that this was an extraordinary situation and plugging into a spare channel in the keyboard amp, this player chose to take a "prima donna" attitude: "If I can't get the right tone settings and sound, I shouldn't play at all." I can't condone this behavior. It only served to create a further problem for the band. The night had to be completed, so the guitar player had to be convinced to "suffer the indignity" of playing through a different amp. I prefer to take a "Let's do what we have to do for the benefit of the group" approach. In the case of equipment failure, you just have to do whatever you can to carry on and make the best of it. It may not be fun, and it may not sound "right," but there's no sense in making things worse by exhibiting a negative attitude. Besides making your bandmates miserable, such an attitude will quickly be projected to your audience. You're already working under one handicap; why give yourself another?

Specifically with drum equipment, the most disruptive failures generally involve broken heads. (Sticks are expected to break, and most drummers keep spares within easy reach.) Broken tom-tom heads can usually wait until the end of the regular set, because most drummers have several toms and can simply avoid hitting the broken one. Broken snare or bass drum heads, on the other hand, require immediate attention. I don't think there's a more miserable feeling in drumming than losing the bass drum. One *can*, if forced, keep a decent backbeat going on a small tom if the snare head breaks. But there's not much to substitute for the fundamental beat of a bass drum. About the best you can do is pound your lowest floor tom in place of the bass drum and suffer through the rest of the song. Then, politely inform your audience that you need to take a brief break to take care of the problem and will be back on as soon as possible. (If this unforeseen "break" occurs near enough to your regular break to get away with it, just make the repair period your regular break, and don't say anything to the audience. If the problem occurs within the first few songs of the set, however, you'll have to explain the problem.)

No matter what the equipment problem might be, deal with it calmly, quietly, and as efficiently as possible. If it's something that the audience is obviously aware of, you might want to make some comment to them—either a brief apology or some light remark to make the situation humorous. There's nothing wrong with including the audience; sometimes it gains you a bit of sympathy and reduces the amount of aggravation.

Personal Problems

There are those nights when—for some inexplicable reason—things just aren't going well with your playing. You just can't seem to "cut" parts that you've been doing perfectly well for months. Drums that haven't moved a fraction of an inch for six weeks suddenly seem to be in all the wrong places. Fills that you should be able to play "in your sleep" come out sounding ragged and amateurish. In short, you're having what's commonly called a *bad night*.

What do you do? I know several players who generally grit their teeth, gird their loins, and tell themselves: "I will *not* allow myself to have such a night. I *will* overcome this. I will now play *brilliantly*!" They then proceed to attempt fills that they would normally find challenging on even the *best* of nights. They usually fail at these, creating even more frustration and leading to even more futile attempts to play well. The evening is lost in a downward spiral of trial and error—mostly error.

I've mentioned before that a great deal of club playing can often be done on "automatic pilot," when your concentration needs to be involved with other things. In the "bad night" situation, it's sometimes possible to let that automatic pilot take over. There is something that I call "negative concentration" that can sometimes occur with almost all players. Basically, we hear something that doesn't sound right in our playing. That causes us to focus our attention more tightly on the playing, which, in turn, creates a sense of anxiety. We become hysterical, and nothing seems to meet our standards. We're trying too hard.

The solution is simply to sit back, relax, and let the months of rehearsal and hundreds of nights of repeated playing come to the fore. Just play the gig! Don't think about every beat you're playing or every nuance of every song. Don't reach for unusually intricate fills; play what's necessary to get the song across. If it's the same fill you played last night, don't worry about it. It worked fine last night, and it'll work fine tonight. Just get through the set, and get yourself back on track. Concentrating on the problem generally only compounds it. You *know* what to play and how to play it. Just do that—nothing more or less—and you'll be fine.

The other side of this coin is when you aren't paying *enough* attention to the gig. Even the "automatic pilot" must be present and operating in order to get things done. You have to have your mind on your work to the degree necessary to play competently and be entertaining. You owe this to both your bandmates and to your audience. You also owe it to yourself.

Audience Problems

Now we get into some problem areas over which you may have little or no control, but that have a major influence on your performance. Club bands rely a great deal on the rapport created with their audience for the creation of the "vibe" in the club on any given evening. If that rapport cannot be established or is disrupted, the night can very easily be blown.

Probably the most common problem with an audience is the *lack* of one. There's nothing more depressing than playing to a nearly empty room. But how a group handles this is a major indicator of its professionalism. I've seen many groups who simply cannot relate to a small crowd, and lose all interest in playing. They take—and very obviously convey—the attitude that "there aren't enough people here to make playing worthwhile." Other groups take a different approach: "Well, there aren't many people here, so we'll just fool around. There's no sense busting our butts." Often, these groups will just jam, ignoring the regular, rehearsed material. The result is that they sound loose, sloppy, and unprofessional. They are boring, and what audience they do have is very rapidly alienated.

What alternatives does a group have? Several. The first, and easiest, is to simply go ahead with the planned sets, and play them as energetically and competently as on any other night. The people who are in the room—be they 15 or 1,500—have a right to your best work. It doesn't take any special effort on your part to play the same gig you play every other night. That's actually the easy way out.

Another alternative, which is more difficult but perhaps more interesting for you, is to bring your audience into the performance. There's nothing wrong with being a bit informal or unconventional in your approach to the evening, as long as you do it with forethought and with taste (and as long as the act itself—cues, segues, intros, etc.—remains tight). If you have a small, intimate gathering of people out there, get them involved, and make it a more intimate performance. Speak directly to the audience, and see if there's something you might do for them that they'd especially like to hear. Take requests. It's alright to attempt songs that aren't in your repertoire, as long as the audience understands that they aren't and that you're trying the songs just to honor their requests. In a lot of cases, this will give you the opportunity to try material that wouldn't normally be in your style—which can be quite refreshing. Just don't be haphazard about these attempts; do them as well as you possibly can. Even if you can only do a part of the song an audience member requested, that person will likely be flattered that you made the attempt on his or her behalf. You'll have made a friend.

I'd much sooner play to a room of twelve "friends" than to a club full of people who are ignoring my band completely. I think that is probably the most frustrating situation that can occur in club playing. The sad fact is that there's no way to *force* people to be enthusiastic. All you can do—once again—is play your gig the best way you know how and hope that some people will get into it. Find a table of people who *do* seem to be into it, and play to them. Once a nucleus of people who are enjoying themselves has been created, the vibe will usually spread. But for heaven's sake, *don't* try to browbeat or "cheerlead" your audience into a false enthusiasm: "Hey, put your hands together out there…!" And don't beg: "Boy, we sure would like to see some dancers on the floor…." Your audience will respond in whatever way they feel like responding, no matter what you do. Don't be bitter, and don't give up halfway through the night. Do your best, and give a performance that you know is worth responding to.

When it comes to dealing with almost any kind of problem, the bottom line is: Do what you need to do to get through it, and go on from there. And remember, the bright side to any problem is how much better you feel when you've solved it.

Apples In An Orange Crate, Part 1

When we arrived at the club, the first thing we noticed was the number of motorcycles parked in front of it. They stretched, side by side, for the better part of two blocks.

Playing in a club band can be one of the most comfortable gigs in the entire music business. That's because club bands generally perform in rooms for which their music is appropriate, their performance fits the requirements of the room, and their own personalities are compatible with those of the clientele. And because club bands often work the same rooms for extended periods of time or for multiple repeat engagements, a certain sense of "homey-ness" can often come with the gig.

That is, of course, until you get a booking for which all the wonderful characteristics listed above don't apply. This doesn't happen often—thank goodness—with full-time, professional club bands, because they generally have a pretty good idea of their own musical and visual image, and either book themselves into appropriate rooms or rely on agents who share their understanding and will do the same. Unfortunately, weekend bands or club bands just getting themselves off the ground may not be so organized, and as a result may encounter inappropriate bookings with alarming frequency. The nasty thing about that is, a pro band is more likely to have the experience necessary to cope with such a situation; a semi-pro or newly formed band may be really thrown by it.

I've been playing in clubs over twenty-five years now. And I mean *all kinds* of clubs, with *all kinds* of bands. I've played in situations that weren't to my personal liking any number of times. (That sort of goes with this business.) But fortunately, I've only been in situations where the *whole band* felt like "apples in an orange crate" a very few times. Some were humorous, some were quite serious—but all of them were learning experiences. I thought I might share some of that learning, in the hope that I may help you to avoid having to get it "the hard way."

The Show Must Go On?

In 1975 I joined a theatrical show called Bonnie & Clyde & the Hit Men. It was an act that was born in an environmental dinner theater, where the show's characters were "on" from the moment the audience came in the door until they left. In other words, it was "showtime" all evening long. When this act was taken on the road, however, it was booked into hotel lounges trying to promote themselves as nightclubs. We did two shows a night, opening with three band numbers, and then bringing on the two "front" artists for the next forty-five minutes or so. Our first booking was a tremendous success, and we were elated, since this was the first time any member of the act had ever been on the road.

That elation was short-lived, however. At our very next booking, the manager informed us that he was happy to have the two shows each night. Then he asked what sort of music the band did during the dance sets in between shows. *Dance sets!?* Who said anything about dance sets? We were a *show act!* We weren't prepared to do anything "between shows." Needless to say, there was a bit of consternation as a result of this unforeseen development. Should we insist on doing things our way? Or should we swallow our pride, woodshed like crazy, and see how many songs we knew between us that could be whipped quickly into a couple of acceptable dance sets? Economics won out, and we did our best to come up with the dance music.

I wish this story had a happy ending, but it doesn't. The fact that we hadn't gone out prepared to do both dance music and our show turned out to be a fatal flaw. Although we struggled through that one gig, we were unable to get any further bookings within a short enough time to keep us solvent. Consequently, we had to return home and disband.

This was a simple situation of taking too much for granted, and not being prepared to react to unforeseen situations. Had we communicated better with the various employers at the time that our bookings were lined up, we would have understood their requirements and could have taken steps to meet them. At the very least, we could have informed them in advance that we did *only a show*, and discussed each booking further on that basis.

However, the experience was not without educational value. Eight months later, I got a call from the leader of the Bonnie & Clyde show. He had put together a new band—complete with dance material—and had updated the show as well. Bookings were already lined up across the country, and things looked great. Would I come back out on the road under those circumstances?

I did, and we had a wonderful time for the next ten months—generally speaking. As long as we performed in reasonably "classy" rooms where theatrical-style shows were familiar—or at least comprehended—we were very favorably received. But we learned another lesson on this second "tour," which was that sometimes a room can be too casual to accept a polished show. (Or, perhaps, your presentation can be too slick for its own good. It all depends on which side of the stage lights you're on, I suppose.)

We left a tremendously successful engagement at the Hyatt Regency Hotel in downtown Denver, and were rejoicing at the fact that our next booking was only a little over 100 miles away in Colorado Springs. (We were used to fourteen-hour treks between gigs; specialty acts are sometimes hard to route.) The club we were to move into was called "The Godfather's," and we thought that sounded like a good omen, since we had a gangster theme to our show. It wasn't to be.

When we arrived at the club in mid-afternoon, we found it all but deserted. The stage was adequate in size, but the only source of illumination was two floodlights dangling from the ceiling by their cords. The club itself was large, and probably would have accommodated a large crowd of dancers and/or seated audience members—were it not for the four pool tables placed directly across the dance floor from the stage. As a matter of fact, from stage level, we were looking not at our audience, but straight into a row of imitation Tiffany-style pool table lamps emblazoned with *Coca-Cola* logos.

Undaunted—well, *almost* undaunted—we set up our equipment (which included a great deal of stage decoration and props) and prepared for the evening's engagement. We were told that the crowd liked fairly loud rock music, which was okay with us, since the band was now prepared for that. What we were *not* told was that the "crowd" generally consisted of a dozen or so hardcore pool players and their dates, two or three passing truck drivers, and five "regular" ladies—who turned out to be topless dancers from the go-go bar down the block. None of these people had ever seen a nightclub act before.

We opened our first night with an optimistic outlook. The band played every rock tune we knew, and seemed to go over well enough. Nobody *danced,* but we did get a certain perfunctory acknowledgment from the patrons that we interpreted as approval. When it came time for the first show, we asked the manager how we could turn out the lights over the pool tables and direct the audience's attention more toward the show. He looked at us as though we'd asked him for directions to Mars.

Suffice it to say, we played the rest of the engagement to accompanying whacks, clicks, and thunks from the pool tables, and pretty much to the backs of our "audience." If they understood that we were trying to do a show, they were keeping that understanding to themselves. We took our leave at the conclusion of the week, secure in the knowledge that we had failed to raise the cultural level of Colorado Springs. But we had also learned another important lesson, which was that our booking agent needed to understand the nature of the clubs he was putting us into a good deal better before signing us up.

The Little Band That Wasn't There

Following my experience with the Bonnie & Clyde show, I took some time off at home. Then in 1976 I joined a Top-40 trio, consisting of acoustic and Fender Rhodes piano, bass, and drums. We all sang, and we could cut a surprising variety of material quite well, due primarily to the talent of the keyboard player and a certain cocky confidence that we all shared. Basically, we were willing to attempt almost anything, putting our own arrangement to it and coming up with our own sound.

Owing to the small size and musical versatility of this group, it should have been fairly easy to book us into small to medium-sized hotel lounges. And that proved to be the case—except in one instance. As can happen at any time in a band's career, a booking fell through at the last minute. Now, when you're at home and can just sit tight for a week, a situation like this generally is inconvenient, but not disastrous. However, when you're out on the road, as we were, it can be catastrophic, since you have to put yourself up at your own expense on top of not making any income. As a result, one tends to jump at any lifeline that is offered.

Our "lifeline" came in the form of an 11th-hour offer from a club about 100 miles away from where we were (which happened to be Yakima, Washington). Our agent informed us that it was a small club in a lumbering town called The Dalles, on the Columbia River, in Oregon. He couldn't tell us too much more about it, except that it wasn't attached to a hotel, and we would have to put ourselves up in a motel while we played there. He did know that they had a trio performing in the club at the present time that had been held over for a second engagement. That sounded encouraging—and besides, we were a little desperate. So we agreed to take the gig, even though it wasn't exactly what we were used to.

We closed our Yakima gig on a Saturday night. The club in The Dalles ran bands Tuesday through Sunday. So we had the opportunity to drive to The Dalles, check into a motel, unpack, and go out to the club to catch the departing band's last night. (This was quite a novelty for us, since we were used to coming into a new room "cold," after the previous band had left.) I'll never know what beneficent spirit was watching over us and made that situation possible, but I'll be forever grateful.

As I said earlier, we were a lounge trio. We did not use synthesizers, we had no lead guitar, and we put our vocals through a Shure *Vocal Master* PA system—not exactly megawattage or stadium volume. We played rock music, to be sure, but it was lounge-oriented rock, tempered by tasty arrangements and polished presentation. We were nobody's hard rock band.

When we arrived at the club, the first thing we noticed was the number of motorcycles parked in front of it. They stretched, side by side, for the better part of two blocks. From where we were parked, at the far end of that two-block distance, we could hear the band. Clearly. As clearly as though we were standing inside the club. We were almost afraid to *go* inside the club, but we did.

Our agent was right: There was a trio playing there. But having three musicians in the band was where their resemblance to us ended. You could hardly see them behind the mountains of equipment they were using, including a PA system that would do justice to a 5,000-seat arena, and synthesizers stacked to the ceiling. We entered at the end of an ear-splitting, pre-break closing number—just in time to hear a burly patron shout from the dance floor: "Hey, can't you guys get *heavy?!*"

As we scurried into a booth in the rear, one of the band members spotted us. Recognizing the panic in our eyes, he came over to our table and asked if we were the incoming band. When we said—weakly—that we were, he replied, "Thank God! We thought we'd never get out of here!" When we commented that we thought his band had been held over, he told us that they had been "requested" (in no uncertain terms) to stay when the band booked to replace them had taken one look at the club and kept on driving. He went on to say that if we were smart, we'd do the same.

He informed us that the clientele of this club consisted of two factions: white lumberjacks and Native American lumberjacks. Most of them were "bikers," and all of them hated each other. He also warned us against trying to make polite conversation with any female in the room, since, as he put it, "Every woman here has a husband, an ex-husband, a boyfriend, and an ex-boyfriend. And they're all here, too!" As a matter of fact, the keyboard player had had his bath interrupted one night when his motel room door was kicked down and three massive individuals stormed in with a greeting that went something like: "Stay away from my woman if you want to stay alive!"

Our newfound friend's story was interrupted when a scuffle arose on the dance floor. Someone broke a bottle, threatening a patron with the jagged end. It turned out to be the *manager*—a lady who looked as if she did this regularly—putting a rowdy customer out of the bar! Somehow, we knew that our first-set opener of "Java Jive"—and probably our last-set closer of "Free Ride" as well—wasn't going to make it with this crowd. We thanked our musical compatriot for his sage advice, and quietly left the club. We returned to our motel, packed and checked out, and drove 100 miles toward Seattle. Only then did we stop and call the club to let them know that we could not accept their booking after all.

This was the only time in my career that I, or a band in which I was a member, literally walked out on a booking. But the prospect of a week's stay in that threatening environment seemed to justify our decision. In this instance, we learned that "desperation" is a relative term, and that even though we were desperate for a source of income, we weren't desperate enough to risk our personal safety for it.

Not all bookings that turn out to be different from what the band expects are as dire as this last one. Not all are negative experiences that result only in lessons learned "the hard way." In fact, some even offer opportunities to overcome a challenge and emerge victorious. In the next chapter, I'll relate the story of such a booking, and how what could have been a very unpleasant weekend was turned into a successful and enjoyable gig.

Apples In An Orange Crate, Part 2

It was definitely a "class A" room. We immediately wondered what the heck *we* were doing there.

The preceding chapter offered some anecdotes from my past experience that illustrated what can happen when a band is faced with an unfamiliar or inappropriate situation on a gig. Some of those situations were humorous, and some were downright scary. But all of them provided some sort of learning experience for me.

In this chapter, I want to describe an episode in which a band I was in once again faced a classic "apples in an orange crate" situation. But this time, instead of being overwhelmed by the circumstances that created the situation, we were able to stop, evaluate the problem, and take action to correct it. Let me set the scene for you, and then I'll elaborate on what happened.

To begin with, my group was a '50s/'60s rock 'n' roll party band. We played a bit of contemporary music as well, but only tunes that still retained the fundamental '60s rock character (Bruce Springsteen, Billy Joel, Bob Seger, etc.). The instrumentation consisted of lead and rhythm guitars, a bit of '60s-style keyboard (heavy on the Farfisa and Hammond *B3* sounds), bass, and drums. We used no sophisticated synthesizer sounds, no electronic percussion, and no sequencers. We stressed vocal harmonies, as employed by the Beatles, Beach Boys, and countless generic doo-wop groups. Our approach was loose and easygoing, with an emphasis on classic tunes played for the sheer fun of hearing and dancing to them. Within this context, we were quite good at what we did and were pretty popular in the clubs we normally played. Those clubs were generally neighborhood taverns and bars in the northern New Jersey area, where the age group was basically thirty and up. The patrons of these clubs grew up with the '50s and '60s music that we played. And since so much of that music was back on the charts at the time (either in original form—from the soundtracks of movies like *The Big Chill*, *La Bamba*, and *Dirty Dancing*—or as cover versions from artists like Billy Idol and Phil Collins), the club patrons could get into our performances on both a contemporary and a sentimental level.

However, once in a while we would be booked into a room patronized by a different age group—or people who were into a different style of music entirely. In the situation of my story, we were faced with two completely different audiences at two different times in the evening, with a manager who wanted us to please both groups while attending to his specific instructions—which actually presented a third set of requirements!

The First Night

Instead of a local tavern, we were booked into a fairly classy floating restaurant built into a converted steam ferryboat. With dining rooms on several decks and a dance lounge up two staircases to the topmost level (naturally!), the boat offered fine food, entertainment, and a breathtaking view of the Manhattan skyline and other sights along the Hudson river. It was definitely a "class A" room. We immediately wondered what the heck *we* were doing there.

We were aware that the early part of the evening was going to require a "dinner set," since the lounge also included several tables and people would be eating dinner until well past 10:00 P.M. We certainly weren't a lounge band, but we were prepared to do some of our nicer ballads and quieter, medium-tempo tunes during this period of time. It called for a little restructuring of our set list, but that wasn't really much of a problem.

What we weren't prepared for was the fact that we were to alternate our sets with a DJ. Apparently, this room featured live bands only on weekends, and a DJ for the balance of the week. As a result, it had gained more of a reputation as a dance club than as anything else. We found out (after we had already arrived for the gig) that the manager had hired us because *he* liked '50s/'60s music. As far as the regular crowd was concerned, we were likely to be perceived as pretty alien.

Upon our arrival to set up on Friday night, we were met by the manager. Predictably, his first words were, "Keep it down guys; I've got people eating dinner." As I said, we were prepared for this. But we found ourselves wondering just how far "down" he meant, since the DJ was already playing music that seemed fairly loud by "dinner music" standards. At any rate, we set up at one end of the small dance floor, using what appeared to be the stage as best we could. It was only four feet deep, so I put my drum riser top on one end (extending out a foot or so), and we put the amps on the rest of the stage. The guys in the band stood in front on the dance floor. We played our first set, being excruciatingly careful to keep the volume down. We received a smattering of polite applause from the diners at their tables, and one or two couples actually got up to dance to the ballads. Other than that, there wasn't much response.

When we took our first break and the DJ took over, we were immediately made aware of our "alien" status in this environment. The recorded dance music kicked in with a vengeance—and at three times the volume at which we'd been playing. The bass was thunderous and inescapable, in classic "disco" tradition. (As it turned out, our "stage" was actually sub-woofer cabinets built along one wall!) The material being played was quintessential 120-BPM disco, segued from one tune to the next in a seemingly endless medley of indistinguishable songs. By this time the diners had left and had been replaced by the dance crowd: young people very much into trendy dancing, clothes, and personal image. This was not our normal type of crowd.

When we went back on after about twenty-five minutes of this competition, we were a bit daunted. We played what we thought was strong material from our repertoire, but it didn't seem to generate much enthusiasm in the crowd. We were also still trying to adhere to the manager's dictum to keep the volume under control. (He only seemed to be around our part of the boat when we were playing; where was he when the dance music was blasting?) While a few dancers seemed enthusiastic about our "different" material and its correspondingly different dance style, the majority of the crowd seemed to be waiting on the sidelines for the "real music" to begin again—when we took our next break.

Suffice it to say, the evening went on pretty much like this. Friday night's score was definitely: DJ 1, band 0. However, we were determined that this would not be the case on Saturday. We all tried to evaluate Friday's performance with an eye to what could be improved the next night.

The Second Night

We realized that we had come in on Friday as an "unknown quantity." The crowd didn't understand what we were about, and only found out when we actually started playing. At that point, all they discovered was that we were radically different from what they were used to. They weren't preconditioned to enjoy that; they only saw us as annoyingly unfamiliar. It was up to us to inform them—as soon and as often as possible—that we were something new and different—something that offered an exciting element of variety to the evening's entertainment. So on Saturday night, from the very start of the evening, we announced that "Tonight's music will feature the best of both classic rock 'n' roll and contemporary dance music," indicating that we would be providing the classic rock, while the DJ would handle the balance of the music. Instead of our differing repertoire giving us a handicap, we promoted it as an advantage.

We also checked with the DJ to see if he had any original or cover versions of '60s tunes. It turned out that he did, so we arranged for him to put those tunes on for a half-hour or so before we started playing (thus subtly "setting the stage" for our opening). During the balance of the evening, he continued to mix '60s tunes into his normal repertoire. He tended to rely more on the contemporary cover versions, but that was fine with us, as long as the material still tied in with ours.

In terms of our own playing, we realized that we had adhered a bit *too* closely to the manager's request to keep the volume down. Once the DJ's music had established an intensity level in the audience's perception, we had to at least match that, or seem wimpy by comparison. We still kept the volume down for the first set while people were eating. But after the first break (and following the first DJ dance set) we came back on much stronger, with tunes that were guaranteed dance motivators.

Once again, this called for restructuring our set list, but the strategy worked marvelously. This time, the dance crowd got into the idea of rock 'n' roll dancing, and we all had a good time. (Interestingly enough, we never heard a comment regarding our increased volume from the manager. He only approached the stage area once, noted the packed dance floor, nodded approvingly, and turned away.)

We continued in this mode throughout the evening, constantly reinforcing the "variety factor" of our appearance in that room, and constantly "pushing the envelope" when it came to performance intensity. As the DJ's music got hotter, so did ours. The crowd seemed to enjoy this "competition," and responded by dancing feverishly, buying a significant number of drinks (which made the manager even happier), and actually starting to request classic rock tunes from us. The final score on Saturday night was: band 1, DJ 0.

I guess you could say we "broke even" for the weekend. But by doing so, we were able to prove to ourselves that we could overcome the obstacles inherent in an "apples in an orange crate" situation if we applied a little thought and musical skill towards the problem. The happy ending to this story is that we were booked for several more engagements in that room!

Part 2: Dealing With Equipment

Concepts In Tuning

You simply cannot tune the drums exclusively for yourself, and not take your audience into account. After all, they're the ones keeping you on the gig in the first place.

Trying to advise people on how to tune their drums is a risky affair. Tuning is generally a very personal matter. There are no hard and fast rules, no absolute rights or wrongs. But I've received a lot of letters over the years inquiring about the best tuning for club work, and many drummers have come up to me on my gig and asked me how I got the sound I use. So I thought I'd pass on some of my general thoughts about tuning so you can take them under advisement for your own consideration.

Facing Reality

Any time you hear a drummer on record or in a live concert situation, there are mic's on the drums. Often there are electronic effects in use as well. If you're playing your drums unmiked, with no additional effects, you simply *cannot* hope to duplicate those sounds. You will only inhibit the projection, quality, and musicality of your drums if you try to radically alter the natural tuning the drums create for themselves. Remember that the audience should hear the drums clearly, with a pleasing sound, and with adequate power to balance with the rest of the band. Undue muffling and padding to get a "studio sound" will only force you to work twice as hard to get any projection, or simply make it impossible for you to project adequately at all.

A very good, funky drummer I know once came to me at the end of his set and asked how I had enjoyed the music. I had to tell him that the music was fine, but I hadn't been able to hear him play at all. He was genuinely surprised, and said he thought the drums sounded great. His exact description was, "just like the Steely Dan sound." I told him the drums might sound that way from where *he* heard them, but that the sound was incapable of carrying to the audience. He was understandably disappointed.

Tuning For The Audience

This brings me to a consideration that often seems to escape club drummers. When you're tuning your drums, from what position are you listening to them? In a live situation (again speaking of unmiked drums), you've got to be concerned with what the drums sound like *out front,* where the audience hears them. So many drummers describe the tuning they've achieved by saying how great the drums sound to *them,* seated *behind* the kit. It's physically impossible to have any idea of the projection, depth, or roundness of sound produced by the drums when you're listening from a player's vantage point. You have to listen from out front to hear the influences of the shell and bottom head, which combine to give a drum so much of its tonal quality. From behind, what you mainly hear is the sound of the top head reflected back at you. From in front, the audience hears the sound of the top head as modified by the depth of the shell, the resonance of the shell and bottom head, and the further influences of distance, room ambiance, and dozens of other acoustical factors.

Things you *can* hear from behind the set include the relative pitch of the drums as created by the tension of the top heads, how much ring is in each drum, whether a batter head is wearing out or suffering from a loosened tension lug, etc. But to get an accurate idea of what your audience is hearing, you have to have someone else hit the drums, and *you must go out into the room and listen.*

If possible, you should do this at rehearsal when the rest of the band can play a little too, so you get an idea of how the drums blend in. It doesn't have to be fancy. Anyone who can hit the drums in steady rhythm and step on the bass drum pedal will do. I usually have another bandmember do it for me, while the remaining players play through a tune. It isn't perfect, but it gives me some idea to work with. You simply cannot tune the drums exclusively for yourself, and not take your audience into account. After all, they're the ones keeping you on the gig in the first place.

I hasten to mention that if you *are* miked, then a certain amount of this is reversed. If your drums are top-miked, as they usually are with double-headed drums, then the mic's are *hearing* the drums from much the same position you are. In that case, you *do* want to tune the drums for your own ear, because that's the sound that will eventually reach the audience. Of course, you'll want to discuss that eventual sound with your sound engineer, so that the mic's can be EQ'd to favorably enhance the qualities you want from your drums.

Returning to live, unmiked drums, I'm a traditionalist when it comes to tuning. I believe a drum was designed to create a sound with all of its parts combined and working together: batter head, shell, and bottom head. Remove or modify any of these, and you're reducing the drum's ability to produce sound to its fullest capacity. There *are* certain situations where this is desirable, such as studio work and some concert applications, but I firmly believe that club work is *not* one of those situations.

Exploring The Variables

I believe the way to modify the sound of your drums is by the use of variables that still fit into the "traditional drum" formula. That is, by the use of different heads, different tensions, different drum sizes to begin with, different sticks played in different manners, and so on. I don't like heavy taping, padding, or the use of muffling devices in a *live* situation. All of these have their place, but your drumset in a dance club is not it.

Let me give you some examples of what I mean by variables. Look through the catalogs of the various drumhead manufacturers and you'll see several distinctly different models, with explanations of the sound they're designed to produce. It seems more logical to me to use a head that has an inherent muffling quality of its own than to buy a relatively live, bright-sounding head and then tape it up to deaden the ring. Just as an aside, let me mention that most players over-muffle their drums anyway. The "ring" that everyone is so afraid of is a large portion of the natural resonance of the drum created by head and shell. To *completely* deaden that serves only to destroy the drum's capacity to project through amplified music. My drums, especially the bass drum, ring like old field drums when played alone. But in the context of the band's playing, that ring is absorbed into the amplified sound. What the audience hears is a big, fat, highly projecting drum sound. They don't hear the ring, the *band* doesn't hear the ring, and even *I* don't hear the ring.

You should use the type and weight of drumhead that has the qualities you need to achieve the sound you want. If you hit hard, with heavy sticks, start with a heavy-weight head. Then talk about the quality of sound. If you want a good live sound, use a clear head, since coatings have a subtle muffling effect. If you want a flatter but otherwise unmodified sound, then go with a coated head. If you want deep punchiness, the "ring-out-and-die-quickly" sound, go with heads that feature built-in muffling rings. If you want more attack, emphasizing the stick on the top head, then try heads fitted with reinforcing "dots." But be sure in your own mind what you want from your batter head. Then buy the head that best serves to achieve that for you.

Let's not forget bottom heads. The bottom head is the primary resonator. It takes the sound produced by the top head (fattened and rounded by the shell) and gives it its last modification before projecting it out to the audience. The bottom head can radically affect the final sound of a drum, yet I think it's the most often-forgotten factor in many club players' tuning efforts.

Let me state categorically, once and for all, that unless your drums are miked, there is *no good reason* in the world for removing the bottom head from a drum in a club situation. Period. Some drummers believe that removing the bottom head increases projection. This is a misconception. When you remove the bottom head, you're taking away the drum's main resonating feature, and you're left primarily with the pure "attack" sound of the stick on the top head. The open-bottomed shell concentrates this sound and tends to direct it in more of a linear pattern than would normally occur with a two-headed drum. But remember, this sound is being created by taking *away* part of the total sound the drum is capable of producing, not by adding anything. And there is no way that a drum that has had part of its sound removed can project more than a drum left with all its sound-production capabilities intact.

Additionally, the type of head used on the bottom is the fine-tuning you give to your drum's sound. You can enhance the resonance by using a clear head, or diminish it by using a coated head. A thin head will allow higher overtones to carry, while a thicker head allows only the lower ranges to project. You should note that muffled, dotted, and other special-purpose heads are all intended to be batter heads, specifically designed to modify the sound of the stick striking the drum. They *don't* belong on the bottom of your drums if you intend to get a clear, projecting tone. Of course, since every rule can sometimes be broken to your advantage, be aware that if you have to play a low-volume gig, you might be able to maintain a decent drum sound by using a non-resonant bottom head, rather than padding up the drum or muffling the top head, which generally changes the sound more radically.

I'm a firm believer in using the right tool for the job, and this includes using the right drum sizes for the sound you wish to obtain. I've heard some very unpleasant results from tightening up a 12" tom in an attempt to get a high, concert-tom sound that would have been expected of an 8" or 10". All that was achieved was a 12" drum that sounded like a saucepan. Conversely, I've heard drummers tune a 13" or 14" rack tom very loose and muddy, trying to get a depth that the drum was simply incapable of producing.

Each drum size has its own natural range of pitches you can reasonably expect to obtain. If you try to get higher or lower than the drum can handle, you're defeating the purpose of tuning. Tuning a drum should be an attempt to get the best possible sound out of it—using all of its potential, and varying it only enough to achieve a pleasant variety of sound relative to the other drums.

Michael Derosier, formerly of Heart, once told me he disliked multiple-drum sets with drums only an inch different in diameter, because it simply wasn't possible to achieve a noticeable variety of pitch from one drum to the next. I agree with that. I play a set consisting of 8", 10", and 12" rack toms, and 14" and 16" floor toms. My drums differ two inches in diameter, and at least two inches in depth as well. This enables me to tune each drum to its maximum potential *individually*, and almost automatically achieve a pleasant variety of pitch around the kit.

Remember, your drums are a musical instrument. Let them work *for* you in the manner for which they were designed, and you'll maximize your sound. Don't over-modify them, or try to achieve—in a live situation—sounds that are the products of outside technology. You're live, so let the drums be live, and you'll enjoy a lively reaction from your audience and your musical colleagues.

Cymbals For Club Drummers

The wider the variety of music that you play, the greater the demand is going to be for different cymbal sounds.

"Using the right tool for the job" is especially critical when it comes to the selection and use of cymbals on a club set. After all, you can make your drums work for many different situations through tuning, head choices, and muffling. Unfortunately, there isn't that much flexibility with cymbals—what you hear is what you get. You need enough cymbals to cover all contingencies (though not necessarily all on the kit at the same time). The wider the variety of music that you play, the greater the demand is going to be for different cymbal sounds, which means different cymbal types, weights, and sizes. As your imagination and creativity develop, you'll have to add the cymbals you need to make it happen. There just isn't a way to cut corners here. So let's go back to basics and talk about the selection of cymbals for a club drummer.

We'll assume that you are a good player—one who knows how to use cymbals *tastefully* (i.e., selective use of bell, shoulder, and edge for variety in ride and crash patterns) and *properly* (i.e., glancing blows to avoid cracking crash cymbals). We'll also assume that your band plays a wide variety of musical styles. What do you need to know when considering your cymbal setup?

As far as cymbal sound selection goes, there are two schools of thought—the *individual/variety* school, where each cymbal has a distinct and unique sound quality of its own and doesn't really relate to the others, and the *ensemble* school, where although each cymbal has its own voice, it still is complementary to each of the others, creating a choir-like sound from the total cymbal setup. There are, of course, variations, such as an ensemble setup with a single odd cymbal for effect. Each of these schools of thought has merit. Therefore, you must select your cymbals based on how you wish to project your own sound image, what your band needs from you acoustically, what may have been the original sounds used in the music you tend to perform most, and so forth. Once you have decided what you want to create, you can go about selecting the individual members of your cymbal choir.

Ride Cymbals

The ride is your foundational cymbal. It can carry the beat, propel a soloist, drive the dancers, and color a tune—all depending on what it is and how you use it. Each of the major cymbal companies offers a wide variety of weights, sizes, and types, but be careful when examining cymbal company advertising. Don't be sold on a description of the sound properties of a cymbal unless you know that the properties are what you actually want and need. I don't mean to imply that cymbal ads are misleading. I am only saying that you, as the buyer, need to understand your requirements fully, so that you can evaluate the ads and read the catalogs intelligently.

For example, if you are playing in a situation where the band is amplified and you are not, then you wouldn't want a flat ride or ping ride. These cymbals are specifically designed to reduce the buildup of overtones, and emphasize the sound of the stick against the cymbal. If you have to project in a live, unmiked situation, you'll need a powerful ride cymbal, such as a medium to heavy ride. You may wish to consider a "rock" model, which usually is fairly heavy and generally features an oversized bell. The bell is good for loud bell-ride work, and it also maximizes the spread and sustain. These cymbals *do* build up overtones, but they are absorbed into the general mid-range ambiance of the amplified music, and what the audience hears is good, strong ride-cymbal projection.

On the other hand, don't use a full-bodied cymbal for small-group jazz or quiet lounge gigs. Here, the flat ride or ping ride might be just the ticket. "Dark" or "warm sounding" rides are also good for soft, expressive gigs. They give nice support to a vocalist or instrumental soloist, since they aren't as bright as a standard cymbal of the same weight. For louder applications, the sharper, more piercing sound of the standard variety is generally more desirable.

Hi-Hats

Club drummers do a lot of work on hi-hats, both with their sticks and with their feet. So the hi-hat needs to be clear and precise, with the legendary "solid 'chick' sound." To get a good "chick" sound, you need a medium to heavy top cymbal, a heavy bottom cymbal, and some way to avoid air-lock. Hi-hat stands incorporate tilters to help out, but I prefer using hi-hat cymbals that have some provision in their own design, such as Paiste's *Sound Edge* (with a scalloped edge to prevent air-lock), or Zildjian's *Quick Beats* and Sabian's *Flat Hats* (both of which use heavy, flat-dished bottom cymbals with no bell, and with holes drilled into them to allow air to escape).

An acoustic problem occurs when you need a lighter-weight top cymbal for quick sticking and distinct open-and-closed definition, such as is required for funk patterns. The heavier the top cymbal, the longer the decay and the muddier the sticking response. For straight 8th- or 16th-note ride patterns, the heavier top cymbal works fine. For jazz, funk, or swing, a compromise must be reached between a good "chick" sound and good stick response on the top cymbal.

Crash Cymbals

Any cymbal catalog will offer you an array of crash cymbal types and descriptions. You'll see terms like: "crash," "crash-ride," "dark crash," "fast crash," "splash," "China type," and "swish." These terms are created by the cymbal companies in an effort to describe each model roughly according to its individual sound, size, and weight. A very thin 8"-diameter cymbal would be a splash, a slightly thicker 16" cymbal would be a crash, and an even thicker 18" would be a crash-ride.

I personally place crash cymbals into only three categories: punctuation crashes, sustain crashes, and exotic crashes. I base these categories on the way the player *uses* the cymbals. A "punctuation" crash is any cymbal that is used for a quick accent where the musical statement made by the cymbal is intended to be sharp and brief. A "sustain" crash is any cymbal that is meant to ring out after being struck, in order to support a longer musical phrase rather than a single accented note. In the context of these categories a 16" crash might be a sustain crash for the drummer in a lounge trio, but it would be a splashy punctuation cymbal on a louder rock gig.

The classification of each cymbal must be relative to the other cymbals in the setup. My "exotic" category includes Chinas, pangs, swishes, splashes, bell cymbals, cup chimes, crotales, and the other little goodies the cymbal companies have been offering lately.

Cymbal Setups

Now we come down to it: What sort of cymbal setup do you need in a club situation to get a good variety of sound? You need as many cymbals as it will take to provide all the sounds required in the music your band performs. This isn't as flip an answer as it sounds. There is no hard and fast answer, but a few guidelines do apply. I would say that a club drummer needs, at a minimum, one punctuation crash, one sustain crash, a good set of hi-hats, and an appropriate ride cymbal. I've seen players using a single crash, but even on a small or low-volume gig, a single cymbal of any size can't really function properly as both a punctuation and a sustain crash. Besides, one crash all evening becomes very boring tonally.

When selecting crashes or rides for your kit, keep in mind that weight is critical. Too many club players have inappropriate cymbals—an occupational hazard when you switch styles of music or change bands often. If your cymbals are too thick, they'll sound overly loud and ringy, and they'll lack delicacy. If they are too thin, they'll have no carry or sustain, and you'll risk breaking them.

Let's say your band generally plays in one type of club, where you perform moderately loud dance music. Your cymbals are medium to heavy in weight, and they work just fine for you. But the band occasionally works weddings or parties, and the cymbals just seem overbearing in that situation. You don't necessarily have to go out and buy lighter cymbals, if you can be flexible with what you have. You can use a 17" or 18" medium to heavy crash as a ride cymbal on the lighter gig, and leave the 21" rock ride at home; a 16" splash on your loud gig might serve as a sustain crash at a wedding, and so on.

Unfortunately, it's tough to go the other way. There's no way a complete set of thin cymbals that might be right for a lounge gig is going to cut a loud rock club date, unless you're miked up. In that case, make sure this includes being miked up back *at yourself* (with a good monitor), so that you can control the urge to hit the cymbals too hard. Otherwise, you'll just destroy them, and they will have died in vain, since they can't get through the amps on their own no matter how hard you hit them. This is not to say that some thin cymbals don't have a place on a loud gig—just use them in moments when they can be heard, such as soft crashes in ballads where sustain is not desired, or quick-choke splashes punctuating up-tempo tunes.

Cymbal Placement

Once you've selected your cymbals, no matter how many or what type they are, you should consider their placement on your kit, and how they will integrate with the drums. There are two ways of considering a setup: musically and geographically. You should take both into account.

"Musical" consideration means placing certain cymbals near certain drums, so that musical patterns played on those drums can be supported by those cymbals. I tend to place my larger sustain crashes over my floor toms, so that as I end a fill on the deeper drums I have the power of a large crash immediately at hand.

"Geographical" placement refers to the ability to reach any cymbal easily and comfortably from any drum. I have a couple of examples of this on my kit. The first is my "cymbal tree," which puts my ride and four crashes on one stand to my right. When positioning my hand comfortably to play the ride, I have only to elevate it an inch or so and turn it a few degrees to the left or right to strike the sustain crash on either side of the ride. Another two inches of elevation and a flick of the wrist gets me to my two punctuation crashes placed directly above the two sustains. I don't have to move more than four inches in total to strike any one of five cymbals. The second example of geographical consideration is the placement of a 17" crash-ride, which is sort of an all-purpose cymbal in my setup, directly in front of me, so that I can easily reach it with either hand from the snare or the hi-hat. I do place my one exotic crash (an 18" China) high up and to my left. But I can get away with this because of the infrequency with which I use it as compared to my other crashes.

When it comes to the ride, I believe that a ride cymbal should be placed as low and close to you as the drum setup will allow. I can't think of anything less practical than having to reach up high and away from you to play a sustained ride pattern. It just doesn't make sense physically, considering that you're fighting gravity, time, distance, and muscle strain, all at the same time. Keep the ride low and close, and you'll have much less work to do. This allows you to save your energy for creative ride patterns, instead of having to use it just to keep a steady ride going at all.

Proximity should be a major consideration in crash placement, too. You should never have to lean or reach to hit a crash cymbal, and under no circumstances should you ever lose your balance, or your sense of *center*. The reason they put wing nuts and booms on cymbal stands is to make *them* adjust to *your* needs, so take advantage of that capability. You should be able to sit comfortably, extend your arms in a relaxed and natural manner, and strike everything on your kit (drums and cymbals alike) with as much power as is necessary. I play a large kit (seven toms, snare, bass, hi-hat, ride, and seven crashes). Yet I can sit in the middle of it, close my eyes, and without doing anything more than extending my arm, hit anything on the set.

To me, this is the way every drummer should feel on his or her kit, and the cymbal setup is the key. Most drummers set their drums up first (concentrating on the *drums* being close and comfortable), then go about fitting the cymbals above the drums in whatever way they can. I disagree with this procedure. I think that the cymbals deserve *at least* equal attention, and the setup of the kit should be considered as a total unit. Then, after careful selection of the proper cymbals for your job, you'll be ready to perform at your best!

Taking Stock

> **Your kit isn't set in concrete. The reason drum stands are adjustable is to allow flexibility and experimentation.**

Music is a progressive art. The tools of a musician's trade need to be flexible enough to keep up with the changes. With this in mind, it's important for drummers to periodically take stock of their tools and how they're using them.

You should evaluate your drumset not only from a musical standpoint, but from a physical one as well. Is it comfortable to play on? Does it contribute to your playing, or does it inhibit you? It's sometimes difficult to convince a drummer even to consider changes in his or her setup, and I often hear the comment: "I've played this same setup for ten years...it fits me." That may be true, but my reply is always, "Are you playing the same music you've played for ten years?" If you really make an objective evaluation of how you feel on your set in relation to what you're currently trying to play, you may find that a slight change will facilitate those new licks you've been reaching for. The limitations might not be in your playing, as much as in the way the drums are set up to receive that playing.

Setups aren't the only thing that need periodic evaluation. Sticks and heads, stick grip, and even overall set tuning should be considered for possible change or experimentation in order to achieve a *state-of-the-art* condition in your playing. Here are some ideas you might want to consider when it comes to experimenting with your equipment.

Overall Drum Setup

This includes the height and angle of your drums and cymbals. For many years I played a fairly traditional big band-type setup, with my drums all fairly low and flat. I sat in sort of a Buddy Rich crouch, coming down onto each drum from above in a nice arc. I liked this arrangement for playing R&B, but as I tried to do multiple-tom power fills in newer rock tunes, I couldn't get enough speed and attack on the toms. So I started raising them, about half an inch at a time. In a period of four months I raised them over four inches. I also slightly increased the angle of the rack toms towards me, and in this position I definitely got more punch and projection. The floor toms and the snare also came up, so as to keep the overall plane of the drums the same as they were before relative to each other. I raised my cymbals just enough from their original position to keep the same distance between them and the drums that there had been. I didn't change the angle on my cymbals at all.

When you consider changing your setup, don't begin by actually moving drums. Begin by closing your eyes and playing in the air over your set, to get a feeling in your wrists, arms, and shoulders as to where the drums should be. I call this "forecasting." Give yourself time to come to some conclusions physically, as well as mentally. If you do this for a couple of weeks, you'll have a solid impression of where the drums should go, and when you really put them there you'll discover there is no strangeness in the new position. The drums will feel like you've been playing them that way all along. For example, at one point in my career I wanted a pair of high-pitched toms over my hi-hat. I practiced on my set as though they were there, and when I finally got them, they were already a part of my playing.

Seat Height

When I needed more projection from my bass drum, I went to a more consistently heel-up style of playing. But when seated low, I found this very fatiguing, because I was literally lifting my entire leg for each beat. When I raised the seat, I found that I could get down onto the pedal with real power and a minimum of overall leg movement. Raising the seat also kept me in good relative position to my new higher snare drum level. I did have a problem playing flat-footed on softer or slower tunes, because of the acute angle created by sitting high and trying to put my heel down. I solved this by wearing shoes with fairly high heels. Thus I could sit high for full leg extension when playing toe-style, but the high heel reached down to the heel plate if I wished to play flat-footed. The higher heel also gave me a feeling of greater leverage for the flat-footed style.

I have talked to other drummers who have experimented with lowering their seat, saying that it gave them more power in their feet and the effect of raising the drums at the same time. Without exception, these were players who played heel-down exclusively, and with great success. If you play that style, then take that into consideration. A higher seat doesn't automatically mean more power, unless you play the kick style I do. I have a very small foot, and I've never been able to get enough raw power with my heel down.

Tom Heads

Head selection is an area where you can experiment widely at minimum cost. Start by objectively evaluating the sound coming from your toms. Is that sound what's happening in the music you're trying to duplicate? If not, try making some changes. Heads not only create sound, but affect stick response, and thus your action around the toms. For many years I used clear Remo *Emperor* top heads on all my toms—tuned fairly tight for good response and lots of resonance. I used smooth white *Ambassadors* on the bottoms. They sounded great for quick sticking in funky music, but they did have a sort of ringy quality. When we got into more rock and I was doing fast fills, my band complained that the toms sounded tinny, with no depth or fatness. So I switched to *Pinstripe* heads on all the rack toms, and put the clear *Emperors* on the bottoms. The *Pins* gave a fatter initial sound, and the thicker heads on the bottom cut out some of the higher overtones—keeping the resonance, but only in the deeper frequencies. I didn't use *Pins* on the floor toms because I found them a bit muddy in the larger sizes. But I got a nice, fat rock 'n' roll sound out of the rack toms, and with the projection afforded by their new higher position, it really made a big difference. I compromised for the R&B that we still played by tuning the heads a bit tighter than I might for rock. In this way, I could play them more lightly and still get a good sound. In the ensuing years I've experimented with dozens of other head combinations—switching brands and models. My object has always been to use whatever best suits the music being played at the moment.

Bass Drum Heads And Beaters

At one point in my career I needed more projection from my bass drum (because my band started working larger rooms and playing stronger music). As mentioned, I raised my seat to give me more pedal power. I also began to experiment with beater balls. For many years I'd used a hard felt ball. When this proved insufficient in volume, I switched to a heavy wood beater ball (and eventually to a hard, clear acrylic ball), with a piece of moleskin to protect the head. The moleskin was insufficient protection, and I very quickly went through the first layer of the twin-ply head. After unsuccessfully trying a series of commercially available protective "impact pads," I eventually wound up taping squares of cut-up drumhead material to the bass drum batter head. As these wore away (mainly due to friction-induced heat created by the acrylic beater) it was a simple matter to replace them. I've utilized this system ever since, whenever my playing situation calls for high-volume playing. For lower-volume gigs, I simply switch back to a traditional felt beater.

Sticks

Sticks are your direct link to the drums. What you do with them, and how they interact with your drumheads and cymbals, make up the greatest portion of your actual sound. Although sticks are the most readily variable tool of our trade, in my early career I subscribed to the theory that if a certain stick fit my hand and I worked well with it, I shouldn't use anything else. This was a misconception that proved extremely limiting. For example, I used the Regal Tip *J.C.* model for several years. It was a fairly light nylon-tipped stick—very fast for quick sticking and very nice on cymbals. But when it came to laying into tom-toms for rock fills, it didn't have the mass I needed to get the fullest tones out of the heads. So I turned the sticks over and tried the butt ends. This worked, but the cymbal sounds were lousy that way, and the tapered ends of the sticks tended to blister my fingers. So I swallowed my traditions and tried a larger stick: the *JoJo Rock* model, with wood tips. (I used the *JoJos*, which are Regal Tip "seconds," to save money while I was experimenting with stick sizes.) I found that the heavier stick and bigger bead let me work the toms to greater advantage, while still getting decent response on my snare and cymbals. I was able to put less force behind my playing (thus tiring less) and yet get greater sound out of the drums. For nights when we played at incredible levels, I could turn them over and play butt-end without injuring my hands, since their taper was less than that of the *J.C.s*. But the larger sticks did not sound good on ballads, nor were they appropriate at all in the earlier sets. So I kept both sizes of sticks on my set, and used whichever was right for the situation. As my career went on, I experimented with lots of sticks, mallets, brushes, and specialty items (multi-rods and the like). The idea is always to have—and be comfortable with—the right tool for the job.

Grip

I was trained traditionally, and I played a sling-mounted marching snare drum for nine years, so the traditional grip works well for me in most applications. But as I began working on power fills (and especially after I raised my rack toms) I found that matched grip gave me more power and speed around the set. I worked on developing my total playing using matched grip, and I eventually reached a point where I could switch grips at will—even within the same song—in order to get the best response out of each pattern or fill. I also experimented with reversing the sticks, not just for added volume, but for the very different sound the butt ends got out of drumheads. By playing this way, I'm always using my sticks to their fullest potential.

These are just suggestions to get you thinking. The whole point is to realize that your kit isn't set in concrete. The reason drum stands are adjustable is to allow flexibility and experimentation. This is the one area in which drummers enjoy a distinct advantage over other musicians. If a guitarist or keyboard player wants to change his sound, it usually requires the purchase of fairly expensive effects equipment, or in some cases, a new instrument. On the other hand, drummers can achieve significant changes in sound for a minimal investment—often at no cost at all. You'll find your playing abilities can progress more rapidly and with less effort if you keep your mind open, and keep your drumset on *your* side.

Periodic Checkups

The breakdown of items that are seemingly insignificant in and of themselves can have a major impact on the function of your drumkit.

I once had an awkward experience while playing a weekend gig: My bass drum pedal broke near the end of a tune. Of course, this wasn't the first time that such a thing has happened; over the years I've broken pedal straps, snapped beater shafts, or simply had the beater slip out of its clamp on the pedal. But this time, there was a new reason. The felt ball on this particular beater was held on by a nut at the top of the shaft, and the nut had come off, allowing the ball to work loose.

The situation was—luckily—easily remedied. I simply replaced the beater ball on the shaft, then put the nut back on and tightened it down securely. But this episode got me to thinking about the various elements of a drumkit that we take for granted, but that can disrupt a performance or damage other equipment if allowed to "go bad." It made me realize how important it is for drummers to perform "periodic checkups" on their kits.

Let me make a distinction between "periodic checkups" and "periodic maintenance." Most people—myself included—generally define "periodic maintenance" as cleaning shells and cymbals, oiling pedal hinges, changing heads, etc. "Periodic checkups" involve going deeper, and really examining all the parts of a kit that are subject to wear, loosening due to vibration, gradually going out of adjustment, etc. As I said earlier, many of these items are often taken for granted; we probably wouldn't even think about them unless—or until—they break. The problem is that, when they *do* break, they can create major headaches. Performing periodic checkups on these parts should eliminate those headaches *before* they occur. Let's take a look at some of the things you might want to examine carefully on a regular basis.

1. Bass drum pedals. A bass drum pedal is a source of several potential problems. Every time you set your pedal up and/or take it down, you should examine it thoroughly. Check to see if the beater shaft is clamped tightly. Make sure the beater ball is still firmly attached to the shaft. (If there's a nut, tighten it. If the ball is machine-fixed, make sure that it isn't loosening up; you'll need to replace the beater if it is.)

Check the pedal linkage. If you use a chain-drive pedal, make sure that the bolts connecting the chain to the axle and the pedal plate are not wearing through, and that their nuts are tight. If you use a leather or nylon strap-drive pedal, check the straps carefully for wear at any point. Straps will wear thin where they bend around the tip of a pedal, and their adjusting holes can stretch out around the bolts that connect them to the pedal and axle. It's much better to replace a strap before a gig than to have one snap in the middle of a tune. If you use a pedal with a metal linkage, such as the Ludwig *Speed King*, be aware that the bent metal "strap" can wear thin where it contacts the pedal and the axle. Remove it periodically and check the points at which that "strap" folds over on itself. Also check the small pins over which it fits; they can become worn as well. If a metal pin breaks on a gig, there's nothing you can do to repair it, so it's critical that you find and correct any weak spots ahead of time.

If your pedal's spring linkage is exposed, be sure to check it. I use a pedal on which the spring is attached to the axle by means of a small, triangular loop of steel that fits over a small pulley. Until I learned to watch out for it some years back, that steel loop used to wear right through the pulley—and once wore partially through the pulley's axle—before I realized what was happening.

While we're talking about the spring linkage, don't forget to examine the spring (or springs). The weak point on a spring is at each end, where the spring connects to the tension adjustment and the axle. If the "hook" of the spring is starting to wear thin, replace the spring.

Hinges need more than oiling. A hinge is designed to move up and down, which is the action that the hinge connecting a heel plate to the rest of a pedal should have. Unfortunately, many drummers don't play exclusively in an up-and-down motion; many move their feet from side to side as well. (This applies to hi-hat as well as bass drum pedals.) Consequently, the hinges—especially the hinge pins—receive a sideways torque that they were not designed to withstand. As a result, hinge pins can become weakened, and the hinges themselves can get "stretched out," causing the connection between the heel plate and the pedal to become loose and sloppy. If left uncorrected, the hinge will ultimately break, rendering the pedal useless. Hinges can easily be replaced if necessary; often the hinge pin is all that's needed.

2. Cymbal sleeves. Most of us cherish our cymbals, and we take great pains to care for them. Yet at the same time, we tend to take for granted the cymbal sleeves that protect our cymbals from grinding against the threads on cymbal-stand tilters. It's easy to sit down at the kit, look up at the tilters and say, "Yup, they're there." But what condition are they really in? If you tilt your cymbals toward you—as most drummers do—you see only the side of the sleeve that receives minimal wear: the side facing you. The cymbal actually rests mainly on the *other* side. It's not unusual to find that one side of a sleeve will be virtually new, while a sizable area of the other will be completely worn away—exposing the threads below. This can happen with rubber, nylon, plastic, or any other type of sleeve material—including the fancy plastic combination-sleeve-and-nut devices that come on many stands these days. I carry a length of clear aquarium hose that works wonderfully as replacement sleeves; I simply cut it with a pair of scissors and install the new sleeve whenever I see any wear on an old sleeve.

And while we're talking about cymbal protection, don't forget about felt washers above and below your cymbals. Make sure they are big enough to prevent any contact between the bell of the cymbal and the metal washers above and below it on your stand. Felt washers do get worn thin after a while; don't neglect this cheap form of protection.

3. Hi-hat clutch. The hi-hat clutch is another item that is heavily subjected to wear, but that we often don't think about until it strips out completely. Pay attention to the "feel" of your hi-hat while playing. If you can't seem to get a secure pull on the top cymbal, examine the clutch to see if it's starting to strip out in the center. You should also be able to tell if you are having to tighten up the bottom nut more and more. Don't wait for the clutch to fail on a gig—leaving you without a functional hi-hat. Replace it when you first notice substantial wear. (This is one item for which I *always* carry a spare.)

4. Cases and straps. Most drummers don't think about their cases very much. The drums go in, the drums come out, and that's the name of that tune. But without your cases, your drums are vulnerable to damage from handling, weather, etc. So treat your cases with the respect they deserve. When giving them a "periodic checkup," you should look for punctures that could develop into rips, rivets that have pulled out, adjusting holes in straps that have stretched, etc. There aren't too many cases around still using leather straps, but if you have such straps on any of your cases, look for places where the leather is wearing thin. This usually happens in the buckle area. Any repairable problem with a case (or drum bag) should be dealt with; otherwise replace the case. (I offer some suggestions for case maintenance and repair in a later chapter.)

5. Miscellaneous items. If you use patch cords of any kind, you should check them from time to time. Modern *XLR* (or "cannon") connectors are pretty sturdy, but ¼" phone plugs are notorious for coming apart. Open up the connector and make sure that the wires are firmly soldered and that the parts of the connector itself (case, leads, pins, body, etc.) are all in good shape. There's nothing more frustrating than losing a microphone or an electronic device on a gig simply because a patch cord got tugged slightly and came apart.

I sometimes use a Tama *Power Tower* drum rack, which has small, black plastic balls threaded onto the ends of all the clamp-tightening handles. I almost lost two or three of them before I discovered that the vibration of normal playing tended to loosen them from their threads and cause them to fall off. Now I simply check each one as I set up the rack. It seems a small thing, but if one of the balls were to come off and the tightening arm fall out of the clamp, the clamp would be useless—and so would be whatever drumkit item it was supposed to hold.

The point of this last example is that the breakdown of items that are seemingly insignificant in and of themselves can have a major impact on the function of your drumkit. "For want of a nail, the shoe was lost; for want of a shoe, the horse was lost; for want of the horse, the rider was lost; for want of the rider, the battle was lost." Don't put yourself into a position of losing your drum battle because you didn't check those small details. Perform your "periodic checkups" thoroughly, and go to your gig with confidence—knowing that your kit is as ready as it can possibly be.

A Drummer's Survival Kit

When you need something, be it a spare part or an aspirin tablet, *you need it now,* not tomorrow night.

Every drummer I know has a collection of small tools, spare parts, and other miscellaneous paraphernalia that he or she carries around in some manner. Usually the stuff is loose in a trap case, which may or may not be accessible during performance. Generally, these items accumulate because at some earlier date, something broke on the set, and the drummer didn't have what was needed right then to fix it. He or she had to jury-rig, or do without the broken piece of equipment for the rest of the night, and then repair or replace it the next day. A spare was brought in as insurance against a similar breakdown in the future.

I'm referring mainly to items like hi-hat clutches, rubber or plastic sleeves for cymbal tilters, tension rods, and other parts subject to constant wear or extreme pressure. Bass drum pedal springs, straps, and hinges are also notorious for inopportune breakdowns. And often the drummer's "collection" will include some non-musical items, like small hand tools, cords, and plugs.

It's great to have all these items, but they're worthless if you can't get to them in a hurry—when you need them. They don't do you any good in a trap case stored in a back room of the club, or worse, in your car or your garage at home. I believe every drummer needs some sort of "survival kit" stored in a small container that can be *kept on stage and is easily accessible.*

I keep my kit in an old-fashioned wooden fishing-tackle box I purchased in the sporting goods section of a local surplus store. The forty-odd dollars it cost was one of the best investments I've ever made. Measuring 13" high, 16" wide, and 11" deep, with a carrying handle on top, it's large enough to hold all the things I need to work with in an emergency, but small enough to keep up on my drum platform. I installed a small hasp and padlock on it, and when I change locations, I use it to carry my microphone and other fragile equipment that I don't want bouncing around in my trap case.

I especially like the tackle box because it's divided into small drawers and sections, so it's easy to keep different pieces of equipment organized as to type and function. The portability of the box gives it another important advantage. I can keep *special use* items in it, such as mufflers and sound effects that I use only for studio work. I know that no matter where I go or what I'm playing, I'll always have whatever I need immediately at hand.

I'm going to describe the items I carry with me, strictly as an example. These are the things I've found useful over many years in clubs—including a long stint of road work, where finding replacement pieces on short notice can be *very* difficult. You probably won't need everything I list here, or you might want to substitute some other things appropriate for your situation. But you'll get the idea of how much can be easily carried, and how well-prepared you can be.

Drum tools: Drum keys, a crank-type "speed key," a hex-wrench, various Allen wrenches.

General tools: Straight and Phillips screwdrivers, pliers, wire cutters, a six-foot measuring tape, a roll of duct tape.

Spare parts: Extra hi-hat clutch, bass drum pedal springs, assorted felt washers, wing nuts, tension rods, rubber and hard plastic cymbal stand sleeves, metal washers, nuts and bolts, nine-volt batteries. (All small items should be kept in individual plastic boxes.)

Special-use items: Various external drum mufflers, large beaded metal chain (for sizzle effect on cymbals), bicyclist's cuff-clip, electric metronome (for establishing tempos during rehearsal of new material).

Personal items: Comb, pad and pencil, knife, fork, and spoon. (Ever play a long rehearsal or session where food was sent in but no one thought of utensils?)

Electrical items: (I handle the lighting for my band.) Various spare lamps, three-way plugs, adapters for grounded to non-grounded plugs, Christmas-tree flasher plugs, electrical tape.

Items transported: (These are items that are carried in the box during moves, but are used on stage during performance.) Microphones, various mic' and speaker cables, six-channel equalizer.

The pharmacy: This is a special section I maintain as a service to the whole band. There's nothing worse than arriving at work facing five hours of performing with a headache, upset stomach, or a cold coming on. And the smoke, dust, and air conditioning in a club can wreak havoc even on a healthy throat and respiratory system. So I try to have something on hand to cover all the minor maladies and injuries that musicians seem especially prone to:

Halls cough drops—for general dry throat and smoke irritation.

Chloraseptic anesthetic lozenges—medicated, for serious sore throats.

Aspirin—for headaches and muscle aches.

Di-Gel—(in rolls) an antacid for upset stomach.

CoTylenol—a cold remedy, and good decongestant for relief of allergy-type sinus problems. It doesn't make you drowsy as some antihistamines can do.

Chapstick—air conditioning blowers can destroy your lips.

Vaseline hand lotion—the same goes for your hands.

Visine eye drops—for eye irritation from smoke and dust.

Band-aids—for minor cuts and scratches. You can get a small box of assorted sizes.

Mercurochrome—an antiseptic for minor wounds.

Tweezers—for splinters, and also handy for minor repair work on tiny items.

Adhesive tape—for creating bandages, and protection from blisters.

Gauze pads—for dressing burns and larger cuts.

The particular brands listed above were selected because of their effectiveness, and the fact that all are available in small, easily stored containers.

Though this may seem like a lot of extraneous stuff to keep on stage, remember, *you're isolated up there.* When you need something, be it a spare part or an aspirin tablet, *you need it now*, not tomorrow night. And you can't run to the local store to get it. Especially if you're traveling, you need to be prepared for all the problems that can crop up during a performance. The survival kit I've described is a way to be self-sufficient and self-contained with a minimum of space consumed.

Dealing With House Equipment

The key to using a house kit successfully is finding out as much as you can about it in advance.

As you progress in your club drumming career and encounter a wider and wider variety of working situations, it's not unlikely that you'll come up against an opportunity—or a requirement—to use a house drumkit. How you approach the use of that kit—and how you prepare yourself—can make the difference between a successful and enjoyable gig and a totally miserable experience.

I want to start by differentiating between using another drummer's kit—perhaps on an off-night gig where a steady band plays the regular nights—and using a "house kit." When playing on another drummer's kit, you generally make any and all arrangements (as to how much of the kit you'll use and what can be removed or readjusted) directly with the regular drummer. Management usually doesn't get involved in these arrangements.

On the other hand, I define a "house drumkit" as one that the club itself has provided for any and all drummers to use on a regular basis. In some cases, the use of the house kit is optional; the club makes it available should the drummer wish to use it. In other cases, use of the house kit is mandatory. If you are given the option, there are pros and cons to be considered before you make a decision. If you *aren't* given the option, there are ways to make the use of house equipment more comfortable and acceptable. Let's examine some various ways to approach each situation.

Optional Use

Some clubs offer a house kit as a convenience to incoming drummers. (These clubs generally have a house PA system, and not infrequently have amplifiers for the other instruments as well.) Obviously, a house drumkit *is* convenient—especially if you're traveling—since you don't have to lug your kit in and set it up. In fact, if your entire tour or out-and-back series of gigs can be booked in clubs with house kits, you don't even have to take a kit on the road with you. This can make your travel arrangements much simpler. The negative side to all this convenience is that, if you don't bring a kit with you, you are *totally at the mercy* of whatever equipment is provided in each club.

Many drummers feel that the worst part of using house equipment is the unfamiliarity; nobody likes unpleasant surprises. One is comfortable with one's own set, and no other set—no matter what the quality—can quite provide that level of comfort. I can't argue with that; all I can say is that you have to balance the value of that familiarity against the convenience offered by the house kit and make your decision accordingly.

If you do decide to use the house kit, the key to doing so successfully is finding out as much as you can about it in advance. If the club is in town, get over there a few days before your gig, and see what the kit is like. If you can listen to someone else playing on it, that would be better; if you can get the chance to play on it yourself, that's better yet. You need to know how well the kit suits you physically, how the hardware adjusts, how the drums are tuned, and generally all the details that will tell you whether or not you can perform to your own satisfaction on the kit.

Even though it may not seem very "artistic" to say so, the actual *sound* of the kit can be fairly low on your list of priorities. After all, tuning can generally be adjusted or adapted. More important is whether or not the drum throne or snare stand will raise or lower to a comfortable position for you, or whether the tom-tom holders are solid—rather than weak or stripped so that the toms will only hang at one angle. You need to know whether the cymbal stands can be positioned in such a way as to put the cymbals where you want them (and whether the stands will support your cymbals if you're bringing in your own). Make sure that the legs on all the drums are secure; there's nothing much worse than playing on a bass drum that slides—or collapses to one side—due to a faulty spur.

Many drummers feel secure about working on a house kit, as long as they are able to make a few changes and/or bring in some of their own equipment. You'll need to discuss this with management to determine their policy regarding such changes. For example, if you can't live with the heads on the kit, can you replace them? If so, who pays for the heads? (If the club does, the heads stay on the kit; if you do, you take them with you when you leave.) What about replacing some items on the kit with your own? Many traveling drummers carry their own snare, cymbals, and pedal, so most clubs are used to that and don't object. But if you want to start dismantling the kit piecemeal and replacing parts of it with pieces from your own, the management may simply prefer that you go ahead and bring in your whole kit.

If you can't physically examine the kit before you arrive at the club to play, you *must* make it a point to call ahead and talk to someone who can give you as much information about it as possible. Management personnel may or may not be qualified to tell you about it; it will be up to you to ask your questions as simply as possible so as to get the kind of information you need. An alternative method is to call ahead while the band currently on the gig is still performing and talk to that band's drummer. This might take a bit of scheduling, but it's certainly likely to get you more accurate and useful information.

The potential for getting a good drum sound easily should be something that you consider before you decide whether or not to use a house kit. Assuming that the house has a sound system and mikes up the kit, it's logical to assume that the house sound tech will have worked with the kit and will be able to offer the best possible mix from it. This is a very positive consideration. The other side of this coin, however, is the possibility that the drum sound that the technician likes and the drum sound that *you* like may be very *different* sounds. The house kit may be tuned with a lot of muffling for miking purposes, while you prefer an open, unmuffled sound (or vice versa). If you and the sound tech can reach a compromise in order to achieve a sound you can both work with, then you'll be in good shape. If the sound tech (or house management) is adamant about not changing the sound of the house kit, you may wish to bring in your own kit as an alternative.

Mandatory Use

Clubs that make the use of house equipment mandatory are usually those that employ more than one band per night. For example, many cities feature "showcase" clubs that present several bands each evening. (It's rare that you'd get a steady booking in such a club; you'd more likely be in for one night or perhaps one weekend.) In "showcase" clubs, the use of a house kit speeds up the changeover from band to band tremendously. (Unfortunately, if you are the second or third drummer in line on a kit on a given night, you're faced with the problem of not having enough time to readjust the kit to make it comfortable for yourself. You're also likely to have little time to re-tune the drums to achieve "your sound.")

I have played steady gigs in extended-hours clubs where the first band played a regular 9:00 P.M. to 2:00 A.M. schedule, and the after-hours band played from 2:00 A.M. to 7:00 A.M. There was no time for a changeover of equipment, so a house drumkit was used. (In one particular case, the club rotated the schedule: One band played early on Friday and late on Saturday. Equipment setups and breakdowns would have created a scheduling nightmare for all concerned, so the club simply had a complete set of band equipment on stage and left it in place all the time.)

It's also possible that you might get a steady booking in a lounge in Las Vegas, Atlantic City, Reno, etc. You're likely to be one of several bands using the same stage—and the same equipment—over the course of an entire day and night. In this type of situation, the management is interested in keeping the entertainment going constantly. This means that the equipment must be miked up the same way at all times, so that one or two sound technicians can have a fair chance at running the sound for a variety of acts.

Your main concern in a mandatory-use situation is practical, rather than musical. The decision of whether or not to use the house kit has been made for you, so now you *must* be concerned with making yourself as comfortable as possible, so that you can do the best possible job with what you've got. Again, discuss with management what items can be replaced on the set. You may be able to use your own cymbals, but only if you don't have to move the existing cymbal stands. You may be able to use your own snare, provided it doesn't create a problem for the sound technician by being too different from the snare the board is set for. I've never heard of anyone objecting to a drummer using his or her own pedal, but be prepared for the possibility that the sound tech might not like the sound your beater produces.

Don't get the idea that I think all sound technicians are uncooperative and demanding. Most are quite the opposite, and the *really* good ones are as concerned with getting a good sound as you are. But there are those who are stubborn about the sound *they* want to hear from the drums—regardless of who the drummer is or what the group's style might be. They are more concerned with controlling the volume and tone of the kit for the benefit of the room's acoustics than they are about the creative quality of the music. There's not much you can do about this, since they are the ones "pushing the buttons." Your best bet is to be as diplomatic as you can, obtain whatever concessions they might grudgingly allow you, and look forward to the next gig.

All of the suggestions I made earlier about finding out about the kit ahead of time go double in a mandatory-use situation. Your basic philosophy here should be "forewarned is forearmed." Keeping an open mind, a sense of humor, and a cooperative attitude will also help to make the best of a given situation. And who knows—you may get to a club and discover that the house kit is the one you've always dreamed of playing! Stranger things have happened.

Simplifying Set-Ups

Let's start by assuming you have achieved the ultimate setup. How do you keep that arrangement for the next gig?

One of the aspects of club playing I enjoy the most is the change of scene that goes along with moving from club to club. But while the constant variety of location, audience, and playing situation is pleasant, the hassles of breakdown and set-up are not. (For drummers who have to relocate on a nightly basis, those hassles are multiplied even more.)

Let's start by assuming you have achieved the ultimate setup. As it stands now, your kit is exactly the way you want it, with all stands at the proper height and angle. All drums at the right spacing, all tripods and legs arranged without tangling. How do you keep that arrangement for the next gig?

Obviously, you have to mark the position of all drums and stands. All of the major drum companies now incorporate some form of locking collar onto their stands. These collars interlock with the stand fitting below, to hold the position of the drum or cymbal at the proper height and angle. If you have this type of hardware, then 75% of your work is already done. But if your hardware pre-dates memory systems (and a lot of mine does), then you have to create your own. There are several methods of doing this:

1. Gaffer's (or duct) tape. This is the cheapest and quickest method. Once your drums are set up the way you want, you simply place a loop of tape around each stand above where it fits into the next stand section. This will give you the point at which the sections meet so you can put them up that way next time. A simple ink mark on the tape, corresponding to the tightening bolt of the section below, will give you the exact horizontal adjustment of the stand as well.

One of the drawbacks to tape is that it can slip under the weight of the stand if the tightening bolt loosens or lets go completely. As the stand section slides down, it can force the tape out of place. It is also aesthetically offensive to some people to see tape on drum hardware (although the piece need not be large). This, of course, is up to you. But this system is quick to install or remove, making it especially good for marking *experimental* position changes that you might not want to keep.

2. Hose clamps. For several years, many drum companies used standard hose clamps to mark height adjustments on stands. These work pretty well for marking purposes, but cannot be relied upon as a second holding device if the main tightening clamp lets go. They also do not lock in the exact angle by fitting into any other part of the stand. Both of those features are exhibited by modern memory collars. But if you have older stands of small diameter, hose clamps work well for marking height settings, and you can install them in such a way that some particular part of the clamp (such as the short space between the two ends of the tightening screw) lines up with the tightening bolt of the section below, giving you the angle setting as well. Hose clamps are very inexpensive and readily available in any hardware or auto parts store.

3. Shaft collars. These are the closest thing to the machined memory collars that come on modern drum hardware, and that's because they are designed for machine work. Shaft collars are small steel "doughnuts" with a specific inside diameter and a set screw fitted through one side. They come in a wide variety of sizes, from quite small up to about an inch in inside diameter. Mark Sanders, formerly with Tower Of Power, once showed me how he uses 3/8" collars on the ends of his floor tom legs to give instant height and leveling adjustment. I'm using several on vintage cymbal stands, and also on some newer stands that don't incorporate memory collars in their design. The shaft collars are sturdy and lock firmly in place. And since they are machined steel parts, they tend to blend in and appear as part of the actual drum hardware. You can achieve the proper angle adjustment by lining up the set screw with the tightening bolt of the stand section below. Shaft collars are available at most well-stocked hardware stores, or you might call a nearby machine shop for other local sources.

Even if your equipment has memory collars now, there are a few places where you might be able to use additional homemade ones. I've already mentioned floor tom legs. I've also installed shaft collars on the inside ends of disappearing bass drum spurs. All I have to do is run them out till the collars stop them, and they're at exactly the right length.

After you've gotten each individual stand set up just the way it should be, you still have to arrange all the stands and drums to assemble the total kit. Once again, you're faced with trying to re-create a combination of legs and tripods that worked perfectly the last time. The way to do this is to employ a technique called *spiking*. This technique comes from the placement of scenery on theater stages, and has been borrowed by stagehands placing equipment onto rock concert stages. These guys have to get the equipment where the artists want it. It must be done correctly and it must be done quickly. What they do is mark on the drum platform, either in paint or with gaffer's tape, little "U"s where the feet of each stand touch down. The open end of the "U" points back along the angle of the stand leg. This achieves the double benefit of putting everything where the drummer wants it for playing, and re-creating an untangled stand arrangement each time. I use the same technique on the top of the drum platform I carry with me. You can also use gaffer's tape on your drum rug. If you don't use either a platform or a rug, I suggest you invest in a carpet remnant and start using it, if only for the ability to spike your stand positions. Even if you play on club stages already carpeted, the addition of one thickness of carpet will make no difference in your stability, while the benefits of having your own personal stage layout to carry with you will be enormous. If you've ever spent the first three nights of a steady gig adjusting stands and drums by fractions of inches, you'll appreciate what I mean.

Memory settings allow the drums to be set up quickly. Spiking the stand and drum positions allows for very quick and automatic kit arrangement, with the added advantage of identical positioning from gig to gig. You can concentrate on playing, rather than spend a lot of effort making those frustrating adjustments that can go on forever.

Beating The Breakdown Blues

The less you have
to take apart,
the less you have
to put back together.

According to most drummers I know, playing in a band is a pretty enjoyable profession. There's a certain amount of glamour involved, even at the local club level. You're doing something that most—if not all—of your audience can't do. You're handling complicated and mysterious equipment, and exhibiting special talents. It's fun, it's rewarding, and—let's face it—it's generally pretty good for the ego.

That, of course, refers to the time when you're performing. We generally don't talk much about the *un*glamorous side: loading in, setting up, breaking down, loading out, driving home...head 'em up, *RawHIDE!* Well, nothing is going to make that part of the job go away, but I can offer a few tips to make it a bit easier. Hopefully these will help you to maximize the "magic time" by minimizing the mundane time.

Drumkit Breakdown

If done efficiently, even the breakdown of a large kit can be accomplished quickly and easily. There are several keys to an efficient breakdown.

1. Start immediately. Assuming you don't have a roadie who can handle the breakdown for you, you're going to be doing it yourself. I suggest that you get right on it, as soon as the gig is over. Don't go off and have a couple of drinks, and then come back. Your energy level is going to be relatively high at the end of the gig—even if it was a rough night—because your adrenaline will have been pumped up over the last set. If you take too much time to "cool off" before you go to work, you'll lose momentum and it will be more difficult to get started. Break down *first.* Then when that work is done, take a moment to relax before the load-up.

2. Break down in a systematic manner. It's important to have a definite system for breaking down. Generally, it's best to start at the top (with cymbals), and work down (following with rack toms, then the snare, then the stands that are now free, then the larger drums, etc.) Breaking down according to the same system every time will give you the efficiency that can only be obtained by repetition.

3. Break down as little as possible. My feeling has always been that the less you have to take apart, the less you have to put back together. This, in turn, means less time spent setting up, and less worry about whether things are back together *correctly.* So, my advice is: Don't break anything down any further than you have to. I deliberately built my trap case extra large, so that I can leave many of my stands—especially those I custom-made using multi-clamps and mini-booms—partially set up. This speeds up not only the breakdown, but also the set-up at the next location, and helps to make sure my setup is the same the next time.

Breakdowns can be shortened immeasurably if everything is memory-locked in some manner, as described in the previous chapter. (If you employ a drum rack, with multiple tom arms and cymbal booms, this becomes even more important.)

Now, some drummers complain that the use of memory collars requires the various parts of the stands to be packed up separately, which defeats the purpose of telescoping stands, namely: convenience. I can't argue with that. If you have stands that telescope into themselves and you wish to utilize this feature, you can mark the various sections at their proper level with crayon, permanent marker, or some other means that will stay on the stands. (This may not be easy, considering the amount of handling that stands normally take.) These marks can be in an "L" or inverted "T" shape, so as to indicate how each section matches with the next one both horizontally and vertically. This system will work well if you have mainly traditional straight or boom stands with no accessory items.

On the other hand, even if you have traditional stands, why worry about whether to telescope them or take them apart? Why not just get a hardware bag long enough to accept the stands set at their full playing height, with only their tripods collapsed? (This could be anything from a professional hardware bag to an old golf bag. It doesn't automatically require a large expenditure.) You might need to rotate a boom arm down alongside the vertical shaft, but the boom's playing position can easily be marked with a bit of tape or a marker, and one adjustment is better than total breakdown and reassembly.

If you have stands that mount multiple items via accessory clamps, *leave the clamps in place*. Again, use a hardware container large enough to accommodate this. If possible, leave whatever the clamp *holds* (tom arm, mini-boom, etc.) in place, too. If you *must* remove that item, be sure to have its position locked with a memory device of some kind.

I would *much* rather have slightly larger-than-usual trap cases (and enlist the aid of band members to load them) than spend precious minutes disassembling and packing up a complicated mass of drumkit components at the end of a long night—to say nothing of having to sort out and reassemble that same mass before the next gig. Being able to do a minimal breakdown and a quick load-out constantly justifies the effort I made in obtaining (or in some cases building) the oversized containers I use. When you think about it, the total weight of the equipment is the same, no matter how much or how little it's disassembled. But the amount of time spent setting up or breaking down the same kit can be very different, indeed, depending on the extremes to which those tasks are taken.

Cables

More and more drummers today are miking their drumsets. Recognizing this, several companies have recently introduced microphones that offer excellent performance in very compact packages. The idea is to keep the mic's as inconspicuous and out of the drummer's way as possible. This is terrific, but it doesn't do a thing about the problem of multiple mic' cables, and how to keep *them* inconspicuous and out of the way. And if a drummer uses triggers or electronic pads, there are even more cables to worry about. All those cables can create a messy-looking kit when they are in use, and a real time-consuming headache to straighten out and pack up after the gig.

The answer to this problem is to bundle the mic' and/or patch cables into a "hod" (or "poor man's snake"). This not only keeps them neat while on the kit, it also makes them easier to break down and travel with. The key to doing this successfully is to employ a method that will keep the cables bundled securely, yet can be easily removed and re-installed if and when you want to add or remove a given cable from the hod.

Start by setting up your kit and installing all the necessary mic's and/or electronics. Next, figure how much slack is needed for all the cable runs. Then, working from the end of the cable farthest from the mixing board, start working the slack backwards toward the board. Using simple wire ties (such as are used to wrap around the necks of trash or leaf bags), bundle the cables every few inches. Each time a new cable is reached, give it a few feet of slack, and then add it to the bundle. If you want any cables to travel down particular stands in order to be even more inconspicuous, put a wire tie on that particular cable (or on the stand) at a point where it can affix the cable to the stand but be easily untied at the end of the gig.

Don't use tape for cable hods. Masking tape is too weak and is conspicuous due to its light color; electrical tape is messy and unreliable; and duct tape is hard to get off in a hurry in order to make changes. Stick with garden-variety wire ties. You can get them in most hardware stores, either pre-cut, or on a 1,000' roll, which you can cut to length as needed. It would be good if they could be in the same color as your cables, but even if they aren't, they're the easiest and quickest method of securing cables into a hod.

If it is easier to reach your mixing board from the drums by starting at the center front of the kit and going around the two sides, it might be necessary to create two separate cable hods. (My mixer is placed immediately behind me, so this is the case.) If, however, the mixer is off to one side and everything must ultimately go in that direction, a single cable hod is usually the best idea; it certainly is easier to pack up and carry.

Efficient Packup

Here's a time-saving tip that I discovered the hard way. I've worked in any number of clubs where the drums were set up on a small stage or riser, against a back wall (and often in a cramped alcove). The stage, in turn, faced out onto the dance floor area. When it came time for me to break down and pack up my kit, I couldn't get my cases on stage behind or near my kit; they had to be placed on the dance floor area in front of the stage. As the drums came off the kit, I was faced with the choice of stacking them up on the stage beside me (taking up room necessary for further breakdown of stands) or walking down off the stage to where the cases were, putting the drums away, and then walking back.

This same problem existed if I tried to start with the hardware. As soon as I put my cymbals in their bag, I had a bunch of stands waiting to be put away, but no easy way to break them down and get them right into their container. Once again, if I piled them up, they created a space problem. If I took them, a few at a time, to the hardware bag, I was doing a lot of walking.

That's a long story to illustrate a simple principle: Get some help! Many drummers—even at the club level—have drum techs. If you do, you're set, and you can stop reading at this point. But if you don't, get someone to help you pass your equipment from where it comes off the kit to where the cases are. This can be a designated drum tech, a good buddy, a spouse, or (as in my case) a bandmate. My bandmembers soon learned that if they helped me get my gear offstage and packed up quickly, we *all* got home earlier.

Here's my breakdown system. I stay behind the kit, first pulling off my cymbals and bagging them. The bag is handed to my helper. Then I remove the drums. As each one is removed, I hand it to my helper, who puts it in its case. This leaves me with bare stands. I break these down—minimally—and give them to my helper, who fits them into my trap cases. When all else is gone, the only things left on stage are my mic's and cables (which I have bundled neatly so that I can just wrap them up quickly and pop them into their container). My helper doesn't have to know anything more about drums or hardware than how to put them in a case or bag, and *I* don't have to spend twice the amount of breakdown time I should walking between the stage and my cases. It's a simple system, but it works wonders.

By the way, I reciprocate for this help from my bandmates by being the first one at each gig and checking out all the technical details (like stage space, power sources, lights, etc.). I also have my drums set up early enough to be available to help set up our PA system. We don't have any roadies, so we employ a team effort to make our setups and breakdowns as efficient and painless as possible—which keeps us all more excited about the time in between!

In Transit

When the gig ends and it's time to break down, load up, and travel to the next location, the scene often begins to look like something out of a Three Stooges movie.

In the last few years, musical equipment has become more sophisticated, lighting and special effects have become more common, and all in all, the amount of gear a band is required to use on stage has increased dramatically. When you see a successful club group on stage these days, you often see a setup that rivals a major arena act. The level of sophistication exhibited by many of today's club groups, in terms of incorporating all that equipment into their stage presentation, is quite remarkable.

But that sophisticated image often falls apart when a gig ends and it's time to break down, load up, and travel to the next location. Instead, the scene often begins to look like something out of a Three Stooges movie. The reason for this is very simple: Most musicians put a tremendous amount of thought into what equipment they need in order to play, and how it should best be arranged on stage for performance purposes. But they often give little or no thought to how all that gear is going to break down, be containerized, and fit into the transport vehicles.

The unfortunate result of this lack of prior planning is major confusion during pack-up (which generally takes place in the wee hours of the morning when everyone in the group is tired, patience is minimal, and tempers are likely to flare). If the group is traveling to another town, such load-up hassles can delay departure—throwing off the entire travel schedule and starting the next gig off on a bad foot by affecting the arrival time and setup at the new location.

The solution to this situation is very simple: Plan ahead. Devote some serious time and effort to figuring out the most efficient way of packing up and loading your gear. I'm going to direct my specific suggestions to drummers, but most will apply to any musician who has to deal with hauling around equipment.

Packing Up

To begin with, have a designated place to put *everything*. Small items that have to be individually carried increase your breakdown time, and they are also very prone to being left behind. Have all the necessary drum cases, trap cases, miscellaneous parts boxes, and tool kits you need, as well as containers for microphones, cables, extension cords, etc. Aside from oversize items like studio-size mic' booms, drums risers, or other such pieces, *nothing* should be carried on its own. Containerize everything you possibly can, and combine things as much as practical (accounting for reasonable weight) to reduce the total number of containers you need.

Loading Up

This is the meat of the whole operation. Even groups that have ATA cases for every piece of equipment sometimes run into snags when it comes to fitting everything into the vehicles. And the average drummer, with many different sizes and shapes of cases and containers, is faced with an especially difficult job. Again, the key here is prior planning, including some hands-on rehearsal. Here are my suggestions.

1. Rehearse your load up. Take an entire day to experiment with loading arrangements in your vehicle. The best time to do this is when the actual equipment is set up on stage, and you are only moving around the empty containers. This saves a lot of energy yet provides you with an accurate idea of the space required by each item. Work with every case, box, and miscellaneous item that is going to have to fit in at the end of the gig. Don't just toss everything in; experiment with different loading patterns until you find the one that gives you the most efficient use of space. Remember, you don't want things to shift while driving, so each case should help hold and support the next one. You also may be adding new equipment later, so if you can come up with an arrangement that leaves some empty space, so much the better. Don't just take the first arrangement that gets everything in and assume it's going to be "the one."

2. Use space wisely. If you have several cases or containers that are similar in dimension, you can use them to create levels within your vehicle. For example, I use my bass drum, floor tom, and large trap cases (which are all the same height) to form a "lower deck" upon which I place the top of my drum riser. This forms a "second deck" to put my smaller drums and other cases on. It's also important that you fill up small spaces wherever possible. If your vehicle has a wheel well that is too small for a drum case, try a tool box, or perhaps a small mic' case. Don't leave any unnecessary air spaces. You'll find that they add up to a lot of space, which you won't have when you need it at the end of the load-up.

3. Make a loading chart. Once you've determined the optimum loading arrangement, make a schematic diagram of it, showing where everything goes: what's on top of what, and which way the cases are turned. Often your load-up will be very tight, and the slightest misplacement of any item can throw the entire thing out of whack. The most frustrating thing about that is that you may not come to realize it until you've almost finished the load-up and the last item just won't fit in! Then it means starting over again, which can be a real downer at five in the morning.

It's often necessary to put things in the vehicle in a certain order so that they can fit in the prescribed position. I suggest you include a sequential loading chart with your diagram. Besides giving you the correct loading sequence, the list also serves two other purposes. First, it speeds up the loading operation because you can read down the list and know just what to put in next (or even better, someone else who's helping you can). Second, it also serves as a checklist. As you load something in, you can check it off, and that way you'll know you haven't left anything behind.

If you are in a traveling act, and personal gear such as suitcases, trunks, ice chests, or portable stereos are to be loaded, be sure to include them in your rehearsal, and show them on your diagram and load list.

4. Be prepared to secure the load. If it is necessary to tie your load down, have bunji cords, rope, chains, locks, or whatever you need as part of your regular traveling gear. *Don't* use them elsewhere when you're not traveling, so that you have to scrounge for them when you need them. Keep them packed in one of your traveling containers.

If you carry any equipment in an open vehicle (such as a pickup truck) be sure to have a tarp or plastic cover available in case of inclement weather. Again, make sure you *always* have it, and make sure it's in good condition. Even a short crosstown trip can be damaging if it must be done in a driving rain.

5. Be consistent. Just as with the breakdown, the key to efficiency in loading up is to do it the same way every time. "Practice makes perfect," and once the load-up is a matter of routine, you'll be surprised at how quick and painless it can be.

Incorporating these suggestions into your personal loading method may not solve every problem you might have in that regard. However, I guarantee it will go a long way towards getting you out of your gig and on your way home (or to the next location) in record time. You'll also be in a much better frame of mind.

Model Setups

I think of myself as a musician and not a stage-hand, so anything that can reduce the amount of load-in work I have to do appeals to me.

See if this situation sounds familiar: You've been playing around town for quite some time with your group, so you've become familiar with the stages on which you perform regularly. Even though your band has quite a bit of equipment, you've managed to work out a fairly comfortable arrangement for every stage. Suddenly, you find yourself booked into a room you've never worked in before. The stage is an unusual shape, and there are some architectural features that prevent you from using any of the setup configurations that you normally employ.

There are some variations on this scenario. One is moving into a familiar club, but having new equipment to add to your setup for the first time. Another is coming into a familiar club, only to find that renovations have taken place, and your comfortable arrangement no longer works. And finally, there's the situation of being on the road, and coming into unfamiliar territory with virtually every new gig. No matter which variation of the basic scenario applies to you, the inherent problems are the same: You have a short time in which to set up a lot of equipment, and a whole new set of circumstances to deal with.

What's the best way to approach this problem? Well, you *could* start with a basic setup that you're familiar with and try to adapt it to the new stage. Of course, this means a trial-and-error process that involves a lot of lifting and carrying, and may ultimately result in a less-than-optimum setup (to say nothing of short tempers, time pressure, and back strain).

You might also try to "eyeball" the space available and come up with an on-the-spot new arrangement, but the risk you run is that what you come up with on the spur of the moment might not be the best possible arrangement sound- and space-wise—especially if the gig is a long-term engagement. Again, it involves a lot of trial and error, with all of the inherent negative aspects that go along with it.

A solution I've employed over the years involves a technique used by theatrical set designers, and also by major tour-support companies that have to deal with getting literally thousands of pounds of equipment on and off trucks, and into and out of various arenas and other concert venues. That technique is the use of scale models.

When I described some of the items I carry in my "Drummer's Survival Kit," I mentioned that I have a 6' measuring tape among my hand tools. In past years I used that tape to create scale models of every piece of equipment my band employed, and also to create floor plans of every stage on which we regularly played. Whenever a new piece of equipment was added, I took its measurements and made a new model to add to the existing ones. On occasions when we were booked into a new club, we wouldn't set anything up until I had a chance to measure the dimensions of the stage and create a quick floor plan.

If this sounds a bit complicated (and perhaps like a lot of extra work), let me just ask you this: Would you enjoy spending lots of time schlepping heavy equipment around on stage, searching for a comfortable and acoustically practical arrangement (that might ultimately still elude you)? Or would you rather sit down at a table for a few minutes, move some cardboard models around on a sheet of paper, and then go right to a predetermined setup that only requires you to move each piece of real equipment once? Personally, I think of myself as a musician and not a stagehand, so anything that can reduce the amount of load-in work I have to do appeals to me.

Making The Models

Creating models of most band equipment is not difficult, since amps, speaker cabinets, electronic equipment racks, sound boards, and similar equipment are basically cubic in design, and call for simple measurements of their various surfaces in order to create the models. Obviously, drums are a different story, but you don't actually need to make models of each drum. What you need to do is figure the amount of floor space that your drumkit takes up and simply make a model for that. I suggest that you also measure how high your stands extend, and make your model a cube, showing the total airspace occupied by you, your drumkit, your riser (if you have one), etc. If other equipment shares space with your riser, or is fitted in around your drum stands, you'll have to make some allowance for that.

It's important to make three-dimensional models, since sound equipment is often stacked, and you need to know what can stack on what and how high it can go. Don't forget that club stages are often tucked into alcoves or have other similar architectural height obstructions, and you need to know whether or not your stack of PA speakers is going to fit where you want it to.

I've found that the easiest way to create models is by the use of a heavy paper called tagboard. It's a material with some stiffness and durability so it can hold a shape, but it also can be drawn on, cut, folded, and glued easily.

To create a model of a piece of equipment, you first have to measure all of its surfaces. Then it's just a matter of using a particular scale to miniaturize those measurements. I've found that a scale of 1" = 1' works very well, because in that scale, it's fairly easy to transfer measurements as small as one inch accurately. (In one-inch scale, $\frac{1}{2}$" = 6", $\frac{1}{4}$" = 3", $\frac{1}{8}$" = 1$\frac{1}{2}$", etc.) Also, this scale works well in conjunction with floor plans on $\frac{1}{4}$" graph paper, which I'll explain later.

In order to make a model of a typical speaker cabinet, the measurements must be laid out—in scale—on your tagboard, creating a pattern such as is shown in Figure 1. This design makes for a fairly strong model, because it's actually one single piece of tagboard, rather than several pieces glued together. For our example, I've used a theoretical speaker cabinet that is 3' high, 2$\frac{1}{2}$' wide, and 1' deep. Thus, our model will be 3" high, 2$\frac{1}{2}$" wide, and 1" deep: Note that on Figure 1 the solid lines indicate where the model is to be cut out; dashed lines indicate where the tagboard is to be folded. Gluing tabs are also indicated; these are used to allow you to glue the various surfaces together. (Before you cut out the model, it's a good idea to label it according to what piece of equipment it represents.)

Cut out the pattern as indicated. Then, crease all the various folds sharply toward you. This should allow you to create the model's three-dimensional shape. Glue the surfaces together where the glue tabs meet an opposite surface, and voilà! You now have a miniature version of your speaker cabinet. Repeat this process for each and every separate item involved in your stage setup. It may be a bit tedious at this point, but it will save you hours of back-breaking labor in the future. Once you have the models, you need never make them again (provided you take care of them); you'll only need to add new ones if and when you add new equipment.

Creating The Floor Plan

A floor plan is nothing more than a diagram of the shape and area of the stage. If you play on several different stages regularly, you'll need a floor plan for each one. All you need to do is measure the periphery of the stage, being sure to take the measurements of any posts, moldings, steps, or other architectural features that affect the area. If you're already set up in a club now, get the measurements while you're there so that you'll be able to make a floor plan for the next time you return. If you know where you're going next, visit that club, get the measurements, and make your floor plan ahead of time so that you'll be able to plan your next setup before you break down from your current one.

Obviously, if you're on the road, you may not have the convenience of being able to run over to the next club and get measurements ahead of time. But I've been on the road, and I know that my days were often quite boring—living in a motel room in a small town for two or more weeks—and I found myself looking for things to keep me occupied. If your next booking is within a reasonable day's round-trip driving distance, it might be an excellent idea to occupy yourself by making an excursion to scout out the premises and get the measurements you need (noting any other problems that you might encounter with your setup, and perhaps meeting the management at the same time). I stress the point that this should *only* be done if the trip is practical for you and does not jeopardize your being back in time for your current gig. But if you can comfortably make the trip, the information you'll gain might save you hours of tension and hard work when you move into the next location. (Even if you can't, the time it will take to measure the stage when you first arrive will be well spent.)

Once you have your measurements, it's a simple matter to lay them out on a sheet of paper, which then becomes your floor plan. I use $\frac{1}{4}$" graph paper, which offers the advantage of breaking the dimensions down into a quick visual-reference format. In one-inch scale, each square on the graph paper represents a 3"x3" square area on stage; four squares equal 1'. Using this scale, it's not only easy to see how the equipment will best fit onto the stage, but it's also easy to determine how much floor space will be available for people to stand and move. (Using graph paper also makes it easy to create a floor plan quickly upon arriving at a new club, without the need for drafting tools.)

If, when you were taking your stage measurements, you found that a low ceiling extended over part or all of the stage, or a fan or lighting fixture blocked a certain area, or any other height limitation existed, that should be notated on the floor plan in the appropriate area of the floor over which the obstruction exists. That way, when you place your models on your floor plan, you can quickly determine whether or not you have the height you need to stack items in that area of the stage. (See Figure 2.)

Using The Models And Floor Plan

The whole idea of using the models and the floor plan is to allow you to design—in advance—the placement and positioning of your equipment. Whenever possible, this should be done before you leave your current gig, when there is plenty of time to experiment and discuss options. If that isn't possible, it should still be done before you begin your setup at your new gig. Any time lost to working with the models will be more than made up in the efficient, organized setup that results. This, in turn, should reduce the pressure that comes with a rushed setup in an unfamiliar situation, along with reducing the sheer physical strain of repeatedly moving heavy equipment.

If you play several clubs regularly, you'll quickly acquire a file of floor plans with which to work as you travel "the circuit." You may discover that, when you come into a new club (either in town or on the road), the dimensions of the new stage will be so similar to one you already have diagrammed that you can use the familiar setup from that club. But you *won't* discover that unless you have the measurements of the new stage, the floor plan of the old one, and the opportunity to work with your models. So take the time necessary to create the models you need to represent your band's equipment, and then make it a point to create floor plans for your stages. Use these tools regularly to help you plan ahead, and you'll find that your load-ins will quickly become "model setups."

Figure 1

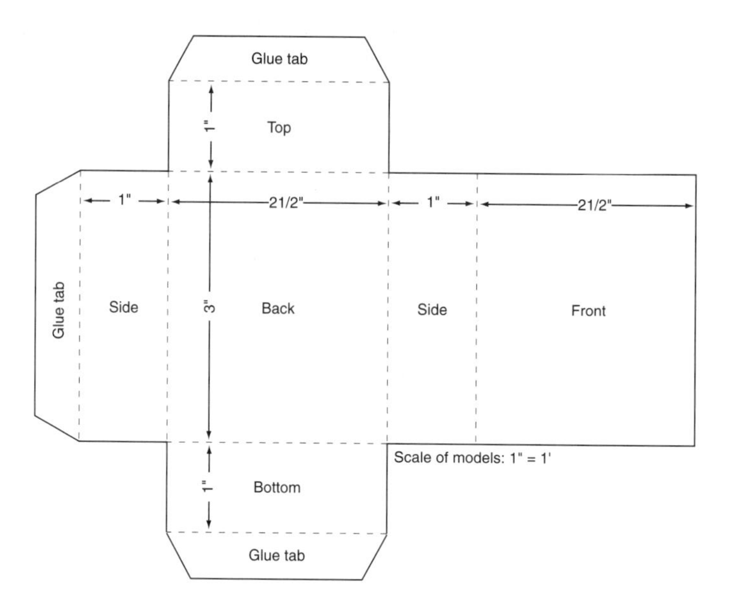

Figure 2

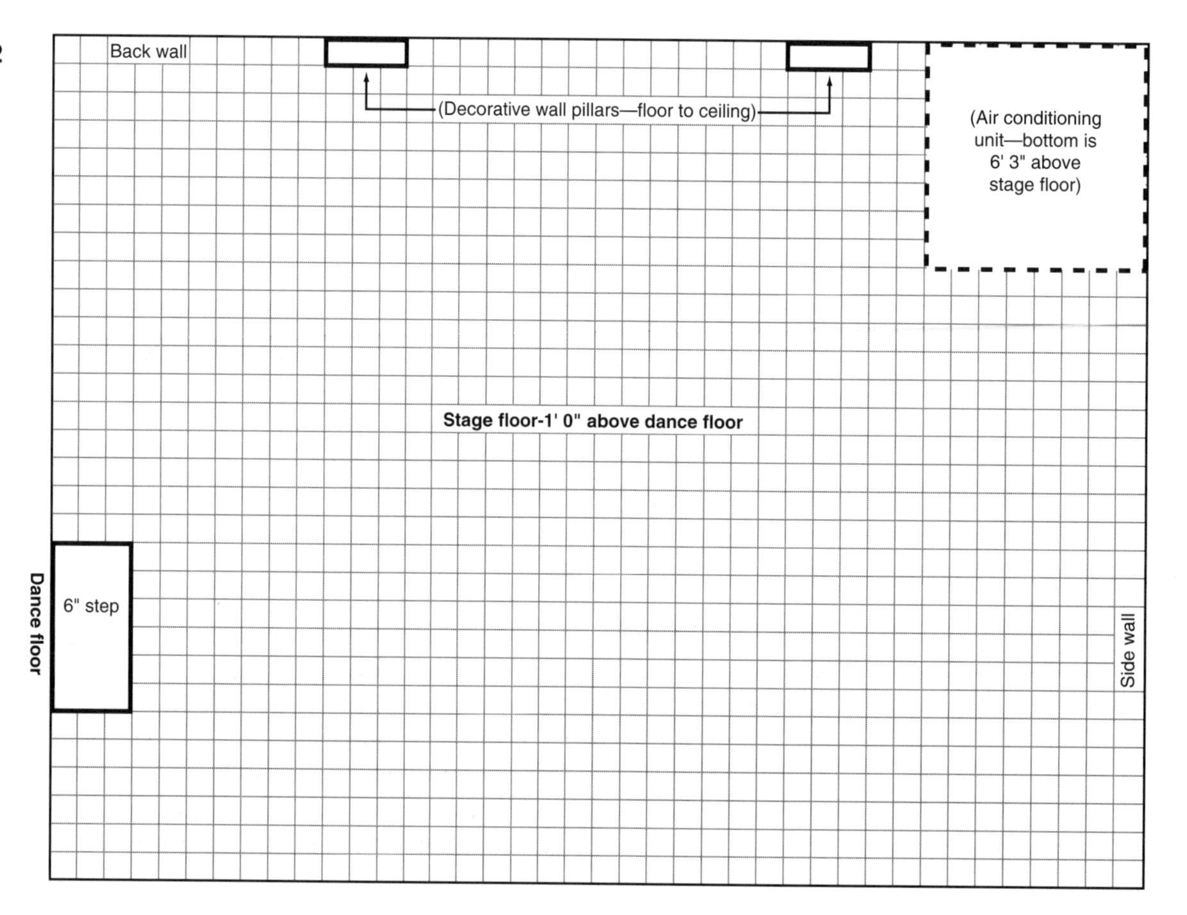

How Much Do You Know?

It is important that everyone knows something about everybody else's equipment.

When you play regularly in a club band, technical things usually go the way you expect them to. The frequency with which you perform serves to establish the best way to do things. The members of your band generally assume specific non-musical duties, and everybody eventually melds into a pretty efficient team. This is all to the good, because the process of setting up and breaking down is made much easier when everybody knows their job and just what is expected of them.

However, there is a downside to all this efficiency. What happens when somebody can't do their job? Suppose a band member is ill or injured, and can't make the gig—or must be late for some reason and is unable to contribute to the setup? What happens if *you* can't handle your own setup or breakdown some night? Does this well-oiled machine fall apart?

Well, it certainly could, but it doesn't have to. There is a fairly simple solution to the problems I've brought up, and that is for everybody in the band to have at least a rudimental knowledge of everybody else's job. Of course, I'm talking about the technical aspects, not the musical ones. No one expects anyone to be able to play everybody else's axe. But it is important that everyone know something about everybody else's equipment, along with how any shared equipment (typically the PA system) is set up and controlled.

PA Systems

In most bands, one individual is responsible for the setting up and operation of the PA system. This may be an onstage band member, or a sound technician. No matter who it is, the rest of the bandmembers should also have a thorough knowledge of how the system is assembled. They don't need to know *how* it works, or *why* a given cable goes where it does; they just need to know where and how everything connects together. The idea is for anyone in the band to be able to get the PA operational. From that point, hopefully, the regularly designated individual (or a qualified substitute) should be able to take over.

Learning how to put together a PA system is really little more than putting together a puzzle: Piece A fits into piece B, etc. All that is required is a clear diagram of the patching system, indicating where each mic' cable comes in, where each speaker cable goes out (and to which speaker cabinet), and where each patch cable connects (and what it connects to). Beyond that, each bandmember should be familiar with the necessary cables, so as to be sure which are mic' cables, which are speaker cables, and which are the appropriate patch cables for each connection. One way to make your patching system virtually foolproof is to label each cable clearly with some sort of tag, and then label your patching diagram in a corresponding manner. (This would make things more convenient for your regular PA person, anyway!)

Other Instruments

Setting up equipment in an emergency can go beyond the PA system. Every bandmember should have at least a rudimentary idea of how each individual's instrumental amps and speakers connect, and how that player likes his or her equipment to be arranged. When it comes to fancy patches for a multi-keyboard player, a diagram might once again be the answer if an emergency setup is called for. At the very least, every bandmember should be able to get the keyboards set up on the appropriate stands, connected to the appropriate amp/speaker setup, and powered up. If the patching is too complex for anyone else to do, that will simply have to wait until the keyboard player can do it.

The same goes for guitar and bass setups. Every bandmember should be able to get the amps and speakers in place, connected, and powered. If the guitar or bass player uses an elaborate pedal or effects setup, that may have to wait until he or she arrives. If a sub is coming in, chances are that that person will be bringing in his or her own, so your bandmembers shouldn't have to worry about them.

Your Drums

"Aha," you say. "But what about my drumkit? It's one thing for me to learn how to set up the PA, but how can I expect other members of my band to set up my drums the way I want them if I need to come late some night myself? My kit is much too personal; it's more than just connecting up some patch cords!" Of course, you can't expect your bandmates to set your drums up perfectly for you. But with a little prior planning on your part, you can make it possible for them to get your kit within 90% of where you need it to be, thereby making it possible for you to come screaming in at the last minute, make a few adjustments, and get on with the first set. (You can always fine-tune as you proceed through the night.)

As we all know, this is the age of the memory-lock. It shouldn't be difficult for anyone to put your drum stands together if they are clearly marked as to what part connects with what other part. This is just a matter of color coding, numerical I.D. tags, or some other identifying system. You should do this for yourself anyway; just make sure that your bandmates know your coding system. As far as which drums and cymbals go on which stands, this is another situation in which a simple diagram would tell all. Just draw an overhead view, showing where you want your drums and cymbals to be placed. (Make sure to show each of your bandmates how your drum mounting system works, and how you wish your cymbals to be placed on their respective stands.) If you happen to use a drum rack, be sure to explain how the rack itself sets up, and then use your diagram to indicate which stand section fits into which clamp on the rack.

Again, I stress that these measures are taken against the possibility of an emergency. In such a case, everybody has to remain flexible and make the best of things. Your drums may not be in tune, and you might be a bit uncomfortable until you can personally set them straight. But at least the gig will be able to start as soon as you arrive, rather than being delayed while you are setting up the drums after arriving late.

Planning Ahead

The bottom line to all of this is that today's equipment is getting more and more sophisticated. As a result, the musicians who use that equipment are turning into specialists. While this specialization works to a band's advantage musically, it can definitely be a detriment technically. In order to overcome this detriment, a band must take appropriate steps to overcome the "mystery" element in each other's equipment, and to make it relatively simple for each member to cover every other member, should the need arise.

Having said all that, I'd like to relate a short anecdote that serves to illustrate two things. First, it underscores the importance of knowing something about other people's jobs in your band. Second, it proves that even when you think you know everything there is to know about club work, you may still be surprised.

Prior to a particular weekend when my band was scheduled to play, our bass player (who normally handled the setup and control of our PA system) had planned a vacation. He gave us plenty of notice, mentioning that he would be flying in on the day of the gig and might be forced to arrive at the club at the last minute. We all felt it wise to distribute the equipment he normally carried among the rest of the bandmembers, so that we could get it to the gig and have it set up without his having to be there. At that point we realized that none of the rest of us really knew the patching system that was employed for the PA. So the bass player created a diagram and gave it to me. Since I normally got to the gig early to set up my drums, it was decided that I would take the PA board, amps, and effects. Our reasoning was that I could set up my drums first, and then cable up the PA. The speakers would come with other members, but all that had to happen with them was to mount them on their stands and plug them in.

We felt very clever and proud of ourselves for all of this prior planning. And, in fact, much of the planning worked out perfectly. However, we did make one classic error: We forgot that the PA board and amps stacked up on the bass player's speaker cabinet. I was unable to carry that cabinet along with my drums and the extra equipment I was already taking. Consequently, when I finished setting up my drums and dutifully got out the diagram to begin patching in the PA, I realized that it would be useless to do so. There were two small, but heavy, racks full of amps and electronic effects, along with a separate mixing board—and no final place to put them. It would have been fruitless to patch them in on the ground and then try to place them on the bass cabinet when it arrived, because the two racks and the board—when connected by all the patch cables—would have been impossible to lift into place. Something would have been dropped, torn loose, or in some other way damaged. I simply had to wait until the rest of the band got to the gig (some forty-five minutes later) with the bass cabinet before I could realistically begin the patching.

All of this goes to show that when planning to cover someone else's tasks in a band, you have to make sure that *every* detail is accounted for. Had I been able to carry the bass cabinet, I could have had the PA ready to go when the band arrived. Perhaps some of my own equipment (which I could certainly have set up rapidly) could have been carried by someone else, while I carried all of the pieces necessary to make the PA setup work. Extraordinary circumstances call for some extraordinary measures—which generally only amount to a little extra forethought.

In Case: Protecting Your Drums

I'm amazed at the number of drummers who walk into club gigs with their drums under their arms and their hands full of stands.

One of the questions asked most frequently by young drummers getting started in regular club work is: *How important are cases for my drums?* My first inclination is to say that cases are the next most important thing after the drums themselves. But I recognize an economic situation today that puts a young drummer between a rock and a hard place. On one hand, if you're talking about drums recently purchased, that means you've just spent some serious money and probably don't have much left over for cases. On the other hand, the very fact that those drums represent such a large investment makes the reason for protective cases that much more important.

It's also important for the aspiring club player to consider the situation in which the drums will be used. If you plan to work locally and to carry your drums in your own vehicle, then you might be able to hold off on the cases until you can earn the money to buy them. If you're lucky enough to get a long-term gig in one place (so that moving the drums is minimized), that too can help put off the necessity of purchasing drum cases. But if the drums are going on the road right away, *even on a local basis* (meaning lots of one-nighters, set-ups and pack-ups), then the cases are necessary right away, and *should* be budgeted into the drum purchase.

Actually, that budgeting would be my initial recommendation to any drummer buying equipment. Think of the equipment and the cases as a total package, and budget accordingly. If it takes a few more weeks to earn the price of both, then wait. No guitar player I've ever known would think of buying a new axe without a case to carry it. And yet I'm amazed at the number of drummers who walk into club gigs with their drums under their arms and their hands full of stands. Invariably, they have been in the business a long time, and their equipment looks it. I believe that respect for one's instrument will manifest itself in how one plays that instrument. Conversely, a lack of respect must also show in performance.

Drums can get pretty roughly handled just getting into and out of your vehicle, depending on how much time you have and who's helping you pack up. If you play a lot of one-nighters and/or you travel a great deal, the wear and tear on the drums builds up quickly. You should be aware of this and take the proper precautions to protect the equipment on which your livelihood depends.

With this in mind, let's take a look at what's on the market in the field of drum protection products. There has been a refreshing growth in the selection of cases in terms of sizes, shapes, styles, and price ranges. At this point, there seems to be something for everyone.

Soft Bags

These are cordura or vinyl covers shaped to fit over the drum. They have a strap for carrying, and open with a zipper. Top-of-the-line bags from companies like Beato, Humes & Berg (*Tuxedo*), Impact Industries, and Tough Traveler (*Drumslinger*) include thick padding to afford some shock protection. Bags are a good, economical choice for a drummer personally moving his or her drums on a local basis. They are not suitable protection for extensive travel.

Fibre Cases

The familiar black cylindrical fibre case such as those offered by Humes & Berg is still the standard of the industry. Fibre cases provide reasonable protection for drums under most conditions. Although available without, most of these cases come with foam linings installed, which is a good form of shock protection. It also adds a little insulation against bad weather.

Modern fibre cases use nylon web straps, and some larger sizes have metal grips with reinforced backing plates to aid in carrying heavier drums. Large drum sizes and trap cases are offered with casters installed for rolling. Keep in mind that if you use deep drums with heavy hardware and thicker-ply shells, you are asking your case to carry substantial weight. Make sure you get a case that can survive sudden lifts and jerks without literally "coming apart at the seams" (leaving your drum sitting on the floor while you hold a bottomless case in your hand).

Plastic Cases

A more recent innovation in the case field has been plastic cases. Cases offered by Impact Industries are similar in thickness to fibre, but are stronger, more waterproof, and still lightweight. Molded one-piece cases from XL Specialty Percussion (*Protechtor*), SKB, and Hardcase are thicker and heavier, and offer seamless construction. These cases come in a variety of design styles, and some colors. Plastic cases offer a high protection in a medium price range, and might serve even a busy traveling drummer very well for all but the most rigorous commercial travel.

ATA Cases

ATA cases are what you see on the stages of concert halls and sports arenas. ATA stands for Airline Transport Association, the organization that sets the standards for safe air travel when it comes to luggage and equipment handling. The ATA case is constructed of plywood, covered on the outside with a plastic or fiberglass layer, and then edged with aluminum and braced at the corners with steel cornerpieces. The cases are strictly box-type, with recessed handles and "coffin-latches" that prevent snagging on mechanical conveyer equipment. These boxes are relatively heavy, and many come with casters installed. These are the Rolls-Royce of cases, and are priced accordingly. They are also *more* than the average traveling drummer needs. But if you regularly have occasion to travel by commercial carrier, and must entrust your drums to the not-so-tender mercies of baggage handlers, the peace of mind given by the ATA cases can be a valuable commodity in itself.

I would like to say something about trap cases in particular. Today's heavy-duty hardware places a heavy burden on trap cases. Fibre cases do not fare well with a lot of weight, unless they are reinforced with a plywood sheet bottom and all the handles are well-backed and securely attached. Even then, most drummers have a tendency to overload them. I've seen innumerable trap cases with broken handles, or holes in the fibre sides due to a carelessly thrown stand. If you have a lot of heavy hardware, either separate it into two or more cases, or consider using an ATA trap case that has the structural integrity to withstand the weight. You'll definitely want it on casters.

Anvil is the largest manufacturer of heavy-duty travel cases in the world, and the name Anvil has come to be synonymous with the ATA case. However, ATA cases, as well as all the other types, are manufactured by several companies throughout the country. And fibre cases are offered by many local outfits. Do some *serious* shopping when it comes to cases. Be sure to get what you need, but not *more* than you need, unless you're investing towards a future goal and have the extra money to spend. And keep in mind, this is the best thing you can do to help your equipment help *you* to be the best possible player.

Case Repair And Maintenance

A big part of preventing case wear is caring for the cases as well as you'd care for the drums inside them.

In the previous chapter I outlined types of drum cases on the market. This time I'd like to talk about ways you can maintain your existing cases. Although it's true that there are several innovative types of cases currently available, I'd be willing to bet that 90% of all club or casual drummers who use cases at all are using familiar fibre cases. Repair problems with these cases seem to fall repeatedly into a few categories. In order of frequency, they are: strap problems, edges pulled apart, handles pulled out, and weather damage. These represent chronic problems for steady drummers who frequently move about from club to club, putting a constant strain on the cases, handles, and straps.

Straps

Since broken straps seem to be the most frequent problem, let's address that first. How best to repair worn straps depends on a few variables:

1. *What kind of straps—leather or nylon web?*
2. *Where are they worn? At the buckle, at the point where they are attached to the case, somewhere in the middle, or all of the above?*
3. *Do you want to keep the existing strap or replace it?*
4. *Do you want to change materials?*

Some of my cases are over twenty years old, and they all came with leather straps. Leather tends to deteriorate with age, and wear and tear only aggravates the condition. That's why, in recent years, manufacturers have gone to nylon-web straps. Nylon is also less expensive than leather. But I like to stay with leather because it's easy to work with and actually pretty cheap to come by if you know where to look.

Let's suppose the strap holding the buckle is in good shape, but the other strap (with the adjusting holes) has worn thin. Some of the holes have ripped out as well, so the strap won't buckle tightly anymore. You need to either replace the entire strap or splice on a new length of leather (into which you can punch new holes).

Your best source of strap leather is the local thrift store belt department. For a couple of bucks you can pick up some good used leather belts, which you can use as raw material for your project.

Be sure to get real leather, not man-made material. And get a belt as wide or wider than your original strap. It should also be about the same thickness. Black is usually available, but if you're not choosy about color your selection will be wider. Make sure the belt you select is long enough to replace the worn strap from wherever you plan to attach it (either from the case or spliced to the existing strap).

For the actual repair project you'll need a few tools, most of which you probably already have. You'll need a hammer, a pair of pliers, an electric drill, and a leather punch. If you don't have the punch, a fairly inexpensive one can be obtained at the local hardware store. Don't go overboard; get only what you need for the job. (I use a pliers-punch with a rotating wheel providing several different punch sizes.) You'll also need some hammer-type rivets, similar in size to those on your case now. If necessary, explain the project to the clerk and ask for help in choosing the right rivets. If all you have to buy is the punch and the rivets, you shouldn't spend more than about $15. If the belt is going to need trimming to size, you'll need a razor knife or sharp scissors and a good cutting board. You'll also need a very hard hammering surface; a concrete driveway worked for me.

If you intend to completely replace the worn strap, first *carefully* drill out the existing rivets attaching it to the side of the case, using a small drill bit. The trick is to loosen the rivets without enlarging the holes in the fibre material of the case. When the rivets have been drilled through, use pliers to collapse them as much as possible and remove them from the case, again being careful not to enlarge the holes.

After the strap has been removed, use it as a guide to make a new strap out of the belt you bought. Match it for length and placement of holes (using, of course, the original hole positions, not the ones that have stretched out due to wear). Use your leather punch to punch holes for the rivets and buckle adjustments. Once the new strap is constructed, rivet it back to the side of the case. Using hammer-type rivets is easiest and neatest, but if you happen to have a Pop-Rivet gun in your shop, that will work too. If you're using hammer rivets, lay the case on its side with the strap in place. Insert the lower half of the rivet from the inside of the case towards the outside and place the cap of the rivet on the outside (on top of the strap). Then position the whole thing on a hard surface and rap the rivets together with your hammer. Make sure the rivets are assembled tightly, or the leather will tend to work them apart.

If you have foam-lined cases, it may be necessary to carefully separate the lining from the side of the case (if possible), or to cut a very small area out to expose the rivet point.

If you prefer to leave the existing strap attached to the case, you can splice a new length of leather onto it and punch the adjusting holes into the new piece. Select a point far enough back on the existing strap so that the splice will not interfere with buckling the buckle. Then lay about two inches of the new strap over the old, punch rivet holes in both, rivet them together, and you're in business. It isn't the neatest job, but it works, and you don't have to drill into the case or damage your foam lining.

If your problem is with the strap holding the buckle, then the same process applies, with the added problem of reinstalling the buckle in the new strap. Just study how the buckle is attached to the old strap and duplicate it on the new one. Be sure to allow enough length for foldover around the buckle.

The use of nylon web has eliminated many of the problems of leather. Webbing is usually so flexible that you don't have the wear problems leather is subject to, and since they use the sawtooth-grip type of buckle, there are no strap holes to wear out. Webbing is virtually unbreakable, so very few straps ever snap in half. But webbing does have its own unique problems. These include rivets pulling out of the straps, ends of the straps too frayed to get into the buckle, and buckles bent or flattened so that they can't grip securely.

Rivets tend to pull through the webbing when the case is lifted by the straps instead of the handle. Even with grommets installed (which is rare) the fibrous nature of the webbing makes it expand around objects inserted through it. The obvious solution to this problem (*before it occurs*) is to never pick up the loaded case by the strap. The solution after it occurs is to replace the strap.

The trick to installing a new web belt is in riveting it to the case. Once again, you drill out the old rivets. But do *not* try to punch rivet holes into the webbing. Instead, use a small-tipped soldering iron or an awl or ice pick heated in a flame to melt a hole for the rivet. The melted nylon will build up around the edge of the hole and create a sort of grommet. Also, be sure to double the strap back on itself an inch or so and melt the holes through two thicknesses of the strap for extra security. If you have plenty of length on your existing strap, it might be possible to back it up a few inches and put new holes in it. If not, nylon webbing is readily available at the hardware store, and rather inexpensive. If you need a new buckle, they go for a few cents at the same store.

The ends of web straps tend to fray with wear unless something holds them together. Some come with metal edging already installed. If yours did not, a piece of tape folded over the end will sometimes work, as long as the strap can still get through the buckle. Melting the fibers into one solid edge works better, but takes a little skill and some source of controllable heat, like a large soldering iron or small propane torch.

Bent or flattened buckles can sometimes be reworked with a screwdriver and a hammer. If not, then they must be replaced. They aren't expensive, and if you study the way in which they were originally installed, it's pretty easy to put in a new one.

Edges

Now let's talk about the problem of edges pulling apart. Usually this happens on the bottom edge of a case due to the weight of the drum repeatedly pressing down when the case is lifted. If the edge starts to pull apart, a quick *temporary* repair can be made by bandaging it securely with gaffers (or duct) tape. Use sufficiently long strips of tape to get support from high up on the side of the case, and reinforce the actual edge with at least two layers of tape. Don't plan on this as a permanent repair; it won't last forever.

The best repair is to obtain some thin, flexible material (I've used very thin sheet metal, and also double-thick denim fabric) and create a new bottom for the case, with enough overlapping up the sides to form a cradle for the drum. You can shape the material to fit the *inside* of the case. Then affix it to the fibre material using contact cement, rivets, or whatever seems appropriate. One drummer I know lined the bottom half of all his cases with fiberglass fabric and resined it to form a reinforced bottom. It added some weight to the case, but he felt the additional strength was worth it.

Handles

Over the last few years, handles have been better-secured in drum cases with stronger rivets and backing plates. As drums became heavier this was a necessity. Problems generally occur when newer drums are carried in older, less well-constructed cases. If you pull a handle out of a case in such a way that only the rivet holes are pulled out, you can re-install it by getting a sheet-metal backing plate, placing that inside the case, and riveting the handle back on. It would be a good idea to glue the plate to the fibre with contact cement. If the handle ripped off a large section of the case, it would be difficult to attach a large enough backing plate to disperse the strain of lifting. In such a situation, I'd recommend a new case.

Punctures

When the side of a case is punctured, it's a simple matter to obtain a flat piece of material (masonite, plywood, sheet metal, case fibre if available) and glue it to the *inside* of the case to cover the puncture. If your case is foam-lined, you may find it necessary to cut out a small piece of foam to get at the hole. With a little luck and care, you should be able to keep the foam piece intact and glue it back in. If not, get a small replacement piece of foam at a fabric or upholstery shop and fit it into the case.

Weather Damage

There is no reason why cases, or the drums inside, should suffer from weather damage. It's a simple matter to weatherproof cases by treating them with polyurethane varnish inside and out. (I also recommend Thompson's *Water Seal.*) You can also use neatsfoot oil on leather straps. This protection should be afforded to any case that is going to move more than three times a year.

Cymbal Cases

Fibre cymbal cases have their own particular problems. One weakness is that their foam lining doesn't really provide much protection to the edges of the cymbals if the case is dropped on its edge. Nor do the sides of the fibre case offer much real crush protection. My suggestion is to line the inside edges of the bottom section of the case with 1/4" plywood, so as to create a solid wall on the four sides of the case. Then, if the case should be dropped, the edge of the cymbal will strike the wood (which is softer than the metal cymbal, and infinitely softer than hard pavement) and run less risk of cracking. The "walls" also help prevent the sides of the case from being crushed if any weight is placed upon it while loading.

An important thing to remember with cymbal cases is not to overload them. Remember, when cymbals are mounted on the central bolt inside the case, they pull down when the case is carried by the handle. This weight pulls that bolt to one side, and can eventually pull it right out of the bottom of the case. Better to have two cases instead of one overloaded one.

A big part of preventing case wear is caring for the cases as well as you'd care for the drums inside them. Keep them out of bad weather as much as possible. Be careful when loading and unloading. Use the handles and not the straps for carrying, and don't overload trap and cymbal cases. A little common sense can save you a *lot* of money.

On The Rise, Part 1

Don't feel that your riser has to be a work of art. This is a club setup, not grand opera.

I've mentioned several times in this book how important the visual element of a drummer's playing is. I've also stressed that that element is virtually negated if the drummer isn't clearly visible to the audience. Because drummers are generally placed at the backs of stages (and invariably behind standing bandmembers), it's essential that they be up on some sort of riser to ensure their visibility.

There are a few commercial sources for drum risers, or for having them constructed. But while buying a stock or custom-made riser is convenient, it is also very expensive, and in some cases may be limited by what is available for sale. The alternative is to build your own riser. In this chapter (and the next one) I'm going to give you some suggestions about do-it-yourself risers. I'll also provide you with a few diagrams to get you started towards your own design.

Let me stress that a drum riser need not be a massive piece of engineering; it just needs to be some sort of construction strong enough to support you and your set safely. Nor does a riser necessarily have to look like something off of a concert stage. To me, a drum riser is a functional item. It's a piece of equipment designed to serve one purpose only: to make *you* more visible when you are drumming. To that end, I feel that the riser itself should be as inconspicuous as possible. Of course, if you wish to have the riser cosmetically consistent with other elements of your band's stage setup, that is another option. But don't feel as if you have to create a work of art. This is a club setup, not grand opera.

Among riser designs created by drummers I've known, one was simply a sheet of plywood supported on concrete blocks; the other was two shallow wooden boxes inverted over plastic milk crates. Both designs were very rudimental and not particularly aesthetic, but they both worked just fine and suited their drummers' purposes satisfactorily. I mention them to illustrate how a little creativity—and a practical outlook—can allow you to obtain what you need in a riser with little or no investment or construction effort.

Riser Designs

For those of you who have the skill, the access to tools, and most of all, the inclination to take on a serious construction project in order to create a custom riser, I'm going to present two design ideas—one in this chapter, and one more in the next. The first of my two designs (and the one we'll discuss this time) is the most basic: a simple, solid-construction box. This unit is relatively easy and inexpensive to build, but has the drawback of being heavy and not collapsible. You'll need to figure out how you'll transport it *before* you start to build it. The second design is for a theatrical collapsing platform called a "parallel." It's a bit more complicated to build, but has several advantages over the box type. We'll go into its design in the next chapter.

As a general introduction to my riser designs, let me say that I've figured a 6'x6'x12" riser as a standard, useful size for most club applications. Of course, you'll need to measure the floor space your kit takes up and adjust your design accordingly. But you'd have to play fairly large club stages regularly in order to be able to use anything much bigger than 6'x6'. Although that size may sound small initially, if you tape out a 6'x6' area on your floor, you'd be surprised at how large it really is, and how much equipment you can fit onto it. (My own riser is 5½'x5½'.) I chose 12" as the height because that height works well for most of the club stages I work on. (An 18" height might be an option, but I wouldn't go higher, since many club stages are tucked into low-ceilinged alcoves and similar tight spots. You don't want to risk a skull fracture every time you step up onto the riser.

As a last introductory word, let me urge you not to attempt any construction unless you are thoroughly skilled at basic carpentry and the use of the tools necessary to do the work. If you aren't, enlist the aid of someone who is. Besides the obvious safety factor, you're going to be making a significant investment in time and materials. You may also need to adapt my designs to suit your own purposes. I want you to be able to obtain satisfactory results without having to start over again several times. That can get frustrating—to say nothing of getting expensive!

Building A Box Riser

Materials required:

1. *¾" plywood.* The design uses two and a half 4'x8' sheets of plywood sanded on one side. It may be possible to actually purchase only two and a half sheets, by paying the lumberyard a small fee to cut a sheet in half for you. (You want it cut *lengthwise,* giving you a sheet 2'x8'.) The cutting charge should be much less than the charge for the unused portion of a full sheet. If the lumberyard cannot do this, you'll need to buy three full sheets. How you cut these sheets into your component parts will be outlined later.

2. *1x3 pine boards.* You'll need some 1x3 boards to create the corner blocks and braces in your riser. The dimensions on the design are based on 1x3 that is milled to an *actual size* of ¾" x 2⅝", which is standard in most areas. Be *sure* to check with your lumber supplier on the actual size of the lumber you are buying, so that you can adjust the dimensions on the design as necessary. Since you want wood that is straight and free of knots, I suggest buying "clear pine." It's more expensive than some other types of board stock, but in the long run the investment should be worthwhile. You'll need a total of 14' of length. Since you'll be cutting the board into individual pieces just under 12" long each, any combination of board lengths adding up to 14' will do. In other words, you could buy one 14' board, or two 7' boards, or one 6' and one 8', etc. The precise cuts will be explained later.

3. *Nails.* You'll need a generous supply of 4d ("four penny") and 6d ("six penny") box nails. (As an option, for extra strength, you might consider using wood screws.)

4. *Glue.* Get a quart of *Elmer's Woodworker's Glue* or its equivalent. This is similar in consistency to the familiar "white glue," but contains resins to make it stronger for woodworking applications.

Tools required:

1. *Saw.* This is the most important tool for this job. A table saw (to cut the plywood) and a radial arm saw (to cut the pine boards) would be preferable, because they can generally provide the most accurate cuts. Failing those, a portable circular saw (such as a *Skil* saw) is the next best thing. A handsaw (crosscut) will also do the job, but the work will be tedious, and you'll have to be extra careful to keep your cuts straight.

2. *Carpenter's square.* This is to ensure square corners and tight joints.

3. *Tape measure.* You'll need this to measure your cuts.

4. *Hammer.*

5. *Screwdriver.* (Only if you've decided to use screws.)

6. *Backstop.* If you're working alone, you'll need something to back the other end of the board you're hammering against. A concrete wall or curb is good; don't use a plaster wall or siding that might be dented or damaged by the impact.

Cuts: (Remember that a saw blade has width; always allow for that width when making your measurements, so that you end up with a piece that has the dimensions you want.)

1. *Plywood.* Cut the first sheet into one 3'x6' piece and two 11¼"x6' pieces. Cut the second sheet into one 3'x6' piece and two 11¼"x5' 10½" pieces. Cut the third sheet (or half-sheet) into one 11¼"x5' 10½" piece and two 11¼"x 1' 10⅞" pieces.

2. *Pine board.* Cut the board stock into fourteen pieces 11¼" long. These are your corner blocks and braces.

Assembly:

1. Starting with a 6' long side, and following the dimensions given in Diagram A, attach corner blocks and braces where indicated, using both glue and 4d nails. Follow the nail pattern shown in Detail Diagram A1, and nail *through* the corner block *into* the side piece. Use your carpenter's square to ensure that the boards are mounted absolutely vertically (square). Also, be sure to attach the blocks to the rough side of the plywood, so that the smooth side faces out. If possible, for this and all assembly operations involving corner blocks or center braces, you should clamp or weight the blocks while the glue is drying, to maximize the strength of the bond. Duplicate this operation for the other 6' side piece.

2. Following the dimensions given in Diagram B, attach a center brace to each of *two* 5' 10½" pieces.

3. Following the dimensions given in Diagram C, attach the two center braces (one on each side) to the 5' 10½" piece that will be the center board of the riser. (See also Detail Diagram C1.)

4. Attach two center braces to each of the two 11¼"x 2' 10⅞" short crosspieces. The braces should be mounted on each board as shown in Diagram D and Detail Diagram D1.

5. Using a backstop, begin to assemble the riser by nailing *through* one 6' side board *into* the ends of the two outer and one center 5' 10½" pieces, using 6d nails and glue. Then nail through *those* pieces into the adjacent corner blocks and braces, as shown in Detail Diagram A2, again using 6d nails and glue.

6. Turn the riser around, and repeat step 5 using the remaining 6' side.

7. Install the two shorter crosspieces, nailing *through* the riser sides *into* the ends of the crosspieces, and *through* the crosspieces *into* the corner blocks and braces. (See Detail Diagram B1.)

8. Lay one 3'x6' sheet of plywood over the riser frame so that it runs parallel to the 6' side piece and the sanded side is up. Note on the top where the ends of the vertical center braces (attached to the short crosspieces and on which the top will rest) meet the top, so that you can nail into them. Then nail the top down to all edges and crosspieces using 6d nails and glue. Repeat this step for the other half of the top.

The box riser is now completed, and may be painted, covered with a rug, or finished in any other way you desire. You may find it convenient either to attach handles or to cut hand-holes in the sides, to make carrying the riser a bit easier.

Before you launch into the construction of a box-type riser, I suggest you examine the parallel type detailed in the next chapter. Then you can decide which design best suits your particular riser needs.

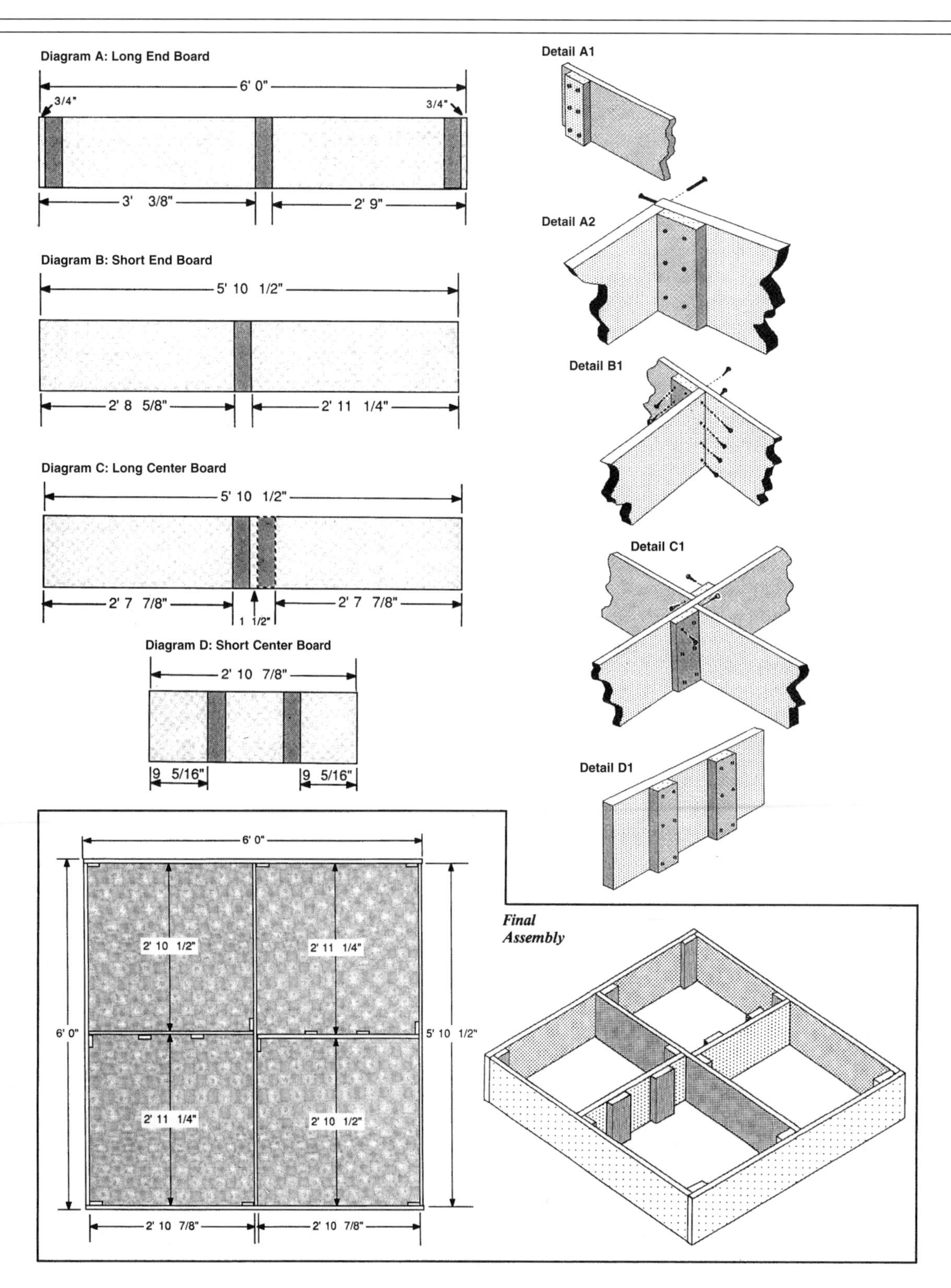

On The Rise, Part 2

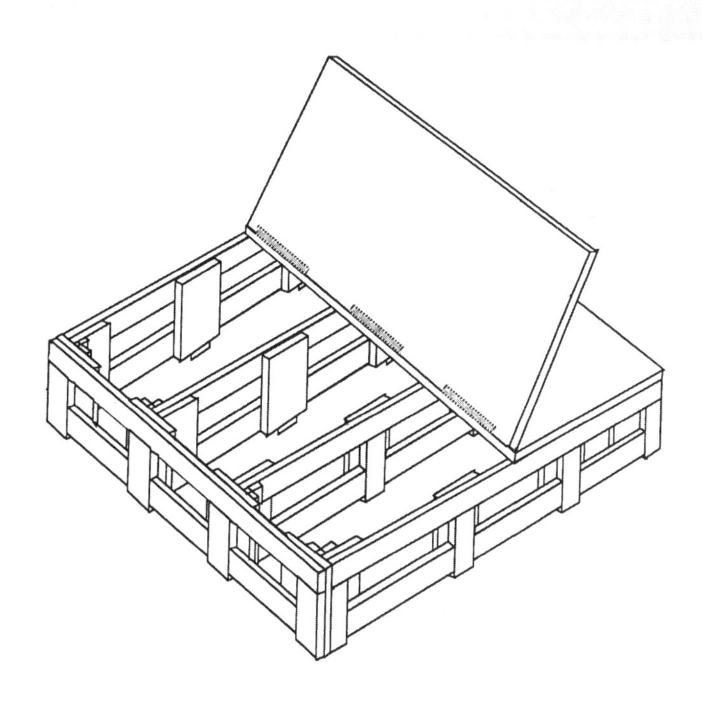

In this chapter we'll discuss a theatrical-style "parallel" riser. It's a bit more complicated to construct than a box riser, but it has the advantage of being collapsible. A parallel is quite strong, and the assembled riser isn't light by any means. But the portability factor is still high, since the riser breaks down into sections, and you can carry as few or as many of those as you wish at a time. The riser is made almost completely of wood; the only hardware involved is a few hinges and the screws necessary to assemble the various pieces. One nice additional feature of this design is that it is very easy to increase the riser's height, if you so desire. All you need to do is refigure the height of the vertical pieces to obtain the final height you wish; all other pieces remain the same measurement.

Before we begin our project, let me reiterate a few cautionary points. First—and most important—if you aren't a skilled woodworker, get help from someone who is. Don't make this your first attempt at carpentry; you're likely to waste time, materials, and money, and you could easily be injured if you aren't familiar with the tools necessary to complete the job. Second, be sure that you (and/or the person assisting you) read and thoroughly understand all the instructions *before* you start.

As with the box riser, I'm again figuring a 6'x6'x12" riser as a standard size for the parallel. If you need a riser of a different size, study my design in order to understand the principles involved, and then adapt those principles to your own specifications.

Building A Parallel Riser

Materials required:

1. *½" plywood.* This will be used for the top of your riser, as well as providing the material needed to create your corner blocks and center braces. You'll need two 4'x8' sheets, sanded on one side. (Note: As an option—to save overall weight—you *may* wish to purchase a half-sheet of ¼" plywood from which to make your corner blocks and center braces. They will do the job as well and will indeed reduce weight. But since my aim is to make this riser design as economical as possible, and since you can get the corner blocks and braces you need out of the same sheets of ½" ply as are required for the top, I've figured the design that way. If you *do* use ¼" plywood, you'll need to refigure some of the design dimensions accordingly.

If you have a particularly heavy drumset, or if you are very heavy or very active when playing, you may wish to opt for a ¾" plywood top. That will increase the strength of the riser, but will also increase the weight of the top section. If you choose to go with ¾" ply and want to keep the riser exactly 12" high, you'll need to reduce all vertical dimensions on my design by ¼". Otherwise, it might be easier just to let the riser come out at a final height of 12¼".

2. *1x3 pine boards.* 1x3 boards will be the basic material for the bulk of the riser. As in the previous chapter's specifications, the dimensions on the design are based on 1x3 that is milled to an *actual size* of ¾" x 2⅝". You want wood that is straight and free from imperfections, so buy "clear pine." If you can't afford that, show the design to your lumber supplier, and ask his or her advice regarding what type of stock to purchase in accordance with your budget.

Lumber is sold in different lengths in different areas. I've figured lengths that would be most common; if you are skilled at figuring total board feet versus necessary cuts, you'll want to determine what lengths to buy for yourself. According to my figures, you'll be able to get the cuts you need (with a minimum of waste) if you buy the following lengths: three at 7', two at 10', three at 12', and one at 12' plus *at least* one inch. (The design calls for two boards that are *exactly* six feet long, so buying a board precisely 12' long won't do, owing to the width of a saw blade. You need a bit extra to cover yourself.) The reason for buying longer boards and cutting them down yourself is economic: Lumberyards charge extra for each cut they make for you.

3. *Screws.* You'll need approximately 500 1" flat-head wood screws. Since this riser will see a lot of set-up and break-down movement, screws are more desirable than nails. If you are going to be putting the screws in with a power drill or "Yankee" type screwdriver, I suggest using Phillips screws.

If the piano hinges you purchase are not supplied with screws, you'll need to buy the correct number and size to correspond with the number of holes in the hinges. (It's not a bad idea to buy a dozen or so *more* than are needed; they always seem to get lost under a workbench.) I suggest using $3/8$" long sheet-metal screws, which are threaded right up to the head. Get half-round heads; they'll handle the easiest.

4. *Nails.* As part of the assembly operation, it may be desirable to "tack" the support frames together with easily removable nails, in order to facilitate the mounting of the hinges. For this, you'll need a supply of 6d ("six penny") double-head nails. It will also be easier to attach the corner blocks and braces to the frames if they are tacked with 1" wire nails before being drilled for the wood screws.

5. *Piano hinges.* The design calls for three piano hinges, each 18" long and at least 1" wide on either side of the pin. Use the hinge type of your choice based on your budget: Steel, chrome, and brass finishes are all available.

Piano hinges are commonly sold in 18" lengths, but you may find it less expensive to see if your local hardware store sells longer hinges by the foot. It may be less costly overall to purchase one 54"-long hinge, and have the store cut it into 18" lengths for you.

6. *Loose-pin hinges.* These are the keys to the collapsibility of the riser. The various supporting frames of the riser are connected by sixteen loose-pin (which means the hinge pins are removable) hinges. When the pins are in place and the top is put on, the riser is very solid; when the top is removed and the pins pulled from the hinges, the riser breaks down into seven separate sections for easy portability. Hinge types vary, but you'll want hinges that are a minimum of 2"x2" on either side of the pin, with holes that will accommodate the heads of the screws you are using.

7. *Glue.* You'll need at least two quarts of *Elmer's Woodworker's Glue* or its equivalent.

Tools required:

1. *Saws.* You'll need a table saw or portable circular saw to cut your plywood, and a radial-arm saw, portable circular saw, or portable jigsaw to cut your 1x3 stock. Hand saws may be used, but extreme care must be taken to ensure that all cuts are straight.

2. *Carpenter's square.* To ensure square corners and straight cuts.

3. *Drill.* A power or hand drill (with appropriate drill bits) will be needed to drill "pilot holes" in your corner blocks and braces, and in the 1x3 below them. A screwdriving attachment for your power drill will make assembling the frames a great deal easier. You'll also need a countersink bit to countersink the screw holes to accommodate the flathead screws.

4. *Screwdriver.* If you're not using a power driver, you'll need some way to drive the screws. It's also a good idea to use a hand screwdriver just to check the tightness of screws put in with a power driver. Obviously, the screwdriver type (Phillips or straight) should match the type of screws you're using.

5. *Tape measure.* You'll need this to measure your cuts.

6. *Hammer.* To assist you in tacking pieces together and removing double-head nails.

7. *Backstop.* If you're working alone, you'll need a backstop to back you up when tacking pieces together. Don't use a plaster wall or a wall with siding that might be damaged by the impact; a concrete wall or curb is best.

Cuts: (Remember that a saw blade has width; always allow for that width when making your measurements so that you end up with a piece that has the dimensions you want.)

1. *Plywood.* From each sheet of $1/2$" plywood, cut a 3'x8' piece. Cut approximately two feet off of one end of each of *those* pieces, so that you are left with two pieces *exactly* 3'x6'. Next, take the two long strips (approximately 1'x8') that were left over from your first long cuts, and cut each of those in half lengthwise, giving you four lengths of plywood, each approximately 6"x8'. (The widths will not be exactly 6", but this is not critical). Finally, from those strips cut twenty-four rectangular pieces approximately 6" wide by *exactly* $10\frac{3}{4}$" long. (See Detail Diagram 1.) These will be your corner blocks and center braces. (If you have opted to use $1/4$" ply for this purpose, a 4'x4' half-sheet may easily be divided into the pieces you'll need.)

2. *Pine boards.* (I'm figuring the following cuts based on my own experience with lumber availability. Again, let me stress that, if you can, you should figure your own cuts from what is commonly available in your area.)

Referring to Construction Diagrams 1A, 1B, and 2, make the following cuts: From the one 12'-plus batten, cut two A pieces 6' long; from two 10' battens, cut twenty-four B pieces $8\frac{7}{8}$" long; from one 12' batten, cut six C pieces 1' $8\frac{1}{2}$" long; from two 12' battens, cut four E pieces 5' $9\frac{1}{2}$" long; from two 7' battens cut eight F pieces 1' $7\frac{5}{8}$" long; and from one 7' batten, cut four G pieces 1' $7\frac{3}{4}$" long. (Pieces indicated as D are plywood corner blocks and braces.)

Construction:

The construction of a parallel looks more difficult than it is. It's really just a big jigsaw puzzle. Simply separate and label the various cuts to correspond with the construction diagrams. Then, take each piece as called for, according to the following instructions.

1. *6' support frames.* Referring to Construction Diagram 1A, lay out the pieces necessary to create one of the 6' frames. Referring to Construction Diagram 1B, place corner blocks and center braces into position. Apply glue to the area where the plywood will meet the 1x3. Then, carefully square up each

corner using the carpenter's square (don't rely on the edges of the corner blocks), and tack the blocks and braces down with 1" wire nails. (Be sure to place the nails in places that the screws aren't going to go.) Once all corner blocks and braces have been glued and tacked into place, *carefully* set the completed frame aside to allow the glue to dry. Remember it's only tacked together, so don't move it any more than necessary (in order to avoid getting the corners out of square). Repeat this process for the other 6' frame.

Once the glue has dried on the first frame, lay it down flat, and drill pilot holes for your 1" wood screws, using a drill bit that approximates the diameter of the shaft of the screw *without* threads. (Refer to Construction Diagram 1B and Detail Diagram 2.) When this is completed, change to a countersink bit, and countersink each hole to accommodate the screw head. (You want each screw to seat in flush with the top of the plywood.) When that step is completed, put the wood screws in, using a power driver on your drill or some other form of screwdriver. Be sure to check with a hand screwdriver to make sure each screw is in tightly. Repeat this procedure for the other 6' frame.

2. *5' 9½" frames.* Repeat the frame construction process for the four 5' 9½" frames, referring to Construction Diagram 2. (The corner blocks and braces are installed in the same relative position on these frames as on the 6' frames, so a separate diagram has not been included.)

3. *Riser top.* Placing the two 3'x6' sheets of plywood with their smooth sides *down*, join them along a 6' length as shown in Construction Diagram 4. Following the dimensions shown, install the piano hinges. (Pilot-drilling with a very small drill bit may be beneficial, but be careful to keep your pilot hole in the center of each hole in the hinge plate. Otherwise, your screws will have a tendency to pull the hinge off center.) When completed, the top should fold up with the smooth side of the plywood to the outside.

4. *Corner hinges.* Note the positions of the loose-pin hinges indicated on Construction Diagram 3 and the mounting method suggested by Detail Diagram 3. There are two ways to install the hinges. The easy way is to set the frames up as indicated in Construction Diagram 3 and nail them together, using 6d double-head nails. Use your carpenter's square to make sure that the corners created between the various frames are all square. Then, either fit the hinges into place and install them immediately, or mark where the screw holes need to go, remove the 6d nails and lay each frame flat again, and install the hinge halves separately.

A method that is a little trickier, but involves fewer operations, is to measure back from the edge of one frame carefully to allow for the thickness of the other, and place the hinge halves accordingly. (Again, refer to Detail Diagram 3 for clarification.)

It's a good idea to code the two halves of each hinge, so that you can assemble the riser the same way each time. In other words, when you install the first hinge, put a clearly visible "A" on each half of that hinge. Put "B"s on the next hinge, and so on, so that the two elements that make up any given corner are clearly identified. Use enamel paint or engrave the code right into the metal, so that the marking is permanent.

Please note that the layout of the hinges is such that the assembled frames cannot all fold up in any one direction; the hinges are placed to work opposite each other and thus prevent that. It is the fact that the hinge pins can be removed and the frames carried separately that makes this a portable unit; it is not a "folding platform." Only the top actually folds up for transport.

5. *Finishing.* When all the pieces are assembled, the riser may be painted (but don't cover your hinge codes), the top may be covered with a rug or painted, special fittings such as cleats or eyebolts may be attached to the top to secure stand legs, etc. (Just remember that any hardware permanently attached to the top may prevent it from folding completely flat.) You may also wish to cut hand holes or attach handles to the top. Be sure to set your kit up on the riser *first,* in order to determine the best location for such holes or handles.

Assembling the riser:

To assemble the riser, simply stand one of the 6' frames against a wall, or have someone hold it upright. Starting at one end, fit the halves of the two hinges on one end of one 5' 9½" frame into the corresponding halves on the 6' frame (according to your coding) and insert the hinge pins. Continue this until all four 5' 9½" frames have been fitted at one end. Then, attach the other 6' frame to the other ends of those pieces. Place the top onto the frames with the hinges down and running parallel to the 6' frames.

It is my belief that you and your kit provide enough weight pressing the riser top down against the 1x3 frames to hold the top firmly in place. However, in order to *lock* the top in place—and also to increase the rigidity of the assembled frames—you may wish to use loose bolts to secure the top of the frames. This is best done by drilling three ¼" holes through the riser top and into the center of the top edge of the two 6' frames and the two outside 5' 9½" frames. (See Detail Diagram 4.) These holes should be about 2" deep into the 1x3. When the riser is set up, simply insert a ¼"x2½" eyebolt down through the top and into the edge of the frame through each hole. The eyebolts are easy to remove, and easy to link together with a piece of string or wire tie in order to travel in your trap case along with the hinge pins.

Building this riser sounds like a lot of work when described on paper, and to a certain degree, it is. But the riser should last for many years if properly handled, and the visual benefit you will gain should make the effort worthwhile.

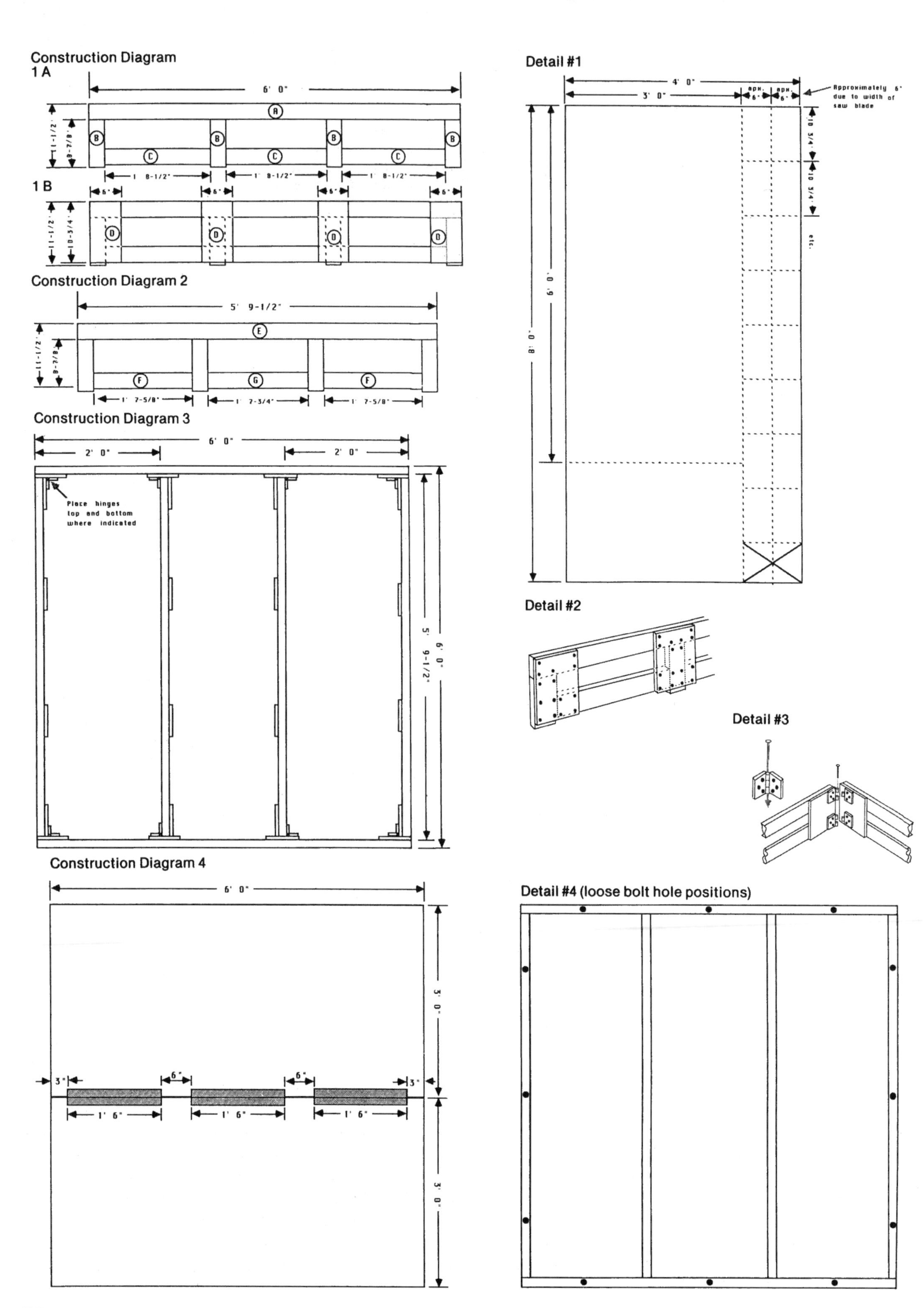
Construction Diagram
1 A
6' 0"
A
B
C
11-1/2"
8-7/8"
1' 8-1/2"
1 B
6"
D
11-1/2"
10-3/4"
Construction Diagram 2
5' 9-1/2"
E
F
G
11-1/2"
8-7/8"
1' 7-5/8"
1' 2-3/4"
Construction Diagram 3
6' 0"
2' 0"
Place hinges top and bottom where indicated
5' 9-1/2"
Construction Diagram 4
3"
6"
1' 6"
3' 0"
Detail #1
4' 0"
3' 0"
apx. 6"
Approximately 6" due to width of saw blade
10 3/4"
etc.
6' 0"
8' 0"
Detail #2
Detail #3
Detail #4 (loose bolt hole positions)

Out Of The Dark

I didn't spend years perfecting my craft as a drummer and entertainer to play in the dark all night!

I've said many times how important I believe the visual element is to a band's entertainment potential. I've encouraged drummers to employ showmanship, shiny equipment, and any other device possible to maximize their visual appeal. But your band could be the best-costumed, best-choreographed, and most enthusiastic act this side of Michael Jackson; it doesn't make a bit of difference if the audience can't *see* you. And that is exactly the situation that once faced my band.

We were booked into a club we had never played before, and that was far enough away from my home to prevent my checking it out in advance. However, I did *call* ahead to ask about the stage size, the position of the stage in the room, the number of outlets available, etc. I also asked if there was any lighting on the stage, and was told that there was.

Well, there were *some* lights over the stage: ceiling lights—not stage lights. And those were only two of the eight fixtures over the entire stage/dance floor area—all operated on the same dimmer. As a consequence, whatever happened to the dance floor lights also happened to the "stage lights." Now, I'll be the first one to admit that a darkened dance floor makes things a bit more intimate, and helps people feel a bit less conspicuous. So I agree with turning down the lights over the floor. However, in this particular situation, the management chose to turn them off completely! This put the band—you guessed it—in *total darkness.*

There is a physio/psychological phenomenon known well by theatrical lighting designers and directors. Simply put, it is that people will not pay attention to what they cannot see. (I was a lighting designer for several years, and more than once had a director tell me, "I can't hear the actors. Turn up the lights!") So I was not surprised when the reaction we got from our audience on the first night of this new gig was something less than enthusiastic.

I very rarely am insulted by the conditions of a club gig; I've been around a long time and have lost most of my illusions. But I didn't spend years perfecting my craft as a drummer and entertainer to play in the dark all night! My background as a lighting designer also came to the fore, demanding that I take some action.

Now, let's take a moment to evaluate the situation. I estimate that fifty percent of today's club bands—especially those playing sizable rock clubs—travel with their own lighting. And most clubs that regularly feature entertainment—especially hotel lounges or other fairly classy rooms—have some sort of stage lighting built in. It's really quite rare to find conditions such as I've described above. On the other hand, if your band plays local taverns, small original-music clubs, and/or the occasional private function in a banquet room or rental hall, you might well be faced with the prospect of little or no lighting dedicated to the stage area (if there is a stage at all). So it pays to be prepared.

Returning to my story: I realized that I was not going to be able to produce a major theatrical setup by the next night's performance; I just needed to provide my band with some basic illumination. And it had to be self-supporting; there was no way to hang, stand, tie, or otherwise secure any lights to any part of the room itself. I didn't have a lot of time, either, since I needed the lights the following night. So the next day I went into my workshop, rummaging for materials with which to solve my problem. I knew I needed lights, cables to power them, a way to mount them, and some means of controlling them. I happened to have a couple of small PAR lights (small theatrical lights using common photoflood lamps and no glass lenses) left over from my days on the road. These came with their own "yokes" (U-shaped flat steel bars designed to hold the light either from above or below). All I had to do was figure out how and where to place the lights so that they could shine on my band without "spilling" light all over the rest of the room. I also had to think in terms of safety, because I knew the lights should be up high somewhere, and I didn't want them falling onto anyone.

I figured that the only high, stable surfaces that I could always count on being wherever my band was playing was the top of our PA cabinets. We use a pair of medium-sized enclosures that are covered in a thick fiber material somewhat like carpet padding. I decided that if I could place one light atop each of the cabinets (which are elevated on tripod stands) and shine it down at the band, that would do the job.

In order to secure each light to the top of a PA cabinet, I needed to provide it with a stable base of its own. I cut two 12" squares of 3/8" plywood, and drilled a 3/8" hole in the center of each. I countersunk the hole on the one side of each base board, so that a flat-head bolt (3/8"x1 1/4") could fit into the hole with its head flush with the bottom of the board. I then put a light, with the hole in the center of the yoke over the bolt, onto each of the base boards, and used a wing nut to secure the light to the base. Voilà—a nice, free-standing lighting instrument, which could be pointed in any direction and angled up or down quite effectively.

But how to affix it to the PA cabinet in a secure, but non-permanent, manner? *Velcro* to the rescue. I glued and stapled several strips of *Velcro* (the "hook" side) to the bottom of each base board. When placed down firmly on the top of the PA cabinet, the *Velcro* gripped the fabric covering quite tightly. The light stayed solidly in place, even when the PA cabinet was (experimentally) jostled and bumped.

So now I had my lights, but how was I to control them? It wasn't hard to figure that I would need to run one or more extension cords from the lights themselves to whatever control switch I planned to use. I chose to use medium-gauge lamp cord onto which I fitted my own male and female connectors, rather than buying ready-made, heavy-duty extension cords. My homemade cords were more than adequate to carry the 150-watt load to each lamp, yet were still fairly flexible and easy to carry in twenty-foot lengths.

For the control switch, I had my choice of a simple off/on switch or a dimmer. I happened to have a pair of standard, household wall switches available, so I used them. I have had experience with household dimmers, and while they are nice from an artistic point of view, they can cause noise in your electrical lines. I simply installed the two switches into an electrical utility (or "quad") box, using a common power line in, and two separate power lines out. In this way, I could control a separate electrical line independently with each switch. (It didn't make much difference with only two lights, but I might want to expand at a later date.) I made sure that each "power line" controlled by one of the switches ended in a multiple female plug.

The end result of all this work is nothing fancy: two floodlights perched on top of our two PA boxes and pointed back down at us. They go on or off—no artsy dimming or changing colors. But they do provide us with our own illumination at a very small cost, and the system can be expanded for greater flexibility in the future.

If you don't have your own lighting instruments to start with, there are several options open to you, depending on your budget and/or how handy you are with tools and electricity. You can, of course, purchase ready-made theatrical lights, yokes and all. A couple of small PAR lights are not terribly expensive, and could be picked up at a theatrical supply outlet, some electrical supply stores, and a few other locations. Check your local yellow pages. Or, you can pick up some outdoor/patio floodlights in almost any building or home improvement store. Get the type with a base made to be screwed onto the side of a building, and with a ratchet to control the angle at which the lamp points. Some of these come with a clip-on "collar" to help prevent the spread of the light. If you don't get that, you'll need to figure some way of partially enclosing the lamp so that you can contain and direct the light only where you want it to go.

I've had success with creating pseudo-PAR lights by mounting a simple ceramic socket base in the bottom of a two-pound coffee can, and then getting some flat steel bar stock and bending it into a yoke. This takes a few extra bolts, nuts, and washers, and a little visualization, but it isn't particularly difficult. What you need to do here is be creative. It's very possible to build a substantial number of perfectly functional lighting instruments for a fraction of the cost of store-bought theatrical lights. Things you need to keep in mind, however, are insulation (making sure that there is space around the lamp for heat to dissipate so that there is no fire hazard), and mounting security (making sure that whatever means you use to place your instrument is safe and solid).

You may find that you need your own lights less than five percent of the time. But as far as I'm concerned, the prospect of performing in the dark is unacceptable, no matter how infrequently it might occur.

Part 3: Taking Care Of Business

Riding The Roller Coaster

Being a professional musician is very much like riding a roller coaster: It has its ups and downs, it can be both exciting and frightening, and it costs you something to ride.

Every so often, I like to stop and reflect on some of the aspects of a career in music—with club drumming particularly in mind. Naturally, I use my own career as a sort of standard by which to evaluate a club drumming career in general, along with comments I've received over the years from colleagues in the field and readers of my column. I've come to the conclusion that being a professional musician who specializes in performing popular music is very much like riding a roller coaster: It has its ups and downs, it can be both exciting and frightening, and it costs you something to ride.

I don't necessarily mean that having a club drumming career is going to cost you money; on the contrary, you're in it to earn a living, which requires that you make a profit. But it is going to cost you in terms of that classic music-biz cliché: paying your dues. And this is where my recent reflections have been focused. I think we all understand that a young player entering the business is going to have to spend some time "paying dues." Many of us came up through various stages of garage bands, teenage dance bands, semipro and wedding bands, and ultimately, full-time professional club bands of one style or another. Many of us have spent time playing in bands that performed music we didn't personally like in order to keep playing, and in order to keep body and soul together. This type of dues-paying is pretty much recognized as a necessity in order to establish a career.

But what some of us fail to recognize, sometimes, is that the dues *never stop*. Unless you get off of it entirely, a roller coaster ride is *always* going to offer both ups and downs, not to mention some unexpected turns. And while I'm sure all of us would like to think that our career moves will always be made in an upward direction, the fact of the matter is that there is a lot of lateral movement in the club scene, and not infrequently a few steps back that must be taken in order to survive the many challenges that the business throws at us.

Let's use a bit of my own career as an example. When I first started playing full-time, I was a member of a typical Top-40 club band, playing weekend gigs on a strictly local level. I was working regularly, but not gaining much in the way of personal esteem or career advancement. My next opportunity came when I got the call to join a traveling show group on a national tour. This was the "big time": nice hotels, paid transportation, seeing the country and getting paid for it! But then a few bookings fell through, and the profit margin declined dramatically. Personality problems added to the tension of the situation, and ultimately I chose to leave. Despite the fact that I had a pretty impressive track record, when I returned home, I had problems finding work. I wound up in a polka trio, playing weekends at a local Polish restaurant. Although that turned out to be one of the most enjoyable gigs of my career, at the outset it seemed like a major step backwards, professionally speaking.

A change of residence caused me to leave that gig, and once again, I was at the ultimate low point on the "roller coaster": I was totally unemployed. I went into the casuals market, playing with a pickup band for weddings and parties. Luckily, this was a group of pretty talented people who were all in the same boat as I was, so we had nothing to be ashamed of musically. But I did feel that my talents were being wasted to a certain extent, since I wasn't working steadily in a club situation.

After about six months of casuals, I got another call to go on tour. My ride was on the upswing again! I joined and toured with a lounge trio doing class hotel gigs over a Christmas season. We made good music and good money, and had a good time. But what goes up must come down, and in our case, the booking agency handling our group folded quite suddenly. Before we could find another agency and get a booking schedule going, financial considerations forced each member of the group to seek more immediate employment elsewhere. So it was back to the casuals market for me.

About a year later, my career took a major step up. I joined a Top-40 band booked full-time on a local club circuit. We worked six nights a week, fifty weeks per year, in a series of very nice rooms—and we never left town. This, to me, was a gig made in heaven. My wife and I had two children and bought a house during the four and a half years I was a member of that band. But all good things come to an end, and that good thing ended when the other bandmembers decided to retire, after some eleven years together. From a position of having had a considerable, regular income, I was once again at the bottom of the roller coaster.

I had taken unemployment fairly lightly in the past; it was a temporary inconvenience that more or less came with the job of being a musician. But after having been steadily employed for so long—and with the additional responsibilities of home and family—I experienced a new attitude. I was discouraged, and a little bitter. After a career now into its eighteenth year, I found it difficult to get work. The disco scene had wreaked havoc on the job market in San Diego, where I was living. The number of clubs that employed live musicians was smaller, and younger bands—willing to work for less money than I could afford to—were filling those clubs. I found myself jumping at the chance to play in a "novelty" band: a '50s rock 'n' roll revival act. This act eventually broadened its musical scope in an effort to appeal to a wider market, but it never attained full-time bookings or a regular, predictable income. In effect, I was back to working casuals, albeit with the same band on each gig. I wasn't meeting my family's financial needs, and I considered taking a day job—something I hadn't had to do in the previous ten years.

As fate would have it, I was spared that necessity, in a totally unforeseen—and pretty drastic—manner. I received a call from a friend with whom I had played in a previous band. He was now playing in Hawaii, and his band needed a drummer. They were the house band in a very popular rock club in Waikiki, with a long-term contract. I would make more money than I had ever made before, work only five nights a week, and play music that I enjoyed. The only kicker was, I would have to lease out my home in San Diego, cut all ties, and move my family to Hawaii—for good, as far as could be seen at the time.

This was a monumental decision for me—involving emotions, finances, and a host of other considerations, and calling for the cooperation and understanding of my family. In the end I did take the gig, we did move, and it turned out to be a very good situation in most respects. I was working well with the group, the money was coming in, and generally speaking, everything looked good for a long run on this gig. It was at this point that one of those "unexpected turns" on the roller coaster took place. I received a call from *Modern Drummer*.

I had been a freelance columnist for *MD* for three and a half years, playing actively in the club market during that time. When the call came, offering me the job of managing editor, I was faced with another major decision. I was coming up on twenty years of playing in clubs. I had what looked to be a pretty solid gig in Hawaii, but it was still a club band. I hadn't become a "star" (as I had told myself at twenty that I would be by twenty-five), and I was facing my thirty-third birthday. Was it time for a career move? Could I be happy working for a drum magazine, instead of drumming full-time? How would my family feel about picking up stakes again, and this time moving from Hawaii, back to San Diego for a brief period, and ultimately to New Jersey? All I can say is, when you have to make decisions like this one, you're paying some dues, psychologically speaking.

I came to *MD* in November of 1983, and although I was thoroughly involved with the magazine, it didn't take long before I began to miss drumming full-time. Unfortunately, it *did* take me a long time to be able to get back into playing *at all.* As an "immigrant" from the West Coast, I had no contacts in the local music scene, and it took me quite a while to link up with a band here. But when I did, an interesting thing happened—something that demonstrates how different a person can feel about the same situation under different circumstances. I became a member of another '50-'60s "oldies" band, playing local clubs on a weekend basis. But this time, instead of being discouraged, I enjoyed myself immensely. The level of musicianship in the band was excellent, and we played tunes that I first played as a teenager myself (so there was a certain amount of youthful nostalgia in it for me). I played with that group for six years. From there I went to a three-year stint with a high-energy R&B dance band, and now I'm back in the wedding and casuals market.

I'm not sure that every club musician has had a career with as many ups and downs as mine has had. But I do know that keeping a realistic attitude about the ongoing nature of those ups and downs—the fact that the dues never stop—has helped me to weather the hard times, because I've always known that better times would come. That same attitude has also helped to keep me from taking the good times for granted, because I've learned that they aren't infinite either. I'm still riding my roller coaster, and I'm going to keep on riding it, as long as I've got the fare.

Customer Relations

Part 1: Dealing With People

In the club, the audience members are your guests, and it's your job to make them comfortable.

In club performing, public relations is a major portion of the business. But many musicians tend to ignore this vital element, choosing to take breaks away from the audience or step out to the parking lot for a smoke. I don't dispute that breaks are your time, to do with as you see fit. But I do encourage you to examine the value of cultivating an intimate rapport with your audience. Table-hopping and congenial conversation can create a camaraderie with your customers that will make them feel more at home in your club. This is what helps to create regulars and the kind of following that every band appreciates. Even if you aren't a brilliant conversationalist, just being present and visible in the room can help, because then an audience member can approach you with a request, a compliment, or some other comment. You don't necessarily have to initiate conversations if you aren't comfortable doing so, but you can be available for someone else to do so.

It's a simple matter to approach a table and say "Good evening," or to ask if they're enjoying the music or if there's anything special they'd like to hear. I find it helpful to make eye contact with someone during the set, and then approach that person during the break. It's an easy way of establishing a small opening for conversation.

It's also important to remember that, like it or not, a band is a representative for the club in which they work. You may only be on a one-night engagement, or you may be on a long-term stay. In either case, your audience sees you in *this* club, at *this* time, and they'll judge the club according to the impression you make. You may not see this as your responsibility, but the club certainly will, so it is to your benefit to accept the responsibility and act accordingly. This simply means to have a polite, friendly, and businesslike attitude on behalf of the club. Whether or not you get along with the manager, or think you're underpaid, or hate the decor, these are not topics for conversation with customers. They are items pertinent only to business between you and the club. Keep your social conversation on a social level, and tailor it to the atmosphere of the club itself. For instance, if you're working in a blue-jeans-and-T-shirt beer bar, you can be more casual than if you're in a major restaurant or hotel lounge catering to family or traveling business professionals. The basic rule to keep in mind is: *Whatever helps business in the club helps your business.* If you make a favorable impression on your audience socially as well as musically, the club management will become aware of it. This, in turn, can mean a return engagement, or a better bargaining position for salary increases on a long-term stand.

There are some specific areas of customer relations I'd like to examine, because they are things that occur repeatedly on every engagement. How you handle them can make or break your social standing in the club.

Requests

This section applies primarily to cover bands who play "Top 40"-type gigs. If your repertoire is wide and you can field just about any request, you're way ahead. If it isn't, simply say something like, "If we know your song, we'll be happy to play it, and if we don't we'll sure try to get something close for you." Or you can add a little humor: "If we don't know your song, we'll play something with a whole lot of the same notes in it." If a customer makes a request to you personally, then you can immediately say whether or not you do the song, and if not, offer an alternative. If the request comes up on a napkin, then you can ask who sent it and offer another choice over the microphone—something by the same artist, or in the same musical style. If you don't have any reasonable alternative, then politely say so. It's no shame not to know every song in the world. Often the requester will offer another choice that you might know.

Unless you have so many requests that it just isn't feasible, you should acknowledge every one. The customer made the effort to correspond with you, and you owe him or her the courtesy of a reply. On the other hand, try to avoid getting trapped with one customer who keeps yelling out requests that he probably knows you don't do. Most bands tend to favor a few styles of music in their repertoire. It never fails that some customer decides you should be doing *his* favorite music instead.

The same kind of situation can occur on a one-to-one basis on your break. I must admit to being terribly frustrated when approached, on my third or fourth break, by a customer who says, "Do you play this? Do you play that? Well, what *do* you play?" I'm tempted to say "What the hell do you think we've been playing for the last three hours?" But again, this is a no-win situation. You alienate that customer and anyone else who might overhear the exchange. Your best bet is to try to get out of the conversation and away from him as diplomatically (and as *soon*) as possible. *You can't please everybody.*

Tips

Tips are great. They are a tangible means for the audience to show their appreciation for your work. You needn't have any qualms about accepting and even encouraging tips. Of course, I don't mean asking for them over the microphone. The simple presence of a tip jar in a conspicuous place is an obvious but subtle statement. Once again, it's possible to encourage tips by using a little humor: "If you have a request, just send it up on a napkin, or for faster service use a five-dollar bill." However, be careful with lines like that, to make sure they are received in the humorous manner you intended. If they don't seem to be, drop the line.

Sometimes a request is sent up along with a tip. If you do the song, great. If you don't, you're faced with a dilemma. It doesn't seem right to keep the money for something you can't do. Here are some suggestions: Find out who sent the request by asking the waiter or waitress who brought it, or by asking over the microphone. Offer an alternative choice on the next break. You have the option, when approaching the requester, of keeping the money or returning it. Most customers will not accept the returned money even if you can't do the song. Don't insist, because it diminishes their graciousness in sending it in the first place. They sent the tip because they like your music, and hoped you could do their song. They are not actually buying that song alone, and you are not under any moral obligation to return the tip if you can't perform it. Obviously, if you cannot determine who sent the request, then keep the tip.

Once in a while you'll get a customer who goes overboard. Usually the customer has had too much to drink, and starts dropping bills in your jar every other song. This calls for some judgment on your part. You don't want to insult the customer by refusing the tips, and you can use the money. On the other hand, you don't want him coming back sober at some later date to complain to management or to other customers that you soaked him. The best bet is to bring the situation to the attention of the manager and see what his or her policy is. If this is not possible, I suggest you politely discourage the customer from further tipping, being as good-natured about it as possible. If he chooses to continue, you must take the attitude that he's an adult, it's his money, and he can do with it as he pleases. Enjoy the profit. However, never *encourage* further tipping by such a customer, as this will very likely give you a negative, mercenary reputation with management and customers alike.

Personal Appearance

First impressions are very important, and, depending on the nature of the club, bands can sometimes be severely judged by their wardrobe and personal grooming. (Many hotel lounges and similar venues have dress and grooming stipulations in their contracts.) You don't have to dress like Elton John; each club will have its own appropriate wardrobe requirements based on that of the clientele. The idea is to look professional, not necessarily over-dressed. Hair length and facial hair for men is no longer much of a social issue, as long as their hair is well-styled and clean. The same goes for women. Wardrobe and hairstyle will often be the thing that is remembered about a female performer, long after her singing voice has been forgotten. This is unfortunate, but true, and must be recognized and dealt with by the successful performer.

Stage Presence

This is the part of your performance that reaches your audience on a personal level. If you're in a cover band, the music is familiar; they've heard it on the radio. Thus it almost becomes impersonal when you play. You are absorbed into the song. But between songs, when you converse with the audience from the stage, then it's really *you* in the room with *them*, at *that moment*. How you approach them verbally, and how much you encourage their participation in the evening's performance, will determine how successful the evening is socially.

The situation is exactly the same as being a good host at a party. You can't just set out snacks, pour drinks, put on the music, and then leave your guests on their own. You have to mingle, start conversations, and introduce people. You have to get things comfortable by your own conscious effort. In the club, the audience members are your guests, and it's your job to make them comfortable. If they're really into dancing non-stop, then you can go song-to-song with very little conversation. But that will tend to make you more impersonal and thus more easily forgettable. If you establish yourself and your group as real people whose company may be enjoyed, then you've made the audience your *friends*, not just your customers.

Mailing Lists

Once you've made friends and established a following, you want to keep them. The way to do that is to keep them posted on your whereabouts through a mailing list. This is especially helpful if you tend to work clubs in one general area. But even if you play a larger circuit, the list can be beneficial. To set one up, you simply arrange a means for audience members to leave you their name and address. My bands have had success with pre-printed forms that we made available on the bandstand beside a little mailbox. The customer filled out the form and dropped it in the box. We collected the forms and made a note of which club the customer was in. A week or so before returning to that club, we'd send out postcards with our opening date and an invitation to visit us again—nothing elaborate, but enough to get the "when" and "where" across. We also used the list to promote special events the clubs might be having—holiday parties and so on. At Christmas we'd send cards to everybody on the list. The small expense involved in this effort proved a very worthwhile investment. (It's also tax deductible as a legitimate business promotion.)

If you are on the road, you might just send cards ahead to the customers in the next town. Your customers will appreciate this personal attention, and recognize it as a genuine desire on your part that they come to see you. It can make a return engagement a real homecoming, complete with friendly faces and a ready-made audience.

Customer Relations
Part 2: Dealing With Drinks

Whether or not you drink is your own personal business.
But whether or not you drink on the job *is* business.

One of the most common problems faced by a steady drummer is how to deal with the custom of showing one's appreciation for the music by buying the musicians a drink. This is a social convention that has become accepted in lieu of tipping. The club is a social environment where drinking is the primary activity, so it's not surprising that the purchase of drinks for the band should be part of that activity.

I refer to this as a *problem* because it can be. I'm not necessarily an advocate of teetotalling, but I think it's important to keep your priorities straight. Whether or not you drink is your own personal business. But whether or not you drink on the job *is* business.

I don't think anyone can have worked long in the club scene without suffering through the experience of playing with someone who was out of control due to alcohol consumption. I've also seen the situation of a popular band receiving three or four rounds of drinks before the evening was half over. By the third or fourth set, some of the members were too inebriated to perform competently, much less be entertaining. This only establishes a negative image in the eyes of the customers, and certainly jeopardizes your chances for further employment in that club. Popularity can backfire on you.

Some groups take the attitude that even though they're working in a bar, they are still *working*. The social environment of the club applies to the customers, not the band. The waitresses and bartenders also work in the bar, but they are not permitted to drink alcohol during working hours, and certainly in no other profession would the employees be allowed to freely consume liquor. This attitude may seem a little stringent, but it does have the advantage of eliminating the possibility of alcohol problems on stage. Again, I'm not recommending it for everybody, but it should be considered as an option when you or your group establish policy.

Whether or not you actually drink alcohol on the job, the drinks are going to come, so you do have to have a policy for handling them. When you begin to develop that policy, you need to consider several factors involving your relationship with your customers, club management, and fellow employees. Here are some of those factors:

1. Size of the club. If you work in a large room with a volume sale, then a couple of drinks more or less won't make much difference to the cash register at the end of the evening. But if you work in a small lounge, a couple of rounds for the band may represent a significant contribution to the evening's profit. I've had managers ask me *not* to refuse drinks under any circumstances because they needed the sale. Also, the round might mean a tip to the server who brings it. Consideration to your fellow employees is important.

2. Has the drink already been purchased? It's one thing to politely decline an offer to buy a drink. It's another to see a tray of them appear on the bandstand. Obviously, the money has been paid by the customer, the drink poured, the server tipped, and the customer sees the drink in front of you. Now what do you do? If you intend to keep the drink, then there's no problem; just thank the customer courteously. If you don't, then I suggest you thank the customer and get the drink out of sight as soon as possible. Don't leave an untouched drink sitting where the customer can see it and take offense. Either move it immediately, or leave it till the next break, at which time you can stop by the customer's table to say thanks—and then proceed to somewhere else in the room to dispose of the drink. Give it away, return it to the bar, or dump it out. Remember: You are under no moral obligation to drink alcoholic beverages, no matter what the opinion of the customer. This leads us to:

3. Personality of the customer. This is a tough one, because you generally don't know the person well. Often you get the drink before you even find out who sent it. If you can find out in advance, and can judge that person's attitude, you can more easily estimate how they would react to your accepting or refusing the drink. If the customer is a regular, then you usually have a good rapport and can politely decline (if you wish) without fear of giving offense. The important thing is to be gracious, whether you do or don't keep the drink—because you definitely *do* want to keep the customer. It is unfortunate that some customers are almost belligerent in their insistence that you accept the drink—taking your refusal as a personal affront. But it's *your* body that is going to consume the drink, not theirs. They're not trying to perform—*you* are. Keep that in mind when considering your policy.

Now let's talk about establishing that policy. It should be consistent from night to night. In this way, your customers will eventually get to know it and you may dramatically reduce the whole problem. Let's begin by assuming that management wishes you to accept drinks. You have several options.

1. If you *do* drink on the job, have one particular drink, and make sure the waitresses and bartenders know what it is. Try to make your drink a standard variety, rather than a premium one, so that the customer isn't repaid for his generosity with a twenty-dollar bar tab. There's nothing that destroys good customer relations faster than giving a customer the impression that he's been taken.
2. If you *don't* wish to drink alcohol on the job, but would rather the customer think you do, you can arrange with the bartender to give you a disguised drink, such as a rum and *Coke* (half *Coke*-half *7Up*), or a bourbon and seven (*7Up* with a splash of *Coke*). This may seem deceptive, but it keeps the customer happy and complies with management's request.
3. I find that since sparkling water is currently in vogue, most customers don't object to buying a *Perrier* with a squeeze. This is my drink, because it not only pleases the customer, but provides me with a refreshing way to overcome dehydration (a prime cause of fatigue over a long evening's performance).

If the club is large enough that management does not specifically request you to accept drinks, then you have a few other options in addition to the ones above.

1. If you choose not to drink alcohol, let the bar staff know it. Then if the customer simply asks to "buy the band whatever they're drinking" the server can bring you the soft drink of your choice. If the customer wants to buy a specific drink ("Give 'em a round of kamikazes") he or she can politely inform him that you don't wish to drink, but would appreciate a *Perrier* or whatever.

   Making sure the bar staff knows your order ahead of time also prevents having the momentum of your performance disrupted by a server coming up to the bandstand and asking what you want. Instead, he or she can go directly to the bar, order the drink you wish and bring it to you, telling you at that time who sent it so you may thank the customer.
2. If the customer comes up to you personally and offers to buy a drink, you have the option to order a soft drink, or to politely decline the offer altogether. But try to be as gracious as possible. Let the offer lead you into conversation with the customer so he doesn't get the impression he's being snubbed. He was expressing his appreciation for your work with his offer. You should repay his kindness with some expression of your gratitude, even if you don't actually accept the drink.

Sadly, some customers feel offended if you order a nonalcoholic drink. In their eyes, it somehow cheapens or diminishes their gift. Often, they are aware that you get soft drinks free anyway. However, this fact can be used to your advantage. If a customer approaches me with an offer to buy a drink, I usually say no, and thank him. If he says, "Well, how about a *Coke*, then?" I'll thank him again, but let him know that I get soft drinks free and I would feel it inconsiderate to let him pay for something I'd get for nothing. The customer usually appreciates this candor, and once again, an opportunity for good relations has been realized.

It's important that you acknowledge a drink as you would a tip or any gift. Whether it's a *Chivas Regal* or a *7Up*, it's a token of the customer's appreciation. It's good politics and simple courtesy to say thanks, either immediately over the microphone, or personally on the next break. I think the personal approach is better since it can initiate a conversation with the customer, but even a simple "Salud!" from on-stage will be appreciated.

In the final analysis, drinking in the club is a political issue, and a major factor of good customer relations. I have emphasized how important customer relations are to the overall success of your performance. But I cannot stress enough how much *more* important is the control you must maintain over your playing. The one must be judged in light of the other, and the *playing* must always come first.

Rehearsing

When, Where, And How

> **Frequent and effective rehearsals can be a major determining factor in a band's economic and professional status.**

I've always believed that the ingredients for a successful club band—aside from basic, innate talent—are originality, showmanship, and an excellent repertoire. All of those require hard work, which in our business translates as "rehearsing." Generally speaking, the better-rehearsed a band is, the more polished and professional their performance will be. This, in turn, tends to have a direct effect on how much that band works and for how much money. Consequently, frequent and effective rehearsals can be a major determining factor in a band's economic and professional status.

But just where, when, and how to rehearse can present a club band with a variety of problems. Of course, each band must work out its own rehearsal arrangements among its members. Any restrictions or special circumstances presented by the clubs in which the band performs must also be taken into account. Cooperation among all concerned is the most effective way in which to establish a rehearsal program.

Here are some suggestions for solving the where, when, and how questions, based on my own experience with a variety of rehearsal methods. Most are based on the concept of a band working a full-time club gig, five or six nights a week. However, some of the suggestions will be equally applicable to bands working weekends or other part-time schedules.

Where To Rehearse

1. In the club. Rehearsing at your job site is obviously the best location. You have all your equipment set up already, and it's the equipment you'll be playing the gig with. Additionally, you're rehearsing the tunes in the environment in which they'll ultimately be performed, so you can immediately get an idea of how they'll sound on the job. If you're a member of a traveling act, this is most likely the *only* option you have. The only real disadvantage to this location is the possible difficulty of scheduling a rehearsal time. We'll deal with that in our "When" section.

2. Alternate site with alternate equipment. If you can't rehearse in the club, this method at least offers maximum convenience. It usually involves rehearsing at a bandmember's home, with spare equipment that can be left set up. Garages, basements, and spare bedrooms work well for this type of rehearsing. The convenience is obvious—especially for the bandmember who lives there—but you do lose the advantage of working with your regular equipment and having the club's acoustics. The major problem with this location is generally with the neighbors. Unless you are rehearsing in the warehouse district or in some rent-a-space park, make contact with your neighbors and let them know that you have a band that will be rehearsing. Have a little courtesy and common sense, and don't plan late-night rehearsals. Also, see if anyone in the vicinity has small children or elderly folks in their households who might be day sleepers. If you can schedule your rehearsals around such situations, you'll go a long way toward building goodwill with your neighbors, and thus avoiding complaints about volume.

3. Alternate site with regular equipment. Although in some cases this method is unavoidable, it certainly is the most hassle. This involves breaking down the equipment, taking it to the rehearsal site, setting it up for the rehearsal, breaking it back down, taking it back to the club, and setting it up again for the gig—*very* inconvenient. About the only advantage I can see with this method is that you are rehearsing on the same equipment you'll be using for the gig. But the negative aspect of all that cartage far outweighs that particular advantage, as far as I'm concerned.

When To Rehearse

1. After hours at the club. I'm a firm proponent of rehearsing a couple of nights a week, right in the club, after the doors have closed. Most clubs large enough to employ bands have a cleanup period of at least an hour after closing, when the bartenders and floor personnel are still working. And in many other cases, late-night cleanup or security personnel are present after hours. This affords you an excellent opportunity to rehearse on your regular equipment, in the environment in which you work. And while some musicians feel that they're "burned out" after a gig and too tired to rehearse, it's my contention that the time between the band's final note and the actual clearing out of the crowd and locking of the doors—usually anywhere from half to three-quarters of an hour—should be enough time to "cool down" from even the most high-energy gig. And if you plan ahead and schedule after-hours rehearsals on less busy nights (say Tuesdays and Thursdays on a five-night gig), you really shouldn't have much trouble in the energy department. Now, lets look at some of the advantages:

First and foremost, *you're already there!* Rehearsing after hours requires no additional trips, no additional locations, no additional equipment—nothing but a little additional time on your part. This, to me, is the ultimate in convenience. You have to devote *some* time to rehearsals anyway. Why not make it as painless as possible?

Second, you're already warmed up, both physically and vocally. This means that the keys you select for vocals are likely to be more accurate than those chosen at a daytime rehearsal, and thus you avoid embarrassing situations that occur when a new tune is debuted on the gig and you discover that it's too low or too high for your fully warmed-up voice.

Third, I can't stress too heavily the advantage of rehearsing in the same acoustic environment as that in which you'll be performing. When playing after hours, it's generally possible to play at full volume (when the song is finally put together, that is), so you can get an accurate feeling for dynamics and tonality from all the instruments. And there's something to be said for the input of club employees who might be listening as you rehearse. They hear more of you than anybody; they probably have a pretty solid idea of what does and doesn't sound good for you—and *from* you.

Naturally, you have to have the cooperation of club management in order to schedule after-hours rehearsals. If you've worked in this club for a fairly long period of time or have returned there often, that's likely to be beneficial to your cause. If there is someone working there after hours who can take responsibility for locking up (a late-night bookkeeper, cleanup crew, security guard, etc.), that can go a long way towards making a manager's decision easier. On the other hand, one band I was in for several years had been a regular with one club chain for so long that we were allowed to rehearse after hours by ourselves. It was our responsibility to shut off the lights and make sure the door was locked behind us when we left. Naturally, we took that responsibility seriously, and the system worked very well for us.

2. Afternoon rehearsals. If you can't rehearse in the club after hours, the best alternative is to rehearse there one or two afternoons a week. I personally recommend rehearsing on the first day of your work week. That is, if you play Tuesday through Saturday, rehearse on Tuesday afternoon. That maximizes the time off that you have, and also serves to prepare your chops and your voice for the first work night of the week. (In other words, in addition to the rehearsal, you get an "advanced warm-up" for the gig.) Another advantage to this rehearsal time is that it minimizes the time between the last rehearsal of a new tune and the debut performance on the gig. If your band is like most of mine have been, you probably debut a new tune on a slow night, making sure it's had a few nights to "settle in" before you hit the busy weekend. A final rehearsal on Tuesday afternoon, prior to a debut performance that night, gives you the best opportunity to keep the tune fresh in your mind.

Disadvantages to this time slot include the fact that you may not be at your best in mid-afternoon, either playing-wise or vocally. Unfortunately, unless you spend some time in the morning warming up (when most club musicians would prefer to sleep), this is unavoidable. Try to warm up vocally in the car on the way to rehearsal, and then perhaps run through a couple of your regular tunes—gently—to warm the entire group up and get your minds into a musical frame before attempting new material.

I've already outlined most of the factors involved with alternate-site daytime rehearsals. Scheduling a daytime rehearsal in the club again requires the cooperation of the management. Obviously, a daytime slot will depend on whether or not the club is open for business at that time. If it is, you're probably out of luck. But sometimes a club is divided, and only the dining room is open during the day, while the lounge is closed for cleaning. It's then possible to schedule your rehearsal during that cleaning period. You may have to compete with a vacuum cleaner, but that's showbiz. You may *very likely* have to keep your volume down during the day, so as not to disturb the diners in the other room.

3. Rehearsing on days off. Whether this takes place in the club or at an alternate site, this is the worst possible rehearsal time—with the possible exception of no rehearsals at all. If you're working a five-night gig, an off-day rehearsal makes it a six-night gig. If you already work a six-nighter, rehearsing on the seventh day is out of the question. No matter how well your band gets along, you *need* time away from each other—time for yourself and for your family—in order to keep a healthy mental attitude. Dedication to the band and its future is great, but don't overdo it.

4. Rehearse regularly. This isn't an alternative; this is a general point. No matter where or when you rehearse, it should be scheduled regularly, so that each bandmember knows when and where rehearsal will be each week. That enables each member to schedule his or her personal activities to include that rehearsal time (so conflicts are avoided). Obviously, a same-time-each-week slot is the easiest to deal with, but sometimes changes are unavoidable. When changes in the schedule must be made, be sure everyone gets as much advance warning as possible.

How To Rehearse

There is no preference list here. As far as I'm concerned, there is only one way for a group to rehearse, and that is to make the most efficient use of rehearsal time by coming *prepared.* Each bandmember should have a tape of the new song, and should practice his or her part individually. If there is a difficult drum part, work it out on your own; don't hang everybody else up at rehearsal while you try to perfect it. If you are singing, *know* the lyrics. If there is going to be a key change necessary, get that information to the other players as soon as possible, so that a new key can be established and the necessary transposition done ahead of time. If charts are necessary, work them up and pass them out a few nights before the rehearsal.

The idea is to use group rehearsal time strictly for assembling the final product; all the parts should already be there. Naturally, you'll want to perfect the arrangement and the group sound. You'll also want to iron out any problems that may occur when one instrument's part is played against another's for the first time.

Section rehearsals can sometimes be a real benefit. If time and tempos are a problem in some of your material, work with your bass player to find and correct the trouble spots. Rehearsal time slots are also good opportunities for band discussions and self-evaluation. (Not all "rehearsal benefits" are the result of actually rehearsing.)

Proper preparation and scheduling can make for effective rehearsals. Effective rehearsals are essential to a successful band. So put a little thought into your rehearsal program, and then get out there and succeed!

Contributions To The Cause

> **When it comes to contributing to my band's welfare, I'm very old-fashioned. I believe in a "one for all and all for one" philosophy.**

When I was writing my *Club Scene* column regularly for *Modern Drummer* I received a letter from a club drummer in a four-piece band. His group was successful from a musical and business standpoint, but there was a familiar-sounding internal problem that was bothering him. Let me give you the gist of the letter:

"Much of our equipment, including about 70% of our small PA system, belongs to our guitarist/leader. He is also the one who conceived the concept of the band, does all of the chart transpositions and arrangements, and selects most of the material.

"I've been in a few bands in my relatively short career, and have gone out of my way—many times at my own expense—to make sure that the band has everything it needs to perform professionally (other than the various players' personally owned equipment). These were always considered as purchases that would remain in my possession long after the group broke up.

"The problem is that our 'leader' wants us to reimburse him for the cost of the PA and other band-used equipment—all of which was purchased long before the band was put together. Now, I don't object to his getting extra compensation for his time and effort in arranging and transposing material, or to reimbursing him for long-distance phone bills, recordings, etc. But I do object to paying for someone else's instruments and equipment. He has gone so far as to tell me that, without his equipment, there would *be* no band. He also says that, if the band should break up, we would not receive any money or equipment in return.

"A lot of time and effort have been expended by *all* of the bandmembers, and we have become not only a tight band, but tight friends as well. This problem, however, seems as though it could put an end to both situations in a hurry. In other bands I've been in, it was understood that all members, regardless of financial commitment, have been worth an equal cut. I resent our 'leader's' attitude that his contribution is somehow greater than ours and, therefore, he deserves greater compensation. I also resent the fact that he thinks I would be musically unemployed without him. Can you shed some light on how other bands might deal with the problem of 'who owns what and what's it worth'?"

This is an all-too-common situation that occurs within bands. When it comes to a band's internal business arrangements, there are many ways to approach things, and none are "right" or "wrong." The overriding condition for a successful system—no matter what it may be—is that it be clearly spelled out and understood by all parties concerned. It's not usually the details of a business arrangement that cause problems; it's usually misunderstandings of those details based on different perceptions.

In my experience, there have been two basic arrangements under which my bands have operated. One was a clear-cut employer/employee relationship between the bandleader and the other bandmembers. The second was a totally democratic "team" arrangement. Let's look at each, in light of the points brought up in the letter.

Employer/Employee

This situation exists when a band is made up of a bandleader and sidemen. It isn't really too common in club bands anymore; it dates mainly from the time when someone would hire a leader and the leader would then contract different musicians just for that gig. But there are some very successful club bands that do utilize this system, and it does make things pretty clear-cut. The leader hires the sidemen, who are responsible for their own instruments and personal equipment, and who are paid a certain salary. The leader is paid substantially more, and is therefore expected to cover any and all expenses necessary for the group's performance other than the instruments of the sidemen. That would include a PA and lighting. If any individual member of the group has additional equipment to offer for general band use, the leader generally pays that player for the use of that equipment—just as if the item had been obtained from an outside source.

This all sounds pretty cold, but it's a good, simple business arrangement that leaves nothing to doubt or misinterpret. Everyone understands his or her own responsibilities and financial situation. I worked for several years under an arrangement like this, and was provided with my band clothes, the use of the PA system, transportation expenses when necessary, and any and all non-drum-related expenses. In return, I understood that I was to make about half of what the leader made. It wasn't that he was *worth* more; it was simply that he had the responsibility for all of the band's operating expenses.

The Team

As I said earlier, the general situation in most club bands today is not likely to be the employer/employee relationship, but rather a democratic, "team" arrangement. In this situation, everyone has an equal say in the band's operations, everyone makes an equal amount of money (at least to begin with), and everyone has an equal responsibility for the success or failure of the group.

The problem with this rather idyllic arrangement is that it leaves a great deal undefined. When it comes to equipment, nobody I've ever known expected the other bandmembers to help defray the cost of his or her own personal instrument or equipment. (I've never been asked to help pay for a guitar or a bass amp, for example.) But what about equipment used by the whole band, such as a PA system, electronic effects equipment, or lighting? What about extra time and money spent by individual members preparing material for the band? What about phone calls, mailers, and other promotional expenses incurred by bandmembers in order to obtain work for the band? What about…? The list goes on and on.

As far as I'm concerned, there are some simple ways to approach these problems. But often, what appears simple and obvious to one person is totally unacceptable to another. So I offer my comments as suggestions only, for your consideration. Much of what I feel is based more on my own personal ethics than on solid business sense, so take it for what it's worth.

When it comes to contributing to my band's welfare, I'm very old-fashioned. I believe in a "one for all and all for one" philosophy. I feel that anything I can contribute to the general good of the band is also automatically for my good, because the better the band sounds, the better I sound. The more the band works, the more I work. With that in mind, I have no qualms about offering any personal equipment—over and above my drums—for general use. Most of the musicians I've worked with over the years have felt the same way. Again, everybody provided his or her own axe and amp, and most have provided their own microphones and stands (if they sang). When it came to PA systems, those who owned any or all of the components made them available to the band at no cost. After all, a PA system is useless unless you have a band to use it. In my particular case, I provided lighting equipment I owned. It never occurred to me to ask the band to pay me for its use.

Let me stress that, so far, I've been talking about equipment already owned by the various members of the band. I honestly believe that every member of a band should contribute whatever he or she may own—for use by the entire band—as a natural part of *being* a member of a band. The concept that "the band couldn't work if it wasn't for my PA (or whatever)" is one that I find totally repulsive. That kind of attitude has no place in any band. (After all, a drummer could just as easily say that the band couldn't work without his or her drumset.) It's a team effort, and every piece of equipment used by the team has an equal value as far as I'm concerned.

However, the team approach does have a problem when it comes to the purchase of new equipment that cannot be handled by one individual. Obviously, individually owned equipment comes and goes with the individual who owns it—be it a drumset, a bass amp, a PA system, or whatever. But what if the group decides to buy a new PA system *as a group*? And what about operating expenses such as those I mentioned earlier (phone calls, mailers, band clothes, etc.)? How can they be handled equitably?

The best way I know of to cover group expenses is by the use of a "band fund." This is simply an operating account, into which each member contributes an agreed-upon amount out of each paycheck. The band determines what operating expenses are to be deemed "group" expenses, and then reimburses *whoever* incurs those expenses. The money in the fund is generally considered nonrefundable and remains there even if a member leaves the band. Now, before you start screaming, let me add that the idea of this fund is not to build up a huge surplus. It should be figured in such a way as to be adequate to cover regular, predictable operating expenses. Each player's contribution should be determined on that basis. If the fund goes for quite a while without having to pay for anything, contributions should be halted until the fund is drawn upon and reduced in size. In this way, there shouldn't be so much in the fund at the time of a player's departure from the group that it becomes an issue.

"Ah," you say, "but what about that pesky PA purchase? Surely a small operating 'band fund' couldn't handle that. And what about band clothes? Who should pay for those?" Again, there are no absolutes here, but I'll tell you what I feel can work successfully.

When it comes to a very large purchase, like a PA system, you should *not* get the group involved in a time-payment obligation. This becomes almost impossible to deal with if a member leaves. (Who picks up the departed member's share? Is a replacement member obligated to make payments for something he or she had no say in buying?) I suggest that such a large purchase only be made in cash, with equal parts being paid by all existing members of the band. If this takes some time to save up for, then so be it. A signed agreement between the members should state that, in the event of the departure of one member, the other purchasing members will "buy out" that player for an amount that reflects his or her purchase share, less reasonable depreciation. If the members of the group can't agree on such an arrangement, I earnestly suggest that you don't make such a purchase. If necessary, *rent* a PA system (a band fund expense) until a single band-member can afford to purchase one or until a workable agreement can be reached.

Band clothes aren't too much of a problem today, since very few bands are uniformed anymore. I've always felt that what a person wore on stage was his or her own responsibility, in terms of purchase, alterations, cleaning, etc. But when a band does wear uniforms, the question often arises as to whether they should be considered the personal property of each member—and therefore a personal expense—or the property of the group as a whole. Practically speaking, it never seems to work out that a new member can fit into the outfit of the departing member, so it seems a bit silly for the band to hold on to uniforms. And it's been my experience that finding new band clothes to match those purchased by older members a year or two ago is also nearly impossible. What it boils down to is, when band membership changes, band wardrobe usually has to change, too. To my way of thinking that makes band clothes "expendable items." Once again, expenditures for such items can come out of the band fund or out of each member's pocket, depending upon what the bandmembers have arranged. In either case, it seems only practical and logical that the clothes stay with the individual bandmembers.

I have very little time or sympathy for people who feel that they have to be compensated for every single thing they do in and for a band. *Everybody* has extra talents to contribute, whether it be in acting as a booking agent, repairing equipment, driving the band truck, or preparing arrangements. It's all for the good of the band, and the good of the band is what keeps you employed. When you contribute to the cause, you also reap the benefits.

Conflicts And Compromises

Whether or not your playing is "right" in a purely aesthetic sense makes little difference if you are unemployed as a result.

A club drummer once wrote me for advice regarding some problems he was experiencing with his career. I'm going to paraphrase a portion of his letter, in order to present those problems in the clearest manner possible.

"The number one criticism I've received on my drumming is that I play too loud. My four most recent bands were constantly telling me that, which creates negative rumors in the music grapevine.

"I've always tried to emulate records and to reproduce their sound, style, and feel authentically. Most of today's records have fat, bigger-than-life snare drums, deep, heavy-footed bass drums with attack, and full, resonant toms with a pitch bend. The drums are 'up front' in the mix on most songs. This seems to be the sound that the best producers and engineers try to achieve. With that in mind, I play a kit of all double-headed toms, a deep snare, and minimal muffling. I play the way I hear and feel, and can't imagine approaching the drums any other way without being dissatisfied with the sound. I'm not insensitive; I try to play according to the style of music being performed. I've been playing since I was old enough to reach the floor; my background is in jazz and big band drumming. I rarely break a stick, and I never break heads. I play with wrists relaxed. I'm not a basher. But I'm afraid that, if I muffle the drums more, I will kill the tone, resonance, and fullness.

"The second criticism that I've received is that I don't play the tunes as fast as the band wants them. Most club bands are in a hurry; they don't groove or play in the pocket. They order me to play the songs faster, and it doesn't sound or feel right for the song being played. But since I'm the drummer, I always get the blame for the time problems. My approach and concentration are centered on the groove, while most players on the club scene in my area don't do that. I try to play the speed of the record; playing any faster sounds amateurish, while being in the groove sounds professional.

"I'm no inflated egotist, but my playing can't be *that* bad, because I'm always getting compliments from audiences, recording engineers, and respectable players. But I am at a breaking point. I've been fired from four bands now, labeled as being either too loud or too slow. I'm so frustrated that I'm considering giving it up to protect what sanity I have left, although I wouldn't know what to do without my music. It's my life, and comes from my very soul. I'd appreciate some advice."

Sound familiar? It does to me. I've certainly come up against similar criticisms over the years. I, too, am a fan of full, live-sounding drums, and consequently, I've run into volume hassles from my bands. I've also had my share of tempo disagreements with other bandmembers. But I have been reasonably successful at sorting out these problems, with a few methods that I'll describe in this chapter.

The "Live-Vs.-Studio" Conflict

There's a fine line that must be tread when playing cover music. In an attempt to re-create the sound of the original tune as accurately as possible, drummers have often tried to emulate the recorded drum sounds exactly. Years ago, when the "studio sound" was almost exclusively the flat, deadened, "Steely Dan" sound, club drummers taped up their heads or used Evans *Hydraulic* heads—or both—and then wondered why they couldn't be heard in a live, unmiked situation. This led to the widespread use of drum mic's in clubs. Now, as the "studio sound" has come to be deep, full-sounding drums, with snares that crack, many club drummers are using power toms, extended bass drums, deep snares, and the mic's left over from the "flat sound" days—and wondering why they're getting complaints about being too loud.

I've said it before and I'll say it again: You cannot hope to duplicate exactly in a club environment what has been recorded in a studio. The circumstances, the acoustics, and the basic physics are all very different between the two musical situations. You have to deal with the realities of where you are performing, not the fantasies of what the music "ought to sound like."

For example, our letter writer brings up several points regarding today's music. It's true that current hits often feature the drummer mixed "up front." But that mixing is done on an engineering board after the initial tracks are cut, rather than at the time of original performance in the studio. A studio drummer has the luxury of being able to play as loud and as hard as he or she wishes. How much drum volume the other players hear can be controlled electronically. If they want to hear less drums, they simply ask that the drums be lowered in their headphones. What a person listening to the finished recording hears is a carefully controlled and blended mix artificially created by the record producer, well after all the tracks were laid down.

Unfortunately, this situation does not exist in a live club performance. Even if the sound your audience hears is being mixed by a technician out front (which is still rare for club groups), it may very well be the case that *on* stage, your drums are loud enough to overpower the other players to the point that they cannot hear their own instruments. This generally results in their turning up their amps, which makes the overall band volume louder. If *you* play louder still as a result, *they* turn up again, and the whole thing snowballs into an uncontrolled—and musically unacceptable—din.

When you play behind your kit, you simply cannot judge, either accurately or objectively, how much sound is going out front from the drums. It might be necessary to reduce the power of your playing and instead experiment with the tuning of the drums in order to achieve a sound that is satisfactory from your point of view, but takes less raw impact. Another solution I've seen drummers employ—especially in the lounges in Las Vegas and Atlantic City—is the use of clear plastic baffles between themselves and the rest of the band. These allowed the drummers to play as hard as they felt they needed to, but reduced the projection so that the band was also happy. This seemed to me to be an effective compromise.

The "live-vs.-studio" conflict also applies to tempo. In the chapter titled "Establishing Tempo" I mention the use of a metronome to establish the "correct" tempo for a song, based on the speed of the original recording. Counting off the tunes on stage after watching the metronome for several beats provides an objective point of reference, and can eliminate arguing about what the "right" tempo is for any given song.

But let me point out that many "groove" tunes played at exactly the recorded speed can be too slow for live performance! They can lack the energy and vitality that people like from a live band, and that also motivate people to dance. Remember, you can't always base your live performance on the original record, because that record *wasn't done live.* There's a psychological difference that's critical. When performing live, many recording acts will increase their tempos, boost their energy level, and generally perform their songs with a greater vitality than the original recordings featured. In many cases, club bands need to do the same thing, because they can have a tendency to seem flat and complacent unless a high level of energy is maintained. I've seen some groups that "grooved" like gangbusters—but were terribly dull to watch and to listen to. Again, things shouldn't be taken to extremes; I don't mean to suggest that every tune should rush like a runaway train. But to me, the "life" of a tune—and of the band—is the critical factor. Don't be so unwilling to approach a song with that "live-vs.-studio" difference in mind that you appear stubborn or uncooperative. If you can prove your point by the use of a metronome, then do that. If you can't, admit that you might be mistaken and adapt.

Diplomacy

Whether or not your playing is "right" in a purely aesthetic sense makes little difference if you are unemployed as a result. And while I certainly don't mean to suggest that you give up all sense of musical integrity, I do suggest that you do what you can to achieve a balance between what you think should be played and what your *band* thinks should be played. Don't *argue* about things; *discuss* them during rehearsals. Discuss your concept of drum tuning and balance level with your band at the time you are considering a song for addition to your repertoire. Make a point to establish a verifiable tempo for tunes on which there is a disagreement. Get the points of contention ironed out ahead of time, so they don't create friction during performances.

I think it's important that you stand up for your musical opinions. I also think it's important to realize that music—and especially club playing—is a cooperative venture. You can't make a living as a drummer playing a "single." It pays to stay employed (no pun intended), so that you maintain an outlet for the musical creativity you hold so dear. A bit of personal and musical diplomacy can go a long way toward that end.

It's Your Move

If the grass looks greener somewhere else, it might be a good idea to make sure that that grass is going to continue to grow.

There comes a time in every steady musician's career when he or she is compelled to consider a change of employment—a move to another musical situation. In some cases, the factors requiring the move are beyond his or her control. In other cases, they're the result of deliberate consideration, soul-searching, and careful weighing of pros and cons. On rare occasions a change is made on impulse or "gut instinct." None of these changes can be made without a multitude of ramifications. Musically, economically, and personally, a change of groups for a steady player is a dramatic turning point. It behooves drummers who are currently satisfied with their jobs to ponder the possibility of a change *before* they're under the pressure of having to make one. Let's examine some of the aspects of making a move.

Outside Influences

1. Getting fired. We might as well start with the least pleasant possibility. Unfortunately, this does happen. For any number of reasons, your group might become unhappy with you as a member. It might involve a new musical style that the group would like to develop and which you are either unwilling or incapable of doing. Sometimes a personality conflict becomes intolerable. Bands are in business, and you should keep in mind that, even if the bandmembers are all good friends, a business must sometimes make personnel changes in order to progress. Your band might see it that way.

Under normal circumstances you'll be given reasonable notice. Two weeks is standard, but it's not a lot of time to get a new gig, even in a large town with a wide variety of groups. Usually, a player who's going to be fired can sense it coming, even before the notice is given. Tensions are not created immediately, and if you feel you might be "under the gun" in your group, it would be a good idea to start scouting around for a new position—just in case. Try not to make firm commitments until you have, in fact, been given notice officially. It's possible that a settlement can be reached and you might stay with your group. But be prepared to cover yourself.

2. Retirement/breakup of group. I was a member of a very successful Southern California band for almost five years. The other members had been together for over eleven years, and had played the last seven and a half in the same three-club rotation, six nights a week, fifty-one weeks a year. On a month's notice, they decided that enough was enough; they wanted out of full-time club performing. They sought day jobs, and we continued to play some casuals. Unfortunately, I didn't want to retire, I didn't want to work full-time at anything but music, and I couldn't survive economically on the casual income we were making. I was forced to seek another group.

In other cases, a breakup can happen suddenly, due to personality conflicts, disagreement over musical direction, or a thousand other things. It can occur on very little notice. I once saw a group actually fight, disband, and walk offstage in the middle of a performance. Sometimes it isn't possible to see a breakup coming, but sensitivity to the collective psyche of the group might prevent you from being caught totally off guard.

3. Group unemployment. This is one of the saddest instances of forced change. It occurs when a group loses its job and can't find another before some or all of the members are out of money. Nobody wants to break up the band, but individually they have to find a source of steady income. Often an attempt is made to do casuals or part-time day work so that the group can stay together until new work is found. More often, each member seeks other musical work. If that work becomes steady, then they become unavailable to return to the original group.

The only advice I can give, if this situation occurs, is to sit down together and discuss, realistically, the economic potential for the group. Then evaluate the relative merits of trying to stick it out as a group or calling it quits. The one bright spot in this situation is that if you part friends, with a mutual understanding of what has happened, there's every likelihood that you'll be able to re-form, or at least work again with other members. If, however, some members feel that someone else "bailed out," leaving the group incomplete and forced to disband, animosity will preclude any hope of reformation. Keep all the attitudes open and positive and be honest with each other. If you aren't able to hang in there, tell the group so and tell them why.

4. Better offer. The *offer* may be beyond your control, but the decision whether or not to accept it is not. I'll get into group loyalty, musical maturity, and other reasons for staying with a band later. But this is always a decision that comes down to the individual. Watch out for hidden pitfalls in taking better offers. Make sure that they aren't only better now, but also have long-term potential. Nothing in our business is certain, and even ironclad contracts can be worthless in some situations. Try to evaluate a new offer objectively, in terms of how it will improve your situation over what you have going now. If the grass looks greener somewhere else, it might be a good idea to make sure that that grass is going to continue to grow.

Inside Influences

1. Musical dissatisfaction. Many players get bored with a long-term job. They may become dissatisfied with the lack of progress their group is making in musical style. Perhaps they fear that their own chops are suffering from the lack of opportunity to "stretch out," since in many cases a group is hired specifically to play one style of music.

Let's assume that your group is gainfully employed, and you get along well with all the members. The problem is musical stagnation versus the need to make a living. You have to weigh the importance of each, taking into consideration such factors as family economics. If you're single, you might be in a better position to make a decision based solely on your musical integrity. If you're supporting a family, that decision becomes more agonizing. Possibly a compromise can be achieved. If your work schedule allows, you might find a part-time or off-night gig with a different band, playing a style you enjoy. You can pick up some extra bucks this way as well. Some players enjoy jamming, for no money at all, just for the relief of "breaking out of the mold" established by their regular group. If this can work for you, you'll be enjoying the best of both worlds. If not, you'll need to be sure you have something to go *to*, before you give your current group notice.

2. Economic dissatisfaction. This occurs when a player isn't happy with the progress made by the group in terms of salary or places of employment. You might be happy musically, but if you aren't being paid enough, or you're working in unsavory clubs with no potential for advancement, then you might wish to consider making a change in order to improve conditions for yourself. Of course, if the band also wants to make improvements, but for some reason is being held back, then a group evaluation is in order. This is one thing I feel very strongly about. I don't believe in staying with an obviously sinking ship. If a group has potential (and decent business management) they'll usually realize their goals, at least partially. The future may not be definite, but a sense of hope and positiveness will pervade. On the other hand, a group that's going nowhere can sense that just as easily. I believe in group loyalty to a point, but not when that loyalty becomes a millstone around your neck. You should decide quickly whether the group can offer you anything in the foreseeable future. If not, I'd recommend making a move.

3. Personality conflicts. This is the major reason for group breakups. Club bands spend a great deal of time together playing, rehearsing, and often socializing. Generally a band enjoying good economic times finds ways of overcoming (or overlooking) minor personality hassles. If times get hard, the conflicts take on more importance, because that's all the group has to focus on. I don't enjoy performing when tension is present onstage. So this is another instance where I say: Try to settle personality differences if the quality of the group is good and the effort is warranted. However, if the conflict becomes the highlight of group activities, get out of it. Besides being an impossible situation for musical creativity, such conflict also jeopardizes the economic potential of the group. Club owners quickly become aware of group dissension, and they are reluctant to hire bands that might disintegrate at any moment.

4. Uncomfortability with the job or location. This seems minor, but I mention it because it has been a problem for me and several friends. I once had a job with a country & western band on a long-term contract. The job was okay salary-wise, I could cut the music easily enough, and the players were good people. But the club itself catered to a clientele with which I was uncomfortable, and the atmosphere in the room became so smoky after a couple of sets that I contracted a respiratory illness after two weeks. I lasted nine weeks before I was forced to give notice.

You should *never* work in a place where you don't feel safe. The only time I've ever walked out on a contract took place on a road engagement. We visited the club on the night before we were to move in. I watched the manager eject a rowdy customer, holding the offender in one hand and pressing a broken beer bottle to his throat with the other! When I later saw a burly customer approach a lady and ask her to dance and, upon her refusal, pick her up bodily and carry her over his shoulder to the dance floor, I decided this wasn't the place for me or my low-key group. I'm dedicated, but not suicidal.

5. Dissatisfaction with personal income. This is the most common reason for leaving a group. If you feel you're working for less than you're worth, this can reduce your self-esteem and playing effectiveness. Obviously, this consideration is coupled with the "better offer" I mentioned earlier. You'd better *have one* before you quit this job. Of course, you could ask for a raise on your current gig, but you might not get it. And if you don't have anything to go to that pays more, then there's no sense in leaving this group out of spite. Be a sensible businessperson. Look for a better opportunity, but make the most of what you have until that opportunity comes along.

General Considerations

1. In favor of staying. I've already mentioned group loyalty, and there's much to be said for it. Aside from the ethics involved (working together to build something, each member being dependent on the others to keep the group going and solvent), there is the obvious fact that the longer a group stays together, the tighter it gets as a musical unit. Musical maturity is readily apparent in a group's performance and is a marketable asset. It might be to your advantage to be part of that marketability.

You should be concerned about establishing a poor personal reputation as a "band-hopper." This comes from operating from a "grass is greener" attitude. Some players, especially very hot ones, just can't seem to settle into a group for any length of time. The pressure from other groups to come join them is just too great. Perhaps musical stagnation occurs more quickly in these individuals. At any rate, after making a series of hops, the player becomes an undesirable commodity, despite any ability as a musician. You'll want to avoid this kind of reputation, and sticking with your band is the best way to do that.

There's a certain advantage to staying with the status quo. Even though there may be problems, your current situation is a known quantity. You understand the problems, the people, the job, the audience, and the musical requirements. All of this makes for a sense of psychological security that's a very real and valuable consideration. Fear of the unknown applies to all changes, including job changes, and this has kept many players in the same gig for several years. Of course, if you enjoy challenges or surprises, then perhaps this may be less of an influence for you.

Most importantly, if you have a family, their interests *must* be considered. Would a change of groups mean more or less money initially? Is the new potential group local? If not, would you be going on the road, forcing a family separation, or perhaps even relocating the entire family? How much does the potential change gain for you when balanced against the upheaval it could cause to your total lifestyle? I suggest that you discuss the move as much as possible with your family, so that you can get their input. Seek their support, and become aware of their objections so you can make a responsible decision. This is perhaps the most difficult aspect of being a musician and a family member at the same time.

2. In favor of a change. First and foremost, you should remember that you're in a business. You work to earn a living. If the economics of a change would be to your advantage (and you are as certain as possible that they are likely to remain so), then that's the strongest argument in favor of such a move. I know few musicians who are independently wealthy to the degree that they can pick their jobs solely for musical value, as opposed to the remunerative value. On the other hand, your integrity as a musician has a value of its own. If your current band is stifling you, then you owe it to your career to consider a change. Just make sure that you do the considering *first.* Get a new and better gig lined up, and *then* make the jump.

In any event, whether you are forced to make a change or decide to initiate one on your own, be professional about it. If you are given notice, don't become a "lame duck" and play poorly for your last two weeks. You may want to ask your old group for a reference to help you connect with a new one. Don't mope or pout; you'll only lose time.

If *you* give your group notice, be sure it's a reasonable one. Although two weeks is standard with a non-traveling club band, if you are a performer with a speciality act (especially if it is on the road), try to estimate realistically how much time it will take to find a *suitable* replacement for you. The old saying is that "no one is indispensable." But in show business, people can be damn near irreplaceable in some cases. If you're one of those, maybe you shouldn't leave; maybe you should ask for a raise. But if you decide to leave, do so responsibly. Don't get the reputation of being a prima donna who destroyed a promising group by leaving them on short notice.

As I said at the beginning of this chapter, the time to think about all these considerations is *before* you need to apply them. Combine the suggestions I've given along with your own ideas and philosophy, and you'll be able to establish an operating procedure to follow should the need arise.

"Between Engagements"

As drummers we're faced with one major limitation placed on us by our choice of instrument: We *have* to find a band to work with.

In the previous chapter, I outlined several different sets of circumstances that might cause you to leave a group. Some were based on your decision; some were not. When it was your decision to leave, I stressed that you should have something already lined up to go to, so as not to be out of work. Unfortunately, often the choice is not yours, and the termination of your employment comes unexpectedly. Or you might be a player just entering the steady club field, and looking for your first job. At any rate, you are currently "between engagements," as it is so delicately put in the entertainment industry. So the big question is: Now what do you do? How do you go about finding the work you want, for the money you'd like to make, in the location you prefer? This chapter will give you some suggestions to help you get yourself on the market.

The key element is communication. You have to communicate to the music employment market that you are currently available. Along with that, you must be able to communicate your abilities and special talents, along with any pertinent data that might make you more attractive as a potential group member. (Unfortunately, as drummers we're faced with one major limitation placed on us by our choice of instrument: We *have* to find a band to work with. A drummer just isn't going to cut it as a single.)

There are several ways of approaching this communication process. Some ways might be more effective than others, varying from person to person and situation to situation. My advice is to look over the list of suggestions, and then employ as many of them as appeal to you. The more methods you employ, the better your chances of success.

1. Making the rounds (also known as "hanging out"). This is the old, time-honored method of going from club to club, meeting with the working musicians, sitting in if possible, and just getting the word out among the musical community that you are available. In the "old days," when individual players tended to shift around a lot from group to group, this was an effective method. The various bandleaders and sidemen came to know you, and if somebody needed a sub quickly, you could very possibly get a call. This, in turn, might lead to a permanent position with that group. In other cases, musicians from one group might recommend you to the leader of another group that they sat in with, and thus your name would be spread around.

Unfortunately, that scene doesn't really exist much anymore. Groups tend to be more permanent in their lineups, and individual players don't "get around" as much. Speaking from my own experience, when I was working five or six nights a week in California and someone would come in and ask me, "Know anybody who needs a guitar player?" I'd have to say no, simply because I never got to hear any other bands or visit with other players. All of the other groups worked the same nights and hours as I did, and thus we didn't have much interchange between us. When I lived in Hawaii, I discovered that there was more of musical community happening. However, the majority of the working bands were traveling groups, and weren't likely to have openings to fill while in Honolulu.

I do want to stress that it *is* important to make the rounds if you are a well-known player with a pretty solid local reputation. If you've been with one successful group for quite some time, people automatically assume that you can step right into another gig. (Sometimes you fall into the trap of assuming that, too.) What happens is that everybody either thinks you're still with the old group or that you've already found new work (since you're so hot), so they don't see any point in calling you for their gig. You need to let them know that you would, in fact, be *very* interested in their offer. Therefore, making sure that the "grapevine" knows about your availability is very important. Just don't spend what money you have left going out "clubbing" night after night. Drop in once, speak to the bandleader, sit in if you can, and then leave. Go to as many clubs as possible, once each. Constantly hanging out in the same clubs will not do you much good.

2. Music stores. In many large cities, the pro music stores are centers of communication. In many cases, there is only one such shop in a given town, and thus *all* the local pro players have to come in there at some point or other. Making your availability known to salespeople (who can pass the word personally) and placing a notice on a bulletin board can be a simple way of reaching a very large group of people with very little effort on your part.

As far as the notice goes, try to make it attractive and professional-looking. Obviously, you should include vital data such as name, phone number, instruments played, style of music preferred, travel availability, and years of experience. But don't go overboard with biographical data. Let an interested party call you and ask for that data if they want it. They don't need it just to decide whether or not to audition you, and a cluttered notice does not attract attention.

Be sure to type the notice or print clearly, neatly, and boldly. A scribbled note on a torn-off sheet of notebook paper does not project a serious desire to obtain work, nor does it represent a professional player. The kind of note (and I've seen them scrawled in crayon) that reads, "I play drums. Looking for serious dudes to jam with. John. 555-5309" does not seem as effective to me as one that is neatly prepared and might read: "Professional drummer seeks steady employment. Eighteen years of experience. Free to travel. Prefer Top-40 or lounge group. John Jones, 555-5309." That isn't too formal, and it tells prospective employers what they need to know before they decide to call you for an audition. I've employed the music store/bulletin board method each time I've been looking for work, and I've never failed to receive some calls from that source.

3. Musicians referral services. This is a method available to unemployed musicians, and to groups who are seeking replacement people. The basic idea is that the service puts those two together. You list with them, telling them your name, instrument, traveling status, and certain other required information. They put your information in their file, and supposedly give your name to bandleaders who call in looking for people to contact. The service screens the callers to determine the type of people they need, and then matches them up with prospective players from their files. Some charge a percentage of your first couple of weeks' salary, while others charge a flat rate when you first subscribe to the service. Most of these services deal on a local basis, but there is at least one advertising in the classified section of *Modern Drummer* on a national basis. I subscribed to such a service (local only) in San Diego many years ago. I did not ultimately get a job through the service. However, I did get calls, and I did go out on auditions. I would caution you to investigate any service thoroughly before you lay out money up front. A service that charges only after you get a job through their assistance seems a little more legit.

4. Union local offices. If you are a member of the musicians union, it is recommended that you let your local office know of your availability. Of course, your union office is not a booking agency, and they'll be the first to tell you that. However, they will occasionally receive calls from leaders asking about musicians available to sub or available for casuals. At the very least, you stand to make a little pocket money while you're waiting for something steady, and you always have the chance of picking up a replacement spot in a working group. Once in a great while a traveling act loses a member while on the road in your town, and they need someone to fill out the current engagement. This can sometimes lead to a full-time membership, if you are free to travel. Keep your local posted on your situation. Don't *expect* them to find you work, but make sure they have the information that might *encourage* them to pass your name along.

5. Use your time positively. This isn't really a method of finding work, but it is a method of keeping your sanity and your good spirits while you're looking. A very serious problem that occurs during "between engagements" periods is the depression that can set in as you look for work unsuccessfully. It takes time to find a new gig, no matter how good you might be. And if you're used to working steadily, it is a very uncomfortable feeling to be unemployed. It seems a blow to your self-esteem and musical ego, to say nothing of the financial distress it causes. The most dangerous thing is that this depression can lead to a sense of apathy. After a while, you just begin to say, "There's no point in looking for work today; there's nothing out there," and so you reduce your efforts. This, in turn, reduces the possibility that you will find work, and the whole thing spirals downhill.

My suggestion for overcoming this depression is to make the off-time productive. When I am "between engagements" I spend time doing maintenance work on my equipment, which I cannot do when the drums are set up on a gig. I break down the kit completely, cleaning and making minor repairs where necessary. I polish my cymbals. I patch cases.

This is also a terrific time to get out the method books and do some serious woodshedding. I try to remember the times when I was on the bandstand and was telling myself, "Your chops are going from playing nothing but this Top-40. Gotta get in some serious practicing soon." I never did, because the hours I spent at work and band rehearsals seemed enough. I wanted the rest of the time with my family. Well, here's a golden opportunity to do the practicing you wanted to do, without losing family time to do it. The additional benefit is that not only does it prevent that sense of apathy from setting in, but when you do find work again, your skills will be as sharp as ever, if not improved!

All of the job-seeking methods I've mentioned so far have focused on obtaining work locally. There is another, very successful method I have employed in the past on a national basis, and that is the distribution of résumés. Of course, these work on a local basis too. In the next chapter I'll describe a successful résumé format, and give some tips on where to send it and how to obtain the addresses you'll need.

The Résumé

You can mail a résumé to a heck of a lot more places than you could ever hope to visit for a personal interview.

In the previous chapter I outlined various methods you might employ to help you find a new gig. Most of those suggestions were based on the assumption that you were seeking *local* work—that is, with a band in your own home area. But what if you're looking for work with a good traveling band? How do you make contact with people who might need your services, but are on the road? Or what if *you* are traveling, find yourself out of a gig, and want to make contact with a working group that needs a drummer on short notice?

The method I've found most successful has been the preparation and distribution of a résumé package. The beauty of a résumé is that, although it works very well on a local basis, it works even better on a national basis, since you can mail a résumé to a heck of a lot more places than you could ever hope to visit for a personal interview. The catch is that the résumé must be complete, attractive, and effective in selling you to potential employers. It has to make *them* want to contact *you*, in order to gain further information, set up an audition, or (in some cases) offer you a job immediately.

Where To Send It

Contacting bandleaders, booking agents, and club owners on a local basis generally isn't difficult. But if you plan to distribute your package to out-of-town or traveling acts, how do you reach them? The answer is: You don't. That is, you don't reach the acts directly. It simply isn't possible; you don't know who they are or where they are. So you do something better. You send your package to an address that is not only permanent, but which will also allow you to reach several groups at once. You send it to booking agencies and management companies across the country, especially in the major entertainment cities (L.A., Vegas, New York, Chicago, Nashville, etc.). The beauty of this system is that you send only one résumé to an office that might handle dozens of groups, any one of which might be in need of a replacement. Remember, when a working band suddenly needs a new member, they're just as desperate as you are, if not more so. They're out of work too, and may actually have bookings that they can't fill until they find a new drummer. They'll be counting on their agent or manager to help them find a replacement quickly. This is what you want to take advantage of.

When I'm preparing a mailing list of agencies and management companies, I first turn to the trade papers, like *Billboard*, *Variety*, and the newspaper of the musicians' union, the *International Musician*. Their classified sections contain ads for many different agencies, all seeking talent to sign. Granted, the ads say they want complete acts, bands, and shows, but at least it gives you the name and address of the agency. If they handle bands, they need a line on single players too, for those situations I've already described.

Another source of names and addresses is as close as your nearest library. Go to the largest one near you, and ask for the telephone directories for the cities you wish to approach. Turn to the yellow pages (headings like "Entertainment," "Talent Agencies," "Booking Agencies," "Theatrical Agencies," etc.) and you'll find several potential candidates. The larger ones are likely to have ads; the smaller ones just a phone listing. If an address is shown, just copy it down and you're on your way. If not, you'll have to call the office and ask for their address. If zip codes aren't shown, it's a simple matter to go to the post office and use the national zip code directory. (The library may have one, too.)

Using this method, and selecting only ten cities that I wanted to concentrate on, I have been able to create a mailing list of over one hundred addresses. Each was a major entertainment management office of some kind, representing several different acts or bands. Thus my line of communication ultimately led to over five hundred prospective employers. Not a bad return for an afternoon in the library.

A good résumé package should have several carefully prepared parts in order to maximize its effectiveness. Those parts include: a cover letter, a data sheet, a photo, a demo tape, and a protective mailer. Let's take a look at what you might include in each of these parts.

Cover Letter

The cover letter is what introduces the package (and you) to the addressee. It makes the entire résumé a little more personal, adding a human touch to your presentation. Without it, the package will more or less appear like a list of ingredients on a cereal box—informative, but not very interesting.

The letter (and everything else of a written nature in your résumé package) *must* be typewritten or computer-printed. This is simply a fact of business; nothing else looks professional enough to do the job you want your résumé to do. Individual copies can be photocopied from the original letter, and then each address typed in later. Be sure to allow enough space on the original letter for lengthy addresses. Also, when typing the addresses on the individual copies, align your margins to conform to those of the original, so the fact that you're using a preprinted from letter isn't made more obvious. If possible, use the same typewriter (or at least the same type style and size) that the original letter was typed with. If you do not type, ask a friend to do it for you, or hire someone. You can find typing services (and, in fact, résumé-preparation services) in the yellow pages. Remember, any money you spend in an effort to obtain employment can be tax deductible, so be sure to keep your receipts.

The cover letter should briefly introduce you, outline what it is you do, explain what kind of work you're looking for, and list any special facts or considerations that you think might be of interest to a potential employer. Don't go into a lot of detail; that will come later on the data sheet. And don't give a lengthy biography; they can get that when they call you back. Keep the letter nonspecific in terms of reference to places, since you'll be sending the same letter to many areas of the country. The following is an example of a successful cover letter format:

John Drummer
1234 Cymbal Street
Hometown, CA 92001
(619) 555-5309
October 1, 1996

[allow five lines for address]
To Whom It May Concern:

I am a professional drummer and vocalist seeking employment in your area commencing April, 1997. I have experience in all forms of musical performance, from hard rock concert bands to studio work; from fifteen-piece stage bands to duos. I've been performing professionally for some eighteen years.

My drumming style lends itself best to groups of four or more, playing high-energy dance or show music. I work well with tight rhythm and horn sections. However, I have had success with piano/bass/drum trios, and for over a year was a member of the house band in a major resort hotel, backing up different entertainers each week for their own acts. I read show charts, work quickly into new material, and make an excellent short-notice replacement for a group needing a drummer. I also have experience as a stand-up vocalist fronting a band.

My vocal range is second tenor, with a strong high falsetto for harmonies. I can handle all styles of lead vocals, from power rock to dramatic ballads.

My road experience includes a national tour with The ShowMen, a show group featuring contemporary musical arrangements, as well as comedy dialog and dance routines. I have also toured the Pacific Northwest with a lounge trio.

Most recently I was the drummer and lead male vocalist for The Hot-Shots, completing a nonstop run of seven years in the Los Angeles area at the end of February '96.

I will be available as of April '97 and I am looking for a solid club band or act, or a remunerative concert act or show. If your agency represents an act needing a drummer [or in the case of a letter to a bandleader, "if your group needs a drummer"] or is putting together a backup band for a lead entertainer, I would appreciate your consideration.

Circumstances prevent my being able to travel for audition purposes outside the L.A. area. However, if you are interested, I can provide a cassette demo of my most recent group, featuring my work on drums and vocals. A brief request from you will suffice for me to send the demo. Personal information accompanies this letter.

Thank you in advance for your consideration. I look forward to hearing from you soon.

Sincerely,
[signature]
John Drummer

Naturally, you have to prepare the letter with information that applies to your situation. You may not be a vocalist. You may play other instruments, or have something else to offer. This letter is an overview, designed to get the addressee interested enough in you to read the entire résumé package. The letter should be polite but professional. You are a business person selling a product—your services as a drummer—through the mail. This should be a business letter.

Data Sheet

This is where you can really give detailed information. But this time, you don't use the letter format. Instead, you use a brief outline format, so that you can give a lot of information without making the addressee do a lot more reading. As an example, here is a typical data sheet, with a few brief comments about the items on it:

1. Name. Give your complete name, and any nickname or stage name by which you are known.

2. Age. Don't fib; being young is no particular advantage when you're writing to unknown employers. You don't know how old they or their group may be. You can't do anything about your age anyway, so you might as well be straight about it. List your birthdate, too. Believe it or not, some musical employers are heavily into astrology. I have a friend who got a job over two other candidates because he was the right "sign" and they weren't.

3. Marital status. Again, being married or single could each be either an advantage or a disadvantage. Some traveling groups prefer single members, since there are no problems with loved ones left behind, and the leader doesn't have to worry about someone yearning to get off the road and "back home." On the other hand, some groups prefer married members on the grounds that they are more mature and more stable. Groups that are co-ed often have problems unless personal attachments are clearly defined, and married members make that a lot easier.

4. Travel availability. Naturally, if you are sending this résumé all over the country, we assume you are able to travel. But does that mean you are willing to go "on the road," or that you will relocate your residence for a steady gig in another city? How flexible are you? Are there some areas you don't want to work in, due to health or other personal reasons? This is the place to outline any traveling conditions you may have. Don't go into too much detail; that comes later in contract negotiations after they've called you. But if you do have anything to say here other than "free to travel," do so and state it clearly.

5. Drumming experience. How long have you been playing drums?

6. Professional experience. How long have you been getting paid for drumming?

7. Reading ability. If you are a monster reader, by all means say so, and try to make clear what you are capable of reading. I can cut a simple show chart—one that is basically a road map for the arrangement and doesn't really go much into specific drum parts. I am by no means a great studio-quality sight reader. Don't just say "can read." You should say "strong sight reader," "heavy reading experience," or something along those lines if that is the case. If you don't read, it's no shame. I'd say the majority of club players aren't strong readers, if they do read at all. We usually don't *need* to read, and unless you use it constantly, your reading skill deteriorates rapidly. But by no means should you say "cannot read." Never state what you *can't* do in a résumé. State what you *can* do. Substitute a positive comment like "I have a very good ear and can pick up parts readily."

8. Vocal range. If you sing, state your range (such as tenor or baritone) and whether you sing leads, backgrounds, or both. I include the fact that I can sing high falsetto harmonies as well, and that I can sing lead or background equally well from behind or in front of the drums.

9. Additional instruments. If you double on anything else, say so.

10. Additional talents. If you write music, arrange, do artwork, have experience operating or repairing sound equipment, or work with lights, costumes or other elements of show business, be sure to add that. I did a show on the road for ten months where, in addition to drumming and singing, I portrayed a character all night, in complete costume and makeup, with a partially prepared script and the rest of the show totally improvised. It was as much theatrical as musical. I got the job because I was a theater major in college, and I had experience in the areas of acting, makeup, handling lights, and improvising dialog. My résumé said as much, and it helped me land that gig.

11. Equipment. Briefly list what you normally play on stage. Assume that your prospective employer isn't a drummer. The employer is not likely to care about individual pieces of equipment by brand, dimension, or catalog number. Just list the size of the kit, the number of cymbals, and any other special equipment you normally use. My list would read like this: Nine-piece drumset (single bass), ten cymbals, wind chimes, headset microphone, 6'x6' portable drum riser, self-contained monitor amp and speaker system.

12. Additional equipment. If you have anything that you might be able to contribute to a band, you might list it here. Examples would be PA equipment, lights, microphones, or additional percussion instruments for other people to use (such as congas, timbales, or hand percussion).

13 Educational background. This is optional. I list my attendance at the University of California, Irvine, as a theater major in lighting design and acting. Other drummers I know like to list the teachers they've studied with. Obviously if you're a Juilliard or Berklee graduate, you'll want to show that.

14. Union affiliation. State whether you are a member of the musicians' union, and if so, with what local. If you are not, say so, and indicate whether you would be willing to join the union if required for a job.

15. Physical description. Since a photo is not likely to give a complete indication of your physical appearance, it's a good idea to list your height, weight, hair color, eye color, etc. In some cases you may be taking the place of an individual who wore certain costumes, and you may literally have to fit the same size. Some bands and acts are very image-conscious, and how they blend together physically is a big part of that.

16. Permanent mailing address. This is very important, since you may not always be at home. You may get a short-term gig and be on the road for a brief time when a really good offer comes your way. Use the address of some relative or friend, or even a paid P.O. box, where the mail can always get to you. This is also good insurance for the future. Agencies and management offices often place résumés on file, and pull them out a year or more later when the need arises. Who knows where you'll be when they want to contact you?

17. Permanent message phone. Same idea here. List your current phone number so they can reach you now, because you're obviously eager to hear from them as soon and as directly as possible. But include a permanent message number where they can reach you at some time in the future when you may no longer have your current phone listing.

18. Date available. Give the date on which you could actually start work. If you need a certain amount of advance notice, then state that as well.

The Photo

No résumé is complete without a photo. Your letter has introduced you, and your data sheet has fleshed out the details. Now the employer can put a face with all that information and come up with a person to consider. There are two ways to go when including a photo in a résumé package. You can enclose a separate photo print (the traditional 8x10 black & white glossy), which adds bulk to the package and costs quite a bit for reprints. Or you can take a good, clear snapshot to a photocopy shop that has the capability to do color copying. Prepare your data sheet with a layout that will allow you to place the photo on it as well, and have the whole thing photocopied at the same time. On my last résumé I was able to include a color snapshot on the data sheet, at a cost of 75¢ per sheet. When you figure that I would otherwise have had to pay for an individual reprint (in addition to a data sheet copy) for every package, this method was more economical, and certainly looked professional. As an additional benefit, I could have it all prepared at one time in one place, rather than having to deal with a photo lab for the reprints and a copy shop for the cover letter and data sheet copies.

Whichever method you choose, be sure that the photo itself is a good likeness and has been taken close enough to show your face clearly. A playing shot is fine, as long as your expression isn't unpleasant and you aren't obscured by cymbals or microphones. The idea is to show you as a person, not necessarily to capture your spirit on the drums.

Demo Tape

It is critical that you have some sort of demo available, because no matter how good your résumé makes you sound on paper, the employer needs to know how good you sound on the drums. A tape of your drumming with your most recent band is your best bet. It need not have been done in the studio. A decent-quality "live" tape should suffice. Of course, that means that you had to have made it while you were still working. If you're already out of work and have no tape, you've got a problem. You can make a tape of just you, drumming alone, but that certainly isn't as desirable as a tape demonstrating how you work with a group. Perhaps you could get some friends together, jam a little, and come up with a few tunes that you could record. I've also heard of drummers playing along with recorded music. What they did was record the song entirely on one stereo channel, and themselves entirely on the other. Then the listener can bring the balance up on the "live" drum channel, and get an idea of what the drummer is doing.

Of course, if you have the money, the facilities, and the opportunity, the video demo is highly in vogue these days. But that's usually for entire bands trying to sell their act. They can pool their resources, and they are usually very selective about who they send the tapes out to. Since you want to saturate your potential market, a videotape isn't really very practical, due to the expense of preparation, duplication, and distribution.

Assuming that you have a demo made on a standard cassette, you certainly don't have to include a copy with every résumé you send out. In reality, you can expect not to get any reply to at least 50% of your packages, and a polite "Thank you. We'll hold you in our files" from another 25%. If you're lucky, you'll get responses from the other 25%, so what you should do is state on your résumé (in the cover letter, and again on the data sheet if you wish) "cassette demo available upon request." At least this way someone has to contact you in order to get your demo, and that establishes a line of communication. It also lets you know how many cassettes you actually need to have duplicated. It's likely that your responses won't all come in at once, so initially, all you need is a high-quality master tape, from which you can have dubs run off as you need them. Once again, remember that the costs of making a demo (and the subsequent costs of duplication and distribution), are tax-deductible items, so keep track.

Protective Mailer

You've gone to a lot of trouble to prepare your résumé package, so you should give some thought to its protection while going through the mail. I recommend the use of the padded envelopes available at office supply stores or the post office. By the time you put in a cover letter, a one- or two-page data sheet, possibly a photograph with a couple of sheets of protective tagboard, and a cassette tape in its plastic box, you'll have a fairly bulky package, yet one that contains items of a fragile nature that you don't want crushed or bent. The padded envelopes are available in various sizes, and offer plenty of protection to their contents.

Just before you put your items inside, think about the outside of the envelope, which is the first thing the addressee will see. You should either use typewritten, adhesive mailing labels (you won't get those envelopes into a typewriter) or you should hand *print*, neatly and with waterproof ink, all the pertinent address information. You should also print or stamp on the front and the back: "fragile—do not bend or crush," to further prevent damage to your precious contents.

Following Up

You should follow up on your mailed-out résumés within two weeks. If you have had no reply at all from the addressee, make a brief phone call, simply inquiring as to whether they received the package. This reminds them about it (and you), and may get someone to look it over another time. If you get a form letter stating, "We'll hold you on file," send a thank-you note to the person who signed the letter. This again brings your name to their attention, since they have to go back and find your original letter in order to file the new one. (Working in several business offices has given me a little inside information about things like that.) Naturally, if you get a note or a call asking for further information, or requesting a demo, you should respond as quickly as possible.

The greatest résumé in the world will not guarantee you a job. But the larger the market you can cover, the better your odds will be of making your "sale." A professionally prepared and presented résumé package can cover an infinitely larger territory in a much shorter time than even the most enterprising individual.

Selling Yourself On Tape

You *must* have a tape that makes a good impression upon the first hearing, because it won't get a second hearing otherwise.

In the preceding chapter, I described the sort of package that a drummer seeking employment with a club band might put together to send to management companies, agents, bandleaders, etc. I mentioned that a demo tape should either be included with your résumé, or available upon request. What type of demo would best present a drummer's capabilities for consideration by a bandleader or manager? What elements combine to make a good impression, and what elements might actually work against the drummer? Here are a few thoughts on the matter, based on my own experience at making demo tapes, and on both good and bad tapes I've heard since coming to work at *Modern Drummer.*

Know Your Market

The first thing you need to determine before you ever put anything on tape is what market you are trying to sell yourself in. If you are an extremely versatile drummer willing to accept work in any one of several styles of playing, it might be to your advantage to make several different demos, each highlighting a particular style. Then, it's just a matter of making sure that a band's leader or management gets the demo appropriate to that group's style. If you're sending a tape to a hard rock band or a management company that specializes in hard rock acts, there's no point in demonstrating your best Steve Gadd samba licks. Keep your playing powerful and fundamental. If you're sending a tape to an R&B/funk act or management company, demo your best grooves—solid and funky—and don't blaze away with Neil Peart fills.

If you're planning to create a demo for the Top-40 market you'll want to include a wide variety of styles on your tape. Just don't go overboard with any particular thing; use excerpts and short passages to get the idea across. Demoing the seven-minute dance mix version of each hit tune on the current chart is not necessary; just let the listener know that you can duplicate the feel of anything that is commercially successful.

What To Play

When creating a drum demo, the critical thing to remember is that you are seeking employment, not trying to impress other drummers. Keep in mind that the people who are most likely to be considering your tape are the *other* members of the band—the musicians with whom you will be playing if you are hired. They're going to be interested in how well you can support them as a bandmember, not how many 32nd-note paradiddles you can put into a two-bar tom fill. Don't plan on doing an extended drum solo on your demo. Keep examples of your soloing to bare minimum, and place them toward the end of the tape. If your listeners want to hear more soloing, they can get back to you and ask you for it.

Playing With Music

Any drumming—no matter how fabulous it might be—is generally going to sound dull and/or obnoxious to non-drummers when that drumming is recorded by itself. Your best bet for creating a demo that is both an accurate representation of your playing in a band context and also appealing to a listener will be to demo your drumming *with* a band. If you have tapes of your playing with the band you are currently in (or have just left), it might be possible to excerpt passages from those tapes to create a very representative demo.

What I've done in the past is select a group of tunes that served to demonstrate the widest possible variety of styles. If the intro was an important part of the song, I started the tune there, and then let it play just long enough to establish the groove or feel. Then I faded out the tune on the tape. In some cases, I faded *into* a given tune at a point just ahead of an important passage for the drums, in order to catch my playing at that point. Then, again, I faded out the tune. Sometimes the tunes lasted for a minute or so, sometimes less. But in a ten-minute demo—which is as long as you can reasonably expect a potential employer to listen the first time—I was able to demo my playing on twelve to fifteen tunes in this manner.

If you haven't got any tapes from a previous band and you're not currently a member of one, don't give up hope. It might be possible to gather some musician friends, work up a few tunes in a "jam" format, and create some tapes from those sessions. Just remember to use sections that sound professional; you don't want your demo to sound "loose."

If the "jam" option is also unavailable to you, you can record your playing along with previously recorded music. There are a few "Music Minus One" albums around—although they tend to be in big band and jazz styles—that feature no drums on the soundtrack. You simply add your own playing to these recordings. If you are able to find such records in the styles you're interested in, you should be in good shape.

If you are trying to demo current commercial material, it's not likely that you'll be able to find MMO recordings. However, several rhythm machines available today come preprogrammed with a variety of musical grooves and song patterns. You could easily play (and record) along with such a machine.

If you don't have access to either MMO recordings or a rhythm machine, you'll just have to play along with recordings that already include the playing of the original drummer (or drum programming). This situation isn't great, but it's still better than nothing. Make the demo tape in stereo, putting the record you're playing to entirely in one channel and your drumming entirely in the other. In this way, the listener can adjust the balance to be able to hear the music adequately but concentrate on your drumming at the same time.

Playing Without Music

If you *must* create a demo with only drums, it becomes critical to make your drumming as musical and tasteful as possible. Here especially, the temptation to play blazing solos is strong, since a basic groove sounds pretty dull—even to drummers—when heard by itself. But remember, it's those grooves that your potential employers are most concerned with. With that in mind, don't preface your demo with "Here are some beats I know," and then launch into an unplanned and unguided flurry of licks and patterns. This generally sounds loose and unmusical. It's also very easy to get into time problems that are all too apparent when the drumming is out there "naked."

Plan your demo carefully. Decide what styles you want to demonstrate and what grooves you want to establish. Use some method of timekeeping as a guide. You might use a metronome, a drum machine programmed with a basic cowbell or cabasa beat, or a recording. Personally, I'd recommend playing along to a record, even if you're not recording it, simply to gain the inspiration and feel of working with a complete band.

As with the excerpt of band performances, don't go too long with any one thing on a bare-drumming demo. Establish your groove or pattern, let the listener get into it for a few bars, and then cut it or fade it out. (Fadeouts are generally less abrupt and more professional-sounding than cuts.)

Listen Back To Your Tape

After you have created your demo, play it back to yourself. You need to imagine yourself in the position that your potential employer will be in when he or she receives the tape. The demo is from an unknown person, seeking work in your band. You have no personal attachment to this person; you're interested only in his or her ability to fit your needs as a drummer. With these things in mind, you should be listening for the following:

1. No errors in playing. This is obvious. If you hear stick clicks, dropped beats, sloppy fills, or time problems, you should re-cut the tape.

2. Good time. Is the time solid and consistent (within each tune and each different tempo)? Does the time remain the same between groove passages and fills?

3. Solid grooves and good feels. Is the drumming solid and foundational, or is it overly busy? Would other musicians want to play over these very drum tracks? Does the drumming make you tap your foot and feel good?

4. Recording quality. Most people who will accept a demo tape at all will *say* that they listen to the quality of the playing without taking the quality of the recording into account. However, it's important to realize that human nature contradicts this. What we can hear more clearly and more pleasantly tends to appeal more to us than what we hear poorly or in a distorted manner. When listening to your tape, evaluate its sound quality. Your demo doesn't have to sound like it was made in a 72-track studio, but it does need to be clear, distortion-free, and enjoyable to listen to. It's a simple fact of life: No drummer—no matter how talented—is going to impress potential employers with a scratchy or muddy demo tape. The simplest test you can make to ensure that your tape is "listenable" is to play it for someone else—preferably another musician—and ask that person what he or she thinks about it. If that person expresses a negative opinion, don't waste your money sending out copies of the tape. Do it over again. You *must* have a tape that makes a good impression upon the first hearing, because it won't get a second hearing otherwise.

How And Where To Send Your Tape

Even though your name and address will be on your résumé, be sure that they are also on the demo tape, along with your phone number. Put this information on the cassette itself, as well as on the box or container. Because the various parts of a résumé can become separated from each other, every item should carry complete information.

Be sure to rewind the tape before you enclose it in the résumé package. It seems a small thing, but you want to make listening to your tape as effortless as possible for your potential employer. It's not unusual for a manager or agent to discard any tape that can't be thrown immediately into a tape player upon receipt.

The demo tape is probably the most important element in a résumé package. After all, no matter how good a drummer's references are, how much experience he or she has had, or how attractive his or her photo is, it's what that drummer *sounds* like that's critical to a potential employer. Take the time and effort necessary to create the best possible demo of your drumming, so that you'll have the best possible chance of "selling yourself on tape."

What's Your Alternative?

Don't limit yourself to one musical style, no matter how good you are at that style or how much your personal preference leans that way.

Let's face it: Times are often tough in the club business. Many clubs that used to book entertainment five or six nights a week have cut down to two-night bookings, while others have eliminated entertainment completely. The resurgent popularity of "dance clubs" and DJs has put a further dent into the scene. What's a full-time or even part-time club band to do? Well, when the going gets tough, the tough (or at least the sensible and/or hungry) start examining their alternatives. There's a surprisingly large number of those available to a talented club band willing to take advantage of them. Here are some for you to consider.

Don't Put All Your Eggs In One Basket

Don't limit yourself to one musical style, no matter how good you are at that style or how much your personal preference leans that way. Remember, the object here is not to display trend-setting originality in order to impress a record label; the object is to find remunerative work in the popular music market. Be prepared to play different types of gigs so that you can expand your "potential-work pool."

For example, if you are primarily a Top-40 club band, consider expanding your repertoire with a few ethnic tunes, a few Latin dance numbers, a Broadway show medley, and "Daddy's Little Girl," and go into the wedding and bar mitzvah circuit as well. It may involve some special rehearsing at first, but most of the material that you'd do in a Top-40 club will work equally well at a private function. The money to be made at weddings and other private parties is generally much better than in clubs, and there are often fringe benefits (such as early hours, short sets, long breaks, and meals). You'll need a tux for this scene, but the cost of one can come out of the first gig's wages.

If you have the capability and the willingness, there are gigs to be had in musical styles outside the general Top-40 field. Country music is very popular in most areas, and C&W clubs tend to favor live bands over recorded entertainment (which is in high contrast to the dance clubs that feature recorded music *exclusively*). Today's country music is a far cry from Hank Williams or the Sons of the Pioneers; it incorporates pop, rock, and even some funk elements that offer much more for a drummer to do. And the material is appealing to a wider and wider audience all the time. This music *sells*, and I know several Top-40 groups who have changed over to it completely. I'm not suggesting that you do that, but taking a country gig once in a while (as opposed to having an empty space in your calendar) might be both musically pleasant *and* financially rewarding.

A slightly more limited market, but a viable one just the same, is the "society" gig. This is a polite euphemism for fancy dress dances generally attended by an older clientele. You're going to play standards, and you're going to be using brushes—a lot. But it isn't going to be all Guy Lombardo numbers. Dance standards include a fine variety of tunes from the big-band era that offer opportunities to swing or to syncopate with a horn section, and Harry Connick, Jr. repopularized the whole big-band-with-crooner idiom that made Frank Sinatra a star. If your group has a keyboard player who can cover lush-sounding horn lines, you can make a killing in this market, because those sounds are what make the music authentic—and often a club or catering hall is required to hire a larger group (with real horns) to achieve them. And whereas nothing compares to playing with real horns, if your small group can cover the gig, so much the better for you.

Other booking alternatives include ethnic and/or "theme" clubs. Can you cut a polka gig in a Polish restaurant? (I made a nice living doing this for about a year.) Can you do a night of '50s/'60s material, heavy on the doo-wop? There are still lots of clubs catering to this style. Can you do a (shudder) all-disco night, featuring non-stop, song-to-song marathon sets? In what may be the ultimate irony, I know of at least three clubs in my immediate area that hire *live* bands to play nothing but late '70s "classic" disco music, from "The Hustle" to "Stayin' Alive"—life imitating art imitating life, I guess. But it's very popular, and the bands who can do it work steadily, because there aren't that many of them.

Only The Names Have Been Changed...

If your group has a strong reputation in the Top-40 club market, and you don't want to risk confusion among your regular employers and your customer following, then change your band's name, wardrobe, and general persona when you take an alternative gig. This can be taken to the level of high art, if you want. I know of a band that bills itself three different ways, under three different names. They have separate photos and promotional material, and even use some different equipment on the various gigs. Of course, that's not *just* for show; some of their equipment is more appropriate for one type of gig than another. But it still helps to promote the "difference" between the three groups. They even use different individual names for themselves on stage with each group. They tell me that the customers who are aware of their "split personality" and attend all their various gigs go along with the fun, while others only follow one of the band's identities and have no idea that the other two exist!

Take It On The Road

During the Great Depression, thousands of people left areas of poor employment and sought better opportunities elsewhere. If your band has the ability to travel, that might be a worthwhile consideration—especially if you're currently in a major city with hundreds of bands vying for only a few steady gigs. There is still a demand for quality entertainment in hotels and lounges in less-populated areas across the country. Getting booked into them usually requires the services of an agency, but you could call any major-chain hotel near you (Holiday Inn, Ramada, Sheraton, etc.) and ask to speak to the person responsible for booking the entertainment. Ask that person how bands for the lounge are booked. If an agency is involved, contact that agency with your band promo. Another source of information on agencies who book traveling groups is the *International Musician*, the newspaper of the American Federation of Musicians. Since this is a union paper, you can assume that the agencies will be looking for union groups—but whether or not you're union members, it might be worth a phone call to make sure.

Divide And Conquer...Maybe

Another alternative that may be explored—but takes some intra-band diplomacy—is the "sub-group." There are times when the whole band can't get a booking, but some members working as a smaller group can. For example, if the group is a five-piece (keyboards, bass, guitar, drums, and vocalist), it's possible that the keyboardist, bass player, and drummer could be booked as a pop or jazz trio. Or the guitarist, bassist, and drummer might do a power-trio rock gig. The singer might easily do a happy-hour gig or an evening in a small cocktail lounge with either the guitarist or the keyboard player. The only problem with situations like these occurs if a bandmember who is *not* working resents the fact that another member *is*. This is something that must be worked out at a band meeting ahead of time. The group needs to check everybody's ego, and see whether the policy for unbooked periods will be "If we all don't work, then none of us work," or "When we all can't work, it's every man for himself—with our blessing."

Keep That Team Spirit

I hope that this chapter gives you some ideas for job-hunting that you might not have considered. I also hope that it gets you and your band thinking about alternatives of your own that I have not presented. The main thing is to keep your spirits up, use your imagination, put some effort into promotion and rehearsal, and get out there and get the jobs that are available. If the band works together...the band will *work* together.

Don't Pay To Play

> **Many bands are so desperate for someplace to play—both from an emotional and professional need—that they succumb regularly to exploitation.**

In many places—especially large cities with an overabundance of aspiring bands and a limited number of venues—the music scene is a "buyer's market." Club owners are besieged with bands who want to perform in their clubs. The ethical thing for these club owners to do is to listen to the bands (either live or via an audition tape), decide which ones will go over best with their clientele, and then book them to play one or more dates. These should be paid bookings, at whatever the appropriate rate of pay may be. (It might be a flat rate, a percentage of the door, or some other figure that is agreeable to both parties.) The band plays the date or dates, and if it does well, is asked back.

As I said, that's the ethical way to do it. The *unethical*—and unfortunately all-too-common way—is for the owner to tell the bands, "Look, you all want to play here. I gotta hire a sound system, pay for lights, cover my staff's salaries, and maybe take a loss on all of this if you guys don't sell a lot of drinks (or tickets, or whatever). So you need to put up a $250 deposit with me. If I make more than that on you, I'll split the overage with you. In the meantime, you guys get the benefit of the exposure you'll get playing in my club."

Now, let's figure that this guy is hiring three bands for the night, and giving them all the same spiel. He makes $750 from the bands, which "obviously isn't enough to cover his expenses for the night," so the bands get nothing back and are each out their $250. In the meantime, the owner has received free entertainment for his clientele, and has been able to perpetuate the impression with any musicians in the area that his club is the hot place to play.

Sound like a ripoff? You bet it is. But many bands are so desperate for someplace to play—both from an emotional and professional need—that they succumb regularly to this type of exploitation.

Well, you ask, what can be done? If there are only so many clubs to play in, and many of those are pay-to-play situations, where do you go? My answer is that you have several options, and the choices depend on how ambitious, creative, and downright indignant you are.

Take A Stand

First, if you are indignant (as I am) about such an unethical practice as pay-to-play clubs, you can pass the word around in your musical community, in an attempt to get more musicians not to play there. In other words, organize a strike! Nothing will affect club owners of this breed except a blow to the pocketbook. Put up flyers around town (music stores, record stores, school bulletin boards, and other places where club flyers are often posted) informing the club-going public about the situation and asking them not to frequent those clubs. And make sure to support any clubs that do *not* have such an unethical policy. I can't guarantee that it will work, but it might, and it certainly might gain you some personal satisfaction.

Take Action

In the meantime, look for the ethical clubs, and try to get work in them. If you live in a big city, try traveling to the suburbs or the smaller towns a bit farther out. It might mean spending some traveling time and money, but those clubs might be *eager* for some quality "out-of-town" entertainment. In other words, you could go from being an unpaid, tiny fish in a very big ocean, to a fairly well-paid, big fish in a small pond. It's worth looking into.

Unfortunately, the bands that are the easiest for unethical club owners to exploit are young bands eager for the opportunity to play in front of people in order to gain experience—and willing to pay for that opportunity. While I concur that experience is an essential ingredient of improvement, I feel that a band can gain just as much experience by performing for some organization that isn't gaining additional financial benefit from the band's efforts. That is to say, rather than pay their own money to play in a club that sells drinks for profit, a band should offer its services, gratis, for school dances, fraternity parties, charity functions, or other such activities. The organization gets the music for free, while the band gets the experience and the exposure. It doesn't put spending money in the band's pockets, but it doesn't take it *out* of their pockets, either. And it does give them the opportunity to try their skills in front of a live audience. Once those skills are fully developed—along with the band's popularity—the band will find themselves in a much better negotiating position when it comes to *paying* gigs.

My basic premise for this chapter is that you should never pay to play. I have nothing against playing for free, if you stand to reap some other form of tangible benefit. But don't make a career of playing for free, and don't do it in a club when the owner is making money as a result of your performance. Is he promoting his club by giving away free liquor? If not, then don't help him promote it by giving away your music for free. If you are working together on some promotional campaign, fine; just make sure that everybody's investment and potential benefits are equal.

Take Control

Finally, if you *must* pay to play, you should pay yourself. That is, if you have to spend money, spend it in such a way that *you* stand to gain from your investment, instead of some unscrupulous club owner. Take the money that the club owner is demanding (or pool yours with that of several other bands) and hire your own hall, sound system, lights, etc. There are always old theaters, VFW halls, school gymnasiums, and other sites available for rental. Again, how much energy you have comes into play here, since you might have to do some research into permits, alcohol regulations, sound level restrictions, etc. But it can be done—and done profitably, if you do it well. You might find that "concert promotion" is more rewarding—in several ways—than slogging about from club to club. And when you are the promoter, you'll find that job-related negotiations are amazingly easy!

The bottom line here is: Always make sure that you gain something positive from your musical efforts, no matter what they may be. That gain may be in the form of experience, publicity, or money. (A combination of the three is even better.) Keep your wits about you when dealing with club owners, and make sure that when it comes to working in their club, you are employed, not exploited.

Part 4: Taking Care Of Yourself

Ergonomics

**You can't fight gravity and win.
The earth is a lot bigger and stronger than you are.**

Today's technology has produced its own vocabulary, including a number of terms that are hybrids of words used in science, industry, academics, etc. Among those that I find most interesting is the word "ergonomics." (I looked through several dictionaries to make sure I understood the word's proper usage before basing a chapter on it.) Paraphrased, ergonomics is the science involved with the relationship of the human body to work, including the physics of motion, mechanics, and the design of physical objects (such as tools and equipment).

I've given a great deal of thought to the relationship of a drummer's body to the drumset, and how one element of that relationship can affect another. I've had occasion to speak to some highly qualified medical people on various *Modern Drummer* assignments, and I've received correspondence from readers relating to physical problems that they were having. Adding some reflections on my own past experiences, I've come to one inescapable conclusion: Drummers need to be more concerned with *ergonomics* than do any other instrumentalists.

It's a simple fact that the drumset is the most physically oriented instrument of all. It must literally be built around the drummer, and must fit his or her physical makeup. But there are some nuances of this "tailoring" process that many drummers are not aware of. If not addressed, these nuances can have repercussions such as impaired playing ability, reduced comfort, and physical injury. Let's take a moment to evaluate the relationship of a drummer's body to a drumkit, and discuss a few points that you might not have considered when creating your current setup.

I want to preface the following comments by saying that this chapter is written primarily from the perspective of the full-time drummer—one who plays five or six nights a week, for four to five hours per night. With this in mind, considerations such as comfort, fatigue, and physical impact on the body over a long period of time are of major importance. Part-time drummers, or even top touring professionals (who probably play harder but for much shorter periods of time) may or may not be affected as dramatically as this theoretical club drummer would be. Realize, also, that different styles of music tend to call for different setups, and that visual image is sometimes a large part of a given drummer's drumkit arrangement. But the suggestions that follow still bear consideration by drummers who play in *any* style and at *any* level of the business.

Gravity

You can't fight gravity and win—not for long, at any rate. The earth is a lot bigger and stronger than you are, and consequently can exert a lot more force than you can. The oldest principle of physics is that "what goes up must come down," and any effort to contradict this principle is going to take a great deal of energy to maintain. (That's why jet engines are so big and require so much fuel.) This principle applies to drumkits primarily when it comes to the height and angle of cymbals (and also of rack toms, to a lesser degree). The higher and farther away from you the cymbals are, the more energy (and time) it takes to overcome gravity in order to reach up and hit them. Conversely, the lower and closer your cymbals are, the less energy it takes to play them.

This equation is most important when it comes to ride cymbals and hi-hats (including remote hi-hats). Sustaining a complicated or fast ride pattern is difficult enough without having to do it on a cymbal that's shoulder high or above. You should make every effort (no pun intended) to keep your ride cymbal and/or hi-hat(s) at a level that maximizes relaxation (rather than tension or strain) in your arm. Under most circumstances, the human arm works best for this purpose when held comfortably at the side of the body with a more or less 90° bend at the elbow. I realize that the position of drums on the kit may make this precise position impossible, but the closer you can come to it, the better your endurance will be, and the better time you will be able to maintain over the course of a long, tiring evening. The stick should be able to strike the cymbal in as close to a parallel plane as possible. That means that if the cymbal is absolutely horizontal, you should be able to comfortably hold the stick virtually horizontally above it; if the cymbal is angled slightly, you should be able to angle the stick to the same degree just as comfortably.

Crash cymbals obviously are not played as much as rides and hi-hats are, but they generally must be struck with more force. This means that keeping them within a relaxed and comfortable reach is very important. They should also be angled in such a way that your wrist doesn't have to go into unnatural contortions to get the body of the drumstick into the body of the cymbal. Acute angles are generally good only if you want to *minimize* stick impact (such as on a very soft jazz gig), since it becomes almost impossible to do anything *but* glance off the cymbal with a stick tip.

Rack-tom height and angle relate to gravity as well, since a drummer generally has to lift his or her sticks up above the main "playing level" of the snare drum in order to strike the toms. Again, the higher or farther the sticks have to travel to get up above the toms and back down into them again with sufficient impact force, the more effort is going to be required. It isn't accidental that the big-band drummers of the '40s tended to set their toms fairly low and flat. They were playing long gigs and fighting a lot of other sound on stage. They needed to maximize their efforts while conserving their energy, and the low, flat positions of their drums and cymbals evolved from that need. Today's club gigs are just as long, and the playing often even more strenuous. Consequently, the need to conserve energy is every bit as great.

Anatomy

The human body is designed to operate in a very limited number of ways. It has remarkable flexibility within those parameters, but does not suffer extended abuse without some reaction—usually in the form of injury or impaired performance. With that in mind, let's look at the relationship of the drummer's body to the position of the bass drum—perhaps the starting point of virtually every drumkit setup.

We've been brought up on photos of drummers sitting proudly behind their kits, with their bass drums facing straight forward so that the illustration on the front head (be it company logo, drummer's initials, or painted palm tree) is clearly visible. The drummers, too, are faced directly forward so that we can see their smiling faces. *What's wrong with this picture?*

Most drummers see nothing wrong with it, and that's the way they set up: drums and drummer facing straight ahead. But if the bass drum is facing straight ahead, that means that the bass drum pedal is pointing straight back at the drummer. This creates a need for what I believe is an unnatural "turning in" of the bass drum foot.

Take a moment to do the following exercise: Sit in a reasonably high, straight-backed chair (or on a drum throne if it's handy). Close your eyes, relax completely, and imagine that you have a snare drum on a stand in front of you. Lift your legs so that your feet are off the ground a couple of inches. Remaining totally relaxed, allow your feet to drop to the floor. You should notice that your feet will land with the toes slightly turned out. In fact, most people stand, and even walk, with their feet in this position. It is my contention that in order to maximize strength, speed, and endurance (and minimize potential damage to the musculature of the leg and foot), the angle of the bass drum pedal should conform to the angle of the foot—not the other way around. This means that if *you* wish to face straight forward, the pedal should angle slightly to the outside of your body (left or right, depending on which foot you use) and the bass drum should be slightly offset accordingly. If you want the *bass drum* to face straight forward, you should angle your body slightly to one side or the other in order to maintain a natural foot-to-pedal relationship. (Double-bass drummers have an advantage here; their setup automatically conforms to this principle.) The hi-hat should be positioned in the same manner for the remaining foot.

Some drummers try to get around this situation by setting the bass drum facing straight forward, but allowing their foot to angle naturally across the pedal plate (instead of turning the foot at the ankle to correspond to the pedal). While this may reduce the risk of problems for their bodies, it likely will increase the risk of damage to their pedals, since the forces operating on the pedals are not in accordance with the forces they were designed to withstand.

This particular point of ergonomics has a very practical benefit—which I learned by experience. Several years ago, while playing a six-night-a-week Top-40 gig, I developed a lump behind my left knee that was diagnosed as a "Baker's cyst." There was no obvious reason for its onset; I had suffered no injury to the area. Nevertheless, it grew to a point where it interfered with the muscles in the area, making it difficult for me to play and painful to walk. Two visits to the doctor to have the cyst drained did not prevent its reoccurrence. I was informed that unless the actual cause was found and remedied, I would face surgery.

It was at this time that I realized that my drumkit setup had grown in the previous months, forcing my hi-hat farther and farther to my left. Since my legs are short, I was unable to maintain a natural foot-to-pedal relationship on the hi-hat. Instead, I had been turning my left foot out several degrees in order to operate the pedal, while angling my lower leg slightly down and to the left from my knee at the same time. Thinking that this might have something to do with the development of the cyst, I altered my drumkit to put the hi-hat back into the optimum position: with my foot squarely upon the pedal at the most natural angle achievable. Within a week, the cyst had noticeably reduced in size; within a month it had disappeared.

Physics And Physiology

Nowhere is ergonomics more important to a drummer than the question of seat height. Of course, "correct" seat height is a matter determined by many factors, and has no absolute definition. There has long been controversy over whether a drummer achieves more power by sitting high or low, and questions regarding control and speed also come into the issue. But there are certain physical factors that should also be taken into account when you are in the process of determining what seat height is correct for *you.* In addition to the musical considerations, take into account your body's need for constant, unrestricted circulation. The edge of a too-high seat can cut into the undersides of the thighs, pinching major blood vessels and causing numbness in the lower limbs. A seat too high *or* too low can provide improper balance, causing the body to move in unnatural manners in order to remain balanced. A too-high seat can cause upper and middle back strain (due to resultant "drummer's slouch"), and lower back problems can develop from a too-low seat that puts most of the upper body's weight on the lower spine. I can't recommend a specific "norm" in this area; all I can do is encourage you to examine your seat height with these considerations in mind.

Efficiency

The other part of the body-to-work relationship that makes up ergonomics is the "work" part. It's important to think about ways to make your means of "operating" as efficient as possible. After all, the more efficiently you work, the less energy you expend.

One way of saving both time and energy is to minimize your setup and breakdown requirements. This subject is discussed elsewhere, but let me reiterate that it's to a drummer's advantage to use the largest trap case that he or she can comfortably handle (and that will fit into his or her vehicle). The object is to avoid having to disassemble stands as much as possible. This makes breakdowns faster and easier, and makes setups faster and more uniform.

It's also advantageous to have your setup as much the same from gig to gig as possible (through the use of memory locks, color-coded tape, "spike marks" on rugs and risers, etc.). This allows your body to get used to the setup, and makes movements around the kit more fluid, comfortable, and energy-efficient.

Conclusion

The object of raising all of these points is not to try to tell you how you should set up your drumkit, or why you should change *your* concept of playing to suit *mine.* My hope is that these suggestions will get you thinking about the critical relationship that exists between your body and your instrument—and the work that the two do together that ultimately comes out as "drumming." An awareness of the ergonomics of drumming should help you to keep that relationship harmonious for many years to come.

Creature Comforts

You don't get any brownie points for being uncomfortable on your job.

How many hours each week do you *actually* spend behind your drums? If you work steady gigs, five nights a week, five sets a night, that works out to around twenty-five hours performing. A couple of rehearsals a week adds another six to eight hours per week. Many drummers work six nights a week (I used to), and some might do more rehearsing, so the likelihood of a 40-hour work week is not at all unusual among steady players.

When you spend this much time in your working environment, you owe it to yourself (and to your playing) to be as comfortable as possible in that environment. There should be no outside factors—no physical or psychological inhibitions—to prevent you from doing your best. You don't get any brownie points for "playing hurt," or for having to work harder than necessary, or for being uncomfortable on your job. On the contrary, professional players will do all that they can to ensure their personal comfort while performing, so that their concentration can be entirely on the playing, and not on some nagging discomfort.

I'd like to give you some suggestions, based on my own experience and those of other players I've talked to, on how to make your working environment more conducive to a comfortable, quality performance.

1. The drumset: This is the most basic element in your physical comfort. How you set up the kit—the relationships between the drum and cymbal adjustments and the distance you have to move to reach everything—is the largest factor in how you feel while playing. You should not have to stretch, nor should you ever have to move in such a way as to be out of balance, in order to strike anything on the set. A drumset, large and mechanical as it may seem, is the most personal of all instruments, because it must literally be constructed around the individual player, and tailor-fitted to that player's size, arm and leg reach, etc. Be sure that you can play around your set with economy of movement, without the need for any special gymnastics in order to reach any part of the kit.

2. The drum stool: This is the single most important piece of equipment, relative to playing comfort, on the drumset. There are several features of your stool that you should examine. To begin with, the seat should be well padded in order to prevent backstrain, and also to prevent the "cutting" of the undersides of your thighs by the edge of the seat. If your seat has little or no padding, or the padding has flattened down over the years, then either replace it or re-pad it. You can easily buy a thick piece of polyfoam at an upholstery or fabric shop (many are sold pre-shaped as the padding for sofa pillows) and trim it to fit on the top of the existing seat. Using the fabric of your choice (leather, vinyl, canvas, heavy denim, etc.), cut a piece large enough to cover the new foam and then wrap down and around to the underside of the seat. Staple or tack the new cover onto the wood base that is the seat's bottom, and (if you desire) sew all the folds or pleats into seams to make a good, tight fit. Now you have a nice, plush seat.

Once you have the bottom of the seat comfortable, what about your back? I can't stress enough how important backrests on drum stools are. Fortunately, several modern thrones have backrests available as options. The opportunity to lean back against some solid support, at least between tunes if not during them, is important towards relieving "drummer's crouch" and the seemingly unavoidable backache that results from it. If your stool does not have a backrest, I earnestly recommend replacing it with one that does. The return in comfort will far outweigh the initial investment.

Another way to avoid backstrain is to be absolutely sure

that your stool is adjusted to the optimum height for your body size, and for your style of playing. As your playing style changes to meet new musical demands, your setup should also change to facilitate the different movements you'll be making in the patterns and fills you'll be playing. I used to sit fairly low, with the drums also low and flat—in a very traditional jazz/big band style. As I got more and more into rock playing and needed more impact power on the bass drum and toms, I raised the toms—and found it more comfortable to play if I also raised my seat.

Even if you've been playing for several years at your current seat height, if you feel any pain or tension in your back, legs or feet, try experimenting (only a little at a time, higher or lower) to find a more comfortable level. You might be surprised at how a quarter of an inch one way or the other can make a tremendous improvement for you.

One little added feature that I use on my drum seat is a towel. I sit on it. This does a number of things for me. It keeps my bottom more comfortable when I'm playing, it keeps the perspiration that beads up on the vinyl seat cover from soaking the seat of my pants, and it prevents that perspiration from leeching out the dye in the vinyl and staining my clothing. I have seen seats that were covered in fabric, rather than vinyl, and of course they didn't have the bead-up problem (since perspiration tended to soak through the fabric cover and be absorbed by the foam padding). But the problem with this is that after a period of time the fabric becomes unsightly due to staining, and the foam tends to hold the perspiration odor, making the stool rather unpleasant, if not uncomfortable. The towel I use is easy to remove and wash, so I always have a fresh seat to work on.

3. Perspiration: Let's talk about ways to keep perspiration problems to a minimum. If you perspire heavily (and even if you don't), you should use an antiperspirant before going on stage. You owe this to your band and your customers as a simple courtesy anyway, but it will help to minimize the interference with your playing that heavy perspiration can cause. You should definitely have a towel available to wipe your face and hands if necessary, and that towel should be within easy reach at all times. As a courtesy to others (and as a hygienic protection for yourself), wash the towel often, or keep several going *in rotation*. Do *not* leave used, soiled towels on stage to ripen. You're working in a nightclub—you don't want it to smell like a locker room.

If your wardrobe and appearance requirements permit, the use of wristbands can be helpful to prevent stick slippage. If your palms perspire heavily and stick grip is a serious problem, consider stick wrap tape or drum gloves.

Perspiration can be a problem, but it is one you should deal with reasonably. You should not turn your problem into one for the entire band. I once knew a drummer who insisted on toweling his face, his hands, *and his sticks* between every tune. You can imagine what this did to the momentum of the group's performance. This was an unreasonable and overindulgent solution to the problem. You can minimize the amount of perspiration that actually interferes with your playing by the methods I've described.

4. Air temperature control: One way to minimize perspiration problems is to keep as cool as possible while working. I heartily endorse the use of personal fans on stage. Of course, their effectiveness at reducing the temperature around you will vary with the heat of lights, the size of the crowd, the effectiveness of the room's own cooling system, and many other factors. But at least a fan can keep the air moving around you, and can help to prevent the stifling feeling that can occur in a crowded club. The size of the fan you use will depend on your budget, the amount of space you have for the fan, and how visible you want or don't want it to be. One word of caution: A fan should not be blowing directly on you, no matter how tempting that might be. You risk chilling yourself too quickly after becoming heated while playing. That quick chilling can create muscle cramps and throat problems.

5. Refreshments: It's a good idea to have a cool drink available for sipping between tunes. Whether or not it's an alcoholic drink is up to you, although I'd like to point out that plain or sparkling water will refresh your system more effectively, without any additional effects.

In order to make it easier to grab a quick drink between numbers, you need some handy place to keep a glass within reach. The top of a speaker cabinet, a trap case, or some other tablelike surface is not bad, if it isn't so conspicuous as to seem unsightly. (For safety reasons, *never* place a glass on or near an amplifier, PA board, keyboard instrument, or any other electronic equipment that could be damaged by a spilled drink.) There are also a few commercially available towel-and-glass racks that clamp onto your stands to keep a drink and a towel handy. While I see nothing wrong with keeping your favorite refreshment on stage with you, I do think you should not have more than one glass or bottle. A stage cluttered with empty glasses or beer bottles cheapens the appearance of the band, and makes the performance seem unprofessional.

The air conditioning in a club can dry your lips. This can also happen with the use of a personal fan. To deal with this problem, I recommend the use of *Chapstick* or some similar lip balm. Their containers are small and easily kept near you on stage, or in a pocket. Used on each break, they can make a great deal of difference to the long-term condition of your lips. Seriously chapped lips are painful, and singing with sore lips is no fun at all. Take care of the problem with this simple solution.

6. Hands and feet: Your hands may or may not take a tremendous beating, depending on how hard you play and how much you abuse them. It might be a matter of just a couple of calluses, or you might be blistering your hands consistently. Remember that your hands are your primary tools in your occupation. If they get too sore to work, you're out of a job. The regular use of a good quality hand lotion will soften calluses and prevent dry skin problems.

Blisters are an indication that something is literally "rubbing you the wrong way." There are some mechanical/technical suggestions I would make first, such as: 1) Examine your playing style and grip. If you play traditionally and blister your left hand, perhaps a switch to matched grip would give you more power without blisters. 2) Evaluate the size of sticks you're using to judge whether you are squeezing too hard and/or doing too much of the work. A larger size might be indicated. 3) Consider miking your drums if you have to hit so hard that blisters result.

If, after careful consideration and appropriate action, you still get blisters regularly, then you need additional protection for your hands. Some drummers simply have softer skin than others, and must deal with this problem in order to play comfortably. I've seen drummers tape up their hands in a similar fashion to conga players, but I find this awkward when handling sticks, which conga players aren't concerned with. My suggestion would be to try a drum glove instead.

Aching feet are a regular complaint among loud players, especially those who play their bass drum in the heel-up style. This style of playing calls for a repeated impact of the toes and/or the ball of the foot against a hard metal footplate. Even though I mike my bass drum, I still play hard, and by the second or third night of the work week my toes feel cramped and the ball of my foot seems bruised. I've tried playing in soft-soled shoes, but I prefer to play in a shoe with a fairly high heel—more like a dress boot—and these are generally not available with a soft sole. So I fit my shoes with Dr. Scholl's (famous among drummers for *Moleskin*) *Air-Pillo Insoles.* These are thick, ventilated foam insoles that serve to cushion the foot, as well as to keep it cooler. A pair of these costs a couple of bucks at the local drugstore, and just might be one of the best investments you'll ever make.

7. Clothing: This seems like it should be obvious, but my experience talking with other drummers has been that it isn't. You should wear clothing that is comfortable, cool, and easy to move in. I'm aware that some bands are uniformed, and the choice of clothing is not yours to make. However, if you do wear a band outfit, make sure it is tailored for your playing requirements, not just for good looks. A trimly fitted tuxedo may look great off stage, but if you can't use your arms freely in it and you have to remove it after the first two tunes, what's the point? Have the coat tailored to allow the movement you need. Think of the outfit as a stage costume: It isn't necessary that it *be* perfectly fitted streetwear, as long as it *appears* to be from where the audience sees it. It has to be functional as well as (and to a greater degree than) fashionable.

If you don't wear a band outfit, then keep in mind which fabrics "breathe," and which tend to cling when soaked with perspiration. If you prefer tightly fitting clothes (because of your body shape or the fashions appropriate to your club), get clothing made from stretchable fabrics that will give you free movement capability. Don't bind yourself up unnecessarily.

8. Litter bag: I hate to see a stage floor littered with matchsticks, cigarette butts, broken stick tips, empty guitar string wrappers, old request notes, and all of the flotsam and jetsam that accumulates over the weeks of a steady gig. I find such a trashy environment depressing to work in, and unprofessional to look at from the audience's point of view. So a few years ago I started placing a simple paper litterbag on the side of my trap case within reach from my set. Now when I unwrap a throat lozenge, the wrapper gets thrown away. If I pull a piece of gaffer's tape off of a drumhead, it too gets thrown away—along with used napkins and the other junk that would otherwise litter the floor. When the bag is full, I just empty it into the trash and return it to the stage for reuse. It really keeps me from being psychologically influenced by a depressing environment.

9. Earplugs: Speaking of psychological influences, high noise level is a very important one. A great deal has been printed in recent years about the dangers of loud music relative to ear damage, and of course this is an element of physical comfort you must not overlook. But I'd like to add that high noise levels can also produce increased tension, aggravation, and impatience. Nervous tension affects tempo, grooves, and the interaction between players in a band. The use of earplugs, in addition to their hearing-protection aspect, can be a major contribution to your psychological well-being and comfort, and thus to the quality of your performance.

All in all, you should be very self-indulgent when it comes to providing for your personal comfort while performing. Don't be embarrassed to take whatever steps are necessary to improve your working environment, because doing so can only help to improve your work. Take care of number one, and you'll find that you'll then have greater personal concentration, and a better attitude toward the rest of the group.

Maladies And Remedies

**There are many minor irritations that can make a club drummer's life miserable.
Here are a few things that can be done to reduce that misery.**

While visiting a friend's house recently, I found myself looking through his collection of old *Field & Stream* magazines. In one of them was an article on common minor maladies encountered by campers (insect bites, poison ivy, and the like). It went on to offer several "home remedies" that could either be prepared in advance and carried along, or actually made up from materials available "in the wild." The remedies were suggested by a variety of veteran outdoorsmen (and women) from their own personal experience.

That article got me to thinking about the number of maladies that club drummers face—the "occupational hazards" that just seem to come with the job. After playing in clubs for more than twenty-five years, I'm pretty sure that I've personally experienced most of these maladies. (And any that I haven't, I've heard about from other players.) As a result I've often had to come up with some on-the-spot remedies myself. On other occasions, I've been fortunate enough to receive some very helpful tips from colleagues and co-workers. So I thought I'd devote this chapter to sharing some of these "home remedies."

Let me start by saying that none of the suggestions I offer here are in any way meant to substitute for professional medical treatment. If you have an injury or condition that is serious, you should seek the advice of a doctor. What I'm listing are just some of the minor irritations that can make a club drummer's life miserable, and a few things that can be done to reduce that misery. I also want to state at the outset that anywhere I recommend a specific commercial product, that recommendation is a personal one, based on my own success with that product. It doesn't constitute any endorsement of that product, or a guarantee that it will work in the same manner for anyone else.

Throat Problems

The single most irritating element about club playing is the environment itself, in terms of the effect it has on a person's respiratory system. Think of all the nasty things that are in the air of a club: cigarette smoke, kitchen fumes and grease, cleaning solvent fumes, and the combined exhalations of a concentrated group of people. Then there is the condition of the air itself. This may range from super-arid (in the case of heavily air-conditioned clubs) to dripping with humidity (in the case of poorly ventilated rooms), and from arctic (when the air conditioner is directly over the musicians' heads, as it invariably is when it doesn't need to be) to equatorial (when the air conditioner is at the other end of the room, as it invariably seems to be when the musicians would kill to have it closer).

When you add the strain of singing for extended periods of time to the adverse effects of breathing this less-than-healthy air, you wind up with throat problems. It's just a fact of life in club work. But there are some things you can do to reduce these problems.

The greatest problem faced by singers is dryness. Our vocal mechanism works best when it is lubricated, and can be easily damaged when it is not. One way to keep the throat lubricated is through the consumption of liquids. Fighting general dehydration allows the body to lubricate all necessary areas naturally. However, given the extremely dehydrating atmosphere of the average club, it's very easy to get waterlogged if one attempts to solve the problem strictly by the steady consumption of beverages. It can also be inconvenient to reach for a drink in the middle of a number. And there are those times when a more direct, topical application of lubrication is called for.

My solution to this problem has been the lowly cough

drop. I've found it very simple to tuck a cough drop into my cheek prior to starting a song, and to sing with it there. I've never had a problem "singing around" the cough drop, and my throat receives constant lubrication while the drop is in my mouth. My personal cough drop of choice is a *Halls Mentho-Lyptus*, simply because the eucalyptus and menthol ingredients also help combat swollen nasal membranes and sinuses that can be caused by cigarette smoke irritation. But any commercial drop will do; the idea is to have a constant source of lubrication actually in the mouth.

I must recommend against cherry or grape flavored drops, simply because they very quickly coat the tongue with a bright red or purple color that doesn't look very attractive to your audience when you are singing. I must also caution against the constant use of *Cloraseptic* or any other medicated lozenge. Even though I know some singers who swear by *Cloraseptic* spray or lozenges, these contain an anesthetic ingredient, and they carry a very specific dosage limitation. I have known one or two people to become a little foggy after using too many such lozenges in a short period of time. Stick with the non-medicated cough drops for lubrication purposes, and keep the *Cloraseptic* lozenges for those extreme cases where you must sing while actually ill and in pain from an infected throat.

Other than general dry throat, there is a condition I call "tired throat" or "second-night voice." This generally occurs on the night after you've had an especially "up" performance vocally the night before. Even though your throat may not seem sore, your voice sounds husky and deep, and you have little or no falsetto capability. You try to vocalize, and you find that you don't have that sense of "smoothness" in your voice mechanism; everything seems dry, thick, and rough.

There are several ways to attack this problem. You can start at home, before the gig (or in your hotel room, if you're on the road). Take a hot, steaming shower, and breathe deeply while in it. Your throat and the muscles around it will be bathed in the combination of heat and moisture, and this will begin to relax your voice box. Do a bit of light vocalizing while in the shower, but don't put any strain on your voice at this point.

In terms of something therapeutic that can be applied directly to your throat while you're on the gig, again I recommend heat and moisture. The term "to warm up" is especially applicable here, and you can help to "warm up" your voice by actually warming the throat. If you are able to do so, I suggest you bring a thermos bottle containing a hot, soothing beverage with you to the gig. I personally prefer hot apple juice for this purpose. It is a clear juice, with enough natural sweetness to have a bit of a coating action on the throat, without being sticky enough to cause phlegm. I do not recommend coffee or tea for this purpose, because although both are certainly hot and soothing initially, they are both somewhat astringent (cleansing rather than coating), they are both dehydrating agents, and they both are often consumed with milk or cream, which can cause phlegm.

If you are already at the club and in need of a hot beverage, coffee or tea would be better than nothing. But a concoction that I've found to be very soothing is a simple combination of hot water and *Rose's Lime Juice.* This is a sweetened juice used as a flavoring for many drinks, and it can be found in any bar. It's a bit better than squeezing real lime or lemon slices into the hot water, because the sweetner adds that coating action I described earlier. Pure lemon or lime juice once again tend to be astringent, removing whatever coating the throat may have.

There are some players I know who swear by a shot of their favorite liquor—generally a liqueur or brandy type of drink. These do have a syrupy coating action, and can give a feeling of "heat" to the throat. I won't say they don't work as well as the hot apple juice I use, because I don't have any personal experience with them. But I will venture to say that I can drink a thermos of hot apple juice and remain standing; I'm not so sure someone could do the same with an equal amount of Grand Marnier.

To overcome the cumulative effect of singing night after night in the unhealthy club environment I've described, your only hope is to provide a healthier environment for your throat to live in for as much of the rest of the time as possible. When I developed a throat condition while touring some years back, I visited a throat specialist. He informed me that leaving the polluted environment of a nightclub—and then going back to my heated and/or air-conditioned hotel room to sleep—was just compounding the problem, since the air in my room was artificially maintained in a very dry condition. He prescribed a cool-mist humidifier (available in any drugstore) for my room, left on at a low setting at all times. This gave my throat a more therapeutic environment to "come home to" after each night's exposure to the air of the club. I've maintained that practice since, and I continue to use the humidifier at home. I use it throughout the year on the weekends when I'm gigging; it runs full-time during the winter to combat the drying effect of my radiators.

Hand Problems

I never really had any problems with my hands when I played in Southern California or Hawaii. Neither environment offered much in the way of detrimental weather conditions, and I was playing gigs that only required me to move my equipment every couple of months. About the worst thing I ever had to deal with was the occasional splinter or cut finger. For those purposes, I always keep a pair of tweezers and a small box of *Band-Aids* in my "survival kit."

However, since moving to New Jersey and getting more into a weekend gigging mode, I've had to deal with the elements a great deal more often. Loading in and out of a club in a snowstorm or a frigid 30-mph wind can wreak havoc on one's hands. The drying effects of cold and wind, along with the abrasion of lifting and carrying cases (to say nothing of actual playing) combine to cause chapping, cracking, and pain. This certainly doesn't make for a comfortable gig.

In terms of relief, prevention is the best approach here. Obviously, if your hands are going to be exposed to the elements, you should cover them with gloves. However, sometimes the heavy gloves that are appropriate for bad weather make handling drum cases and equipment a bit awkward. I've known several musicians—myself included—to drive to a gig wearing such gloves, only to take them off when it came time to actually start bringing in the equipment. This may make the load-in easier, but it makes things harder on the hands. So my compromise in this case has been to use drum gloves, which are made of thin, flexible leather and can be worn quite comfortably while carrying equipment. I admit that they are not designed as foul weather gear; they are not insulated and often have a mesh backing. But they beat the heck out of nothing at all, and I don't feel compelled to take them off as soon as I try to pick up a case.

So much for prevention; how about after-the-fact relief? Once your hands are dry and chapped, you need to soothe and moisturize them. Again, there are any number of commercial products available for this purpose, but there is one that I have found far superior to any others, and that's *Corn Huskers Lotion.* I don't want to sound like an advertisement here, but the advantages to this product over most of the others are especially appealing to me as a drummer. It really softens chapped hands effectively; it is absorbed *completely* into the skin very quickly (so there is no possibility of "slippery hands"), and it is available in small plastic bottles that are convenient to keep in a trap case or stick bag.

In the event that you don't have a bottle of hand lotion with you, other items that can help with chapped hands (and that just might be available on short notice in the club) include *Chapstick* (which can be rubbed into the palms and then smoothed over the entire hand), *Vaseline* or other petroleum jelly (which is often available in first aid kits if nowhere else) and even liquid hand soap or dishwashing detergent (when used liberally with very little water).

Other than chapping, the biggest problem that drummers' hands face is blistering. When I was playing five or six nights a week, my hands toughened up and I didn't have any difficulty with blisters. However, now that I'm playing only on weekends, I am experiencing blisters more frequently—especially on those nights when the band is really "cranking" and I'm playing a bit harder than usual.

There are several quick and easy solutions to this problem. Once again, drum gloves may be used. I must admit that I don't normally use gloves for playing, since I don't perspire heavily and have no stick-slipping problem. But I have worn them while playing when my hands were sore. Gloves are especially good for preventing blisters caused by holding the sticks butt-end forward.

If you don't have a pair of gloves handy, or you just cannot play in them at all, don't despair. There are several other methods of avoiding blisters. One of the most common causes of blisters is hitting too hard with a small stick. You have to grip the stick more tightly than you should (increasing friction) while the small diameter allows the stick to rub in your hand. The simplest solution—and the most logical, when you're trying to gain volume—is to switch to a larger stick. But if you don't have such a stick available, or if you wish to stay with your regular size for technique reasons, what you need to do is make the gripping area of the sticks thicker, softer, and more comfortable for your hands to hold. For this purpose, I recommend taping the sticks. There are several commerical stick-wrapping tapes out. Most of these are designed to add friction for grip security (which may not be what you want if your hands are sore already), and are more or less permanent once they are attached to the stick. However, Pro-Mark's *Stick-Rapp* tape is made of a softer, almost rubbery-feeling material, so it provides more of a cushioned grip. It also is washable and reusable, so that if your stick breaks, you can use the same wrapping on a new stick. I've tried *Stick-Rapp* under the circumstances described above, and it provided significant relief. *Regal Grips*, which are reusable gum-rubber sleeves, are also a possible solution.

Once again, there are some alternatives to commercially available products that you can use in a pinch. Electrical tape is often carried by musicians, and most first aid kits in nightclub offices or kitchens contain adhesive tape. And of course, there is always the musician's savior: duct tape. Once or twice in my career I've felt the need to really pound with the butt end of a stick. But I wasn't comfortable with the feeling of doing that while holding the stick by the neck. So on the spur of the moment, I grabbed the band's roll of duct tape and used that to build up the diameter of the stick from the tip down toward the middle. I actually created a gripping area equal in size to the diameter of the stick at its thickest point. Using this jury-rigged "club," I found I had more than enough power and volume, with no risk of blistering my hands. I grant you, the stick was useful *only* for a fat backbeat; all balance had been destroyed. But it served the needs of the moment.

Fatigue And Sleeplessness

It's no fun to come to a gig, whether from home or from a hotel room, feeling like it's time to go back to bed. But every club player I've known has faced this situation. It's just a fact of life that we don't always get the amount of rest we need before every gig. Consequently, most musicians have come up with ways of stimulating their energy reserves to get them through the night. Some are relatively simple and safe; others should be avoided.

Probably the most common remedy for fatigue is caffeine, in one form or another. Many people drink coffee, others drink cola soft drinks. I have to agree that if you are going to rely on a chemical stimulant of any kind, this is the best one to use. I personally prefer soft drinks, because they also contain sugar (which adds to the energy boost) and are not as dehydrating as coffee. On the other hand, if one's throat is tired, a warm beverage is more beneficial than an ice-cold one. So take your pick depending on your physical condition. However, try to taper off toward the end of the night, or perhaps switch to a non-caffeine soft drink that will still give you the sugar boost, but won't keep you up half the night. (The timing of this switch will be different, of course, depending on whether you're simply returning to your hotel room or you have a long drive home after the gig.)

I don't recommend pill-type caffeine stimulants such as *No-Doz, Vivarin,* etc., because they slam you with a concentrated dosage all at one time—which can sometimes be hard to control. Drinking coffee or cola at least administers the caffeine gradually, giving your body a constant nudge rather than one swift kick. Any pills or chemical stimulants stronger than caffeine are out of the question.

Some musicians use alcoholic beverages as stimulants. This is not a good practice, since the stimulating effect of alcohol is quite temporary, and is shortly replaced by an even stronger depressing effect. The only way to overcome that is with yet more alcohol, and ultimately you have a musician who is not only tired, but drunk. (Not a good combination for exciting music-making.)

A not-so-common (but highly effective) remedy for fatigue is exercise. This might sound contradictory, but it's not. Part of fatigue is a reduced blood supply throughout the body, as well as a reduction of adrenaline production. A little bit of exercise can boost both of these conditions significantly. If you are in a hotel, try grabbing a few quick laps in the pool before you go down to play. If there is an exercise room, stop in for fifteen minutes before showering and dressing for the gig. (Don't overdo it.) You'll be amazed at what a change you'll feel in your overall well-being.

If you're at home and have neither pool nor exercise room, try a few calisthenics in the privacy of your bedroom, or jog around the block. You just need to get things "pumped up" a bit. From that point, your body should be able to maintain its energy level long enough for you to "get into" the gig and start to feel better. And don't forget, it's always possible to do a few jumping jacks in a dressing room or some other private offstage area on your breaks.

Sleeplessness is the other side of the coin from fatigue. Whether as a result of too much chemical stimulation, or just the rush that comes from an exciting night's performance, many club players have difficulty getting to sleep after a gig. If you work a steady gig and you live completely on "musician's hours," you may not consider this too much of a problem. But if you are playing only part-time, or if you would prefer not to sleep your days away, you may be interested in some ways to help you get to sleep more quickly.

The first and most important advice I can offer here is *never* to experiment with sleeping pills. There have been enough horror stories and lurid headlines in regards to musicians and pills to support that advice. As an alternative, I suggest some more organic items, such as herbal teas containing chamomile (there are many varieties), or good, old-fashioned milk. It doesn't have to be warm milk *(yech!)* because what you want is an amino acid called tryptophane that occurs naturally in milk and helps to promote relaxation. (If it puts crying babies to sleep, it's good enough for you.)

Other aids to relaxation include soft and soothing music, a not-*too*-interesting book, a warm bath, or a combination of all three. The idea is to take steps to relax both your body and your mind, so that sleep occurs naturally.

And Finally...

Hiccups. Or hiccoughs. Or whatever you prefer to call them. And before you laugh and say, "How serious a problem can hiccups be?" stop and think about how difficult it might be to keep steady time when your body is spasming unpredictably and uncontrollably every few seconds. And take a moment to pity the poor vocalist who must try to *sing* while suffering from this malady.

It's amazing how easy it is to get hiccups. Many people get them after taking two sips of a carbonated beverage. Others get them from overeating or consuming too much alcohol. I get hiccups from bending over in an awkward position (like trying to pick up a fallen wing nut while sitting on my drum stool), which places a sudden and unnatural pressure on the diaphragm and interferes with normal breathing. The diaphragm reacts by going into a spasm, and—*voila!*—hiccups.

We've all heard the usual and even not-so-usual cures for hiccups, including breathing into a paper bag, drinking a glass of water while holding one's breath, and maybe even the one about drinking the water from the opposite side of the glass while bending over at the waist. (My kids learned that one from watching *Sesame Street.*) However, I'm going to close this chapter with a sure-fire cure for hiccups that is the single most effective—yet off-the-wall—remedy I've ever seen for any club-related malady. I certainly don't take credit for it; I saw it first in 1976 in a Holiday Inn lounge in Yakima, Washington, and have the bartender there to thank for it.

The cure is simple: Take a quartered lime, such as are prepared in most bars, and douse it liberally with Angostura Aromatic Bitters. Then simply bite firmly into the lime. I know this sounds horrible, but I've seen it done time and again, and *I've never seen it fail!* And it seems to work *instantly!* So I recommend it highly to you. (Of course, *I've* never tried it....)

Handling The Ups And Downs

> You're excited about playing in this club, so you give it everything you've got–which is about three times more than it needs.

It has always seemed to me that performing musicians face a unique challenge: In no other profession (except perhaps stage acting) is the emotional state of the workers so greatly manifested in their work, nor so readily apparent to the people they are working for. Emotional and physical conditions can affect your playing in ways I group into two general categories: "Ups" and "Downs."

Downs

1. Boredom. This is the single greatest "downer" in club playing. It's also the most obvious to your audience. Boredom is reflected in the polish of the music, the showmanship on stage, the rapport with the audience—in fact with all the elements that combine to create a group's performance. A bored group is a boring group, and I've seen such acts empty a room faster than acts of poorer musical quality but greater enthusiasm. An audience will be far less tolerant of a group that performs perfectly, but gives the impression that they aren't interested in what the audience thinks anyway.

Boredom is the result of over-repetition. The solution is obvious: Create some sort of change to freshen everyone's outlook. Add new material, or rearrange some of the old material. Just the challenge of doing this should keep things interesting. As the drummer, you can use this same approach in your own playing. Find something new to do in the old material, like new fills or patterns. Or try some new aspect of playing, like using your left hand on the hi-hat and your right hand on the snare. Anything that offers something new to think about will be a positive step towards overcoming boredom. It's very important to start this right away, and to keep it up. Otherwise, a group can fall into a boredom-induced state of apathy where nobody has the inclination to rehearse, or the creative spark to come up with new ideas. It won't be long before things simply grind to a halt.

Sometimes a change of location can make all the difference in the world. This doesn't relieve you of the responsibility of updating your material, but it can give you some breathing space in which to do it. A new room presents new challenges in audience appeal, acoustics, stage set-up, etc., and these challenges help keep your musical and technical creativity at a high level. A new audience means a fresher, more enthusiastic response to your playing, and this can give you a lift too.

Any kind of change, such as costumes, lighting, or even the name of the band, can give a temporary lift to everyone's spirits. Use that lift to encourage the efforts towards longer-lasting change.

2. Tension or depression. Personality conflicts within the band, problems at home, or any other emotional downer that you bring to work is going to affect both your attitude towards playing and the actual physiology of your drumming. Tension is manifested in the muscles as stiffness and immobility while depression can actually lower metabolic rates and create a very real lack of energy or stamina. You must overcome the source of the tension or the depression in order to get rid of the drumming-related problems they create. If the tension is caused by some conflict within the band, then it's to everyone's advantage to take whatever steps are necessary to eliminate it. Some kind of band meeting with an open discussion of problems might be in order. Don't let something like that keep stewing within you—your playing will become worse, which will probably only aggravate the problem.

It's very easy to say, "Leave your personal problems at home and don't bring them to work with you," but in reality that's like saying leave one of your arms at home. I've known very few performers with the Zen-like ability to concentrate on what they were doing so strongly as to eliminate all outside thoughts. But you can try to focus your attention on your playing more than usual, as a method of eliminating other, more distracting thoughts. It won't cure the problem, but it might help get you through the night. Being aware of tension or depression is the first step toward overcoming them. Get some help—talk to someone whose judgment you respect—and do your best to eliminate the source of your emotional condition.

3. Illness. Illness is something that simply occurs in life. You can try to maintain a healthy, vitamin-fortified existence, but the longer you work in clubs, the more exposure you have to hundreds of people, and the greater likelihood there is of your coming down with something. Playing while ill calls for a whole new set of ground rules. Obviously, if you are dedicated and responsible, you want to make the gig, and you want to do the best job you can. If you can make it, great, but don't knock yourself out. Try to share the load a little more than usual with the rest of the band, such as having someone else cover your vocals, or not doing some of the tunes that call for high-energy drum parts. Stretch the leads, repeat tunes, even stretch your breaks a little if necessary. (Just be sure to advise management of the situation so you have their cooperation.)

If you are sick enough that you should not be working, then don't. You'll most likely just increase the length of time that you're ill, and handicap the band that much longer (to say nothing of possibly being contagious). Do whatever it takes to get better and get back on the job sooner. If it means getting a substitute, so be it. Drummers are more fortunate than other instrumentalists, in that our substitutes don't have to worry about keys or chord progressions. They don't *have* to know the song in order to play it. If the substitute can just keep good time, the band can get through the night.

4. Chemical factors. Whether you drink on the job or not is your business, but how you handle it *is* business. The same goes for any form of drug usage. I've played with musicians who were obviously out of control due to alcohol, and I've also played with a few who had been indulging in other drugs on their breaks. In both cases, their performance level was dramatically affected. Their playing became sloppy, and their physical posture and attitude was unduly relaxed. This is simply not the way to perform in front of an audience under any circumstances. The boredom I've already discussed is often the excuse for such indulgence, but that doesn't wash with me. Using substances that visibly and audibly reduce your professionalism on the job is not the way to escape boredom—unless you want to escape by losing the job altogether.

Ups

If I had my choice, I'd much rather have problems with being too far "up" on the job than too far "down." But even so, the effects caused by excitement or elation can create real difficulties for you and the rest of the band. If you come to work feeling unusually happy or excited about something, it often causes your perception of tempo to increase noticeably (to others, but not to you). You'll find yourself wondering why the band seems to be dragging, and why they're looking at you with daggers in their eyes while trying to get through a complicated lyric or tricky guitar passage at twice the speed they're used to. Even if you are *aware* of your excitement level, it may be very difficult to "lock in" to the groove you normally enjoy with the rest of the band. In general, control becomes the greatest problem. In contrast to being down, where you lack the energy to play well, in this case you have more than you know what to do with. Here are some examples of how this might occur:

1. Eagerness to please/Showing off. This is a classic situation. You've just gotten a new gig, and you really want to show what you can do. You're excited about playing in this club, so you give it everything you've got—which is about three times more than it needs. Even if you've been settled in for quite a while, if a friend or colleague comes in—someone you'd like to impress, or just someone you're happy to see—your surprise and pleasure at seeing that person can give your energy level a boost.

The most common pitfall of trying to show off for another drummer is that you wind up losing your groove with the band and your control over your own playing. Very rarely do you do the impressive job you wanted to do in the first place. The key to overcoming these problems is being aware how prone you are to them, and letting some objective outside source be a guide to you. If you are constantly being told that you're rushing the band, don't get offended. Analyze why the problem is occurring, and take measures to correct it. A high level of energy can be channeled into more *creative* playing, not just faster and louder playing. Use that energy in your *head* as well as in your hands.

2. Excitement over new or original material. When you've worked hard on a new piece of material, and you put it in for the first time, often you'll find that the excitement you feel about the new song works against you. The first couple of performances aren't as controlled and polished as the song sounded in rehearsal. But it may not be a problem with how well you rehearsed the song. It's just that the novelty of playing something new gives you an energy boost that affects *everybody's* sense of groove, so the song winds up a little rushed, a little too loud, or just "forced." One solution to this is simply to rehearse it a few more times to iron out the problems. Another is to try playing it a little later in the night, when your fatigue factor might help compensate for the novelty factor. The song will soon settle in.

Original material poses a similar, if not greater problem. I've heard several professional, solid, grooving bands play high-quality Top-40 tunes most of the night, and then suddenly sound like a garage band full of sixteen-year-olds on a particular tune. Then they'll go right back to the polished sound they had before on the next few songs. Later I'll discover that the odd tune was an original and that the band was nervous about performing it in front of people. That nervousness took control of the performance. In some cases it was just excitement about doing something they had written and were proud of, rather than performance anxiety. But in either case, it worked against them, because the tune came out sounding amateurish and of lesser quality than the cover material they had been doing.

Specifically for drummers, learning a new fill can pose a problem. I once met a young drummer who had literally mastered most of Neil Peart's intricate fills. This kid was a monster! Unfortunately, when I asked him to sit in with my straight-ahead hard-rock band, he couldn't resist the temptation to put all the fills he knew into the song (which was a very simple, driving arrangement of Eric Clapton's "Cocaine"). Not only did he rush the fills, he also let his excitement over knowing how to play those fills overcome the necessity for "laying it down" for the band. By all means keep improving your technical skills, but maintain the emotional control to know when to use new fills, and how to keep from rushing them in your excitement.

3. Excitement over new equipment. This is a particular problem of mine. I have a tendency to be thrilled by the addition of a new drum, cymbal, or even a new type of stick or head. Besides being tempted to overuse the new item, I usually find my excitement once again causing me to lose my sense of groove. I try to correct this by forcing myself to see the new piece of equipment as just part of the kit that had always been there, and play as I usually would. It isn't easy—it's like giving a kid a birthday present and telling him he can't play with it until tomorrow. But I try once again to channel my enthusiasm into some other direction, such as incorporating the new item *tastefully* into my playing. This generally helps me settle down and just enjoy playing the total kit.

4. Excitement over a new location or situation. I mentioned a change of job location as a cure for boredom. Unless the new situation is radically different from anything they've played before, this kind of change poses little problem for a professional group. But sometimes a club group gets the opportunity to do a large-scale concert or show, and suddenly this new performance situation seems to disorient them. They feel like they just *have* to spread out like the "big acts" do. Unfortunately, they aren't used to this type of spacing, and they lose the perception they normally have of what they're doing and how they are working together. The performance tends to be disjointed and disappointing for all concerned. My advice for this has always been to do on a big stage just what you're used to doing on a small one. Set up in the same way so that you can communicate in the same way. The sound will be different from what you're used to hearing anyway, so there's no need to compound the problem unnecessarily.

Your adrenaline level when doing a special show or concert will be unusually high. It will be very important for you to concentrate on your control, so that the band can offer its polished, professional-sounding performance. If you want to break out of clubs and into the "big time" concert circuit, now is the time to show everybody (including yourselves) that you're ready to handle it. Part of that is handling the excitement, the nervousness, and the physical effects on your body that an adrenaline rush can create. (I've been so excited on occasion that my hands shook, and the muscles of my arms felt like they were in business for themselves.) Controlling extra energy by some form of concentration or redirection is a primary attribute of the really professional players in the large-scale acts.

5. Chemical factors. Just as the depressing effects of alcohol, marijuana, or downers can reduce your abilities, stimulants such as cocaine or amphetamines can create unexpected amounts of energy—which cannot be controlled by even the strongest conscious effort. Even though your rational mind knows that your body is under the influence of a drug, there's nothing it can do about it. The drug takes control. You need to maintain a decent level of energy over four to five hours, and trying to sustain a consistent level with drugs is virtually impossible. The other major fact to remember is the number of deaths and burnouts attributable to drug use among well-known performers. Enough said.

Playing requires energy, and that energy requires control. You're going to need both to be a successful performer, and so you need to take whatever measures are reasonable to develop both. I've offered some suggestions and opinions, but you alone know the demands placed on you by your lifestyle and performance requirements. Take a moment to evaluate how well you handle some of the situations I've described, and see if any improvements might be necessary. Ours is both a physical and an emotional profession—it behooves us to be in good condition on both counts.

Enjoying The Great Outdoors

Unusual circumstances can occur on outdoor gigs. I've been caught in a sandstorm, had ashes from a forest fire settle on my kit, and once had to surrender the bandstand to a skunk.

Over the years, I've performed outdoors for various reasons, and under widely different circumstances. It might have been something as simple as doing an afternoon wedding party on one of my off days in order to pick up a little extra pocket money, or a situation where the club in which I was working decided to do some sort of outdoor promotional night. I played for two summer seasons on what my band called a "patio gig," where we performed from 6:00 until 10:00 P.M. on an open-air patio/dance area. And on a few occasions my band was involved in large-scale outdoor concerts. Each of these situations presented me with physical, emotional, and musical challenges that were tremendously different from those I normally faced on my regular indoor gigs. Let's take a look at some of those challenges, and what you might do to prepare yourself to meet them should you be faced with an outdoor playing situation.

Drum Sound And Volume

The first thing you'll notice when you take your kit outside is that the drums sound very weak. This is simply due to the fact that, when played in the open air, your drums have nothing surrounding them to contain or reflect the sound. Unfortunately, there's really very little you can do to the drums to overcome the problem. If you generally use a very flat, dead tuning, you can tune the heads a bit tighter than usual and remove any muffling, in order to maximize the natural resonance and projection of the drums. But this will likely be only a minimal improvement. As thunderous as drums may seem within the confines of a club, they just aren't designed for loud or long-range projection in the open air. Consequently, depending on the nature of the gig, you may need some sort of amplification for the drums.

If you're involved with a large-scale concert where a pro sound company's system is provided, you can generally rely on the sound technician to mike your drums satisfactorily. If you normally mike your drums in the club, and your regular sound system is capable of handling the increased projection and fidelity demands of an outdoor situation, then you're also likely to be adequately prepared. (In some cases, more or larger amps or speakers are required to augment a band's regular PA in order to create an acceptable outdoor system.) It may also be necessary to add mic's to your drum-miking arrangement. If you normally use only kick, snare, and tom mic's when inside, you may find that outside you'll also need overheads to pick up your cymbals, and either a separate mic' for the hi-hat or the repositioning of the snare mic' to also pick up the hi-hat. Just remember that your kit is virtually naked out there; if you want your audience to hear all of it, you'll need to *mike* all of it.

If you're not used to miking your drums, this may all be very new. It isn't necessary to employ a huge mixing board with multiple channels if that's not what your band normally employs. If there isn't room in your PA for drum mic's, consider renting a decent-sized keyboard amplifier and speaker cabinet, with either multiple-channel capability (the type popular for multi-keyboard use) or with a small mixer as an outboard accessory. Don't use either a bass or lead guitar amp; you need something with a wider frequency response to cover the range from bass drum to crash cymbals and hi-hat. Using this system, you control the amplification of the drums yourself, and put the sound source alongside the other musical instrument amplifiers. This may, in itself, be enough amplification; if not, the "drum amp" can be miked into a single channel of the main PA. This "drum amp" system is a little tricky, since there may or may not be a sound technician out front to balance the sound. If there isn't, try to listen to the amplified drum level, and be sure that it's balanced with the level of the other amplified instruments.

Let me stress that all of the above goes in large open-air situations where additional volume is obviously required. But before you go crazy with amplification, be sure that it's necessary. If you're doing an outdoor gig in a band shell (or some other semi-enclosed or semi-covered area designed for musical performance), you may find that the acoustics have been engineered for the purpose, and the drums may project adequately by themselves. In another case, you may be playing a small private function at a residence (at poolside, perhaps), or in the patio area of a country club or restaurant. In such locations, you may find that enough volume is the *least* of your worries. You may have to be concerned with how to keep the volume *low* enough to avoid disturbing the neighbors and attracting the local constabulary. Remember that when playing outdoors, you don't have the security of four walls and a roof containing your sound; it's out there for everyone in the immediate vicinity to hear—whether they want to or not. Sometimes in our enthusiasm at doing an "outdoor show" (something I'll touch more on later), we forget that it's just a low-key private party and not Woodstock. Keep things in perspective, and keep the volume appropriate to the needs of the situation.

Emotions

As I just mentioned, playing outdoors—when it isn't what you're used to doing—can create some emotional conditions worth considering. Personally speaking, I always get a big kick out of outdoor gigs, primarily because they're something out of the ordinary. So I always approach such gigs with a great deal of enthusiasm, and perhaps a little bit of "pop festival" fantasy. But while enthusiasm for a gig is generally beneficial, it must be controlled so that your playing technique and volume level don't suffer. If the gig is a big-time showcase or outdoor concert, then naturally some hard, flashy playing is called for. Just be sure to pace yourself, and perhaps do a bit more warming up than you'd normally do for an evening in the club so you don't blow yourself out in the first two numbers. Additionally, be aware that your added enthusiasm can create an adrenaline rush that can, in turn, boost the tempos a lot. Don't lose your control or your groove; keep your performance professional.

On the other hand, remember that a small wedding party, whether outdoors or in the local Elk's Hall, is still a wedding party. Approach your playing accordingly, as I mentioned earlier.

The Elements

This is obviously the single greatest factor that you'll find different from your indoor club gig. Dealing with the elements is also what most drummers tend to forget about when they prepare for an out-of-the-ordinary outdoor performance.

Many outdoor performances are held on warm summer afternoons. Assuming that you'll be setting up, playing, and tearing down under the sun, that's a long time to be exposed. You should be prepared against the threats of sunburn, dehydration, eyestrain from glare, and heat prostration—any one of which can serve to ruin the fun of an otherwise "hot" performance. You should dress appropriately, including some covering for your head and face. If possible, try to provide yourself with some sort of shade, as there may be no covering for your playing area. Bring your own supply of thirst quencher; something like *Gatorade* is recommended. Have a pair of sunglasses; it's no fun to play a set while staring into the setting sun. Be sure to have a good supply of sunscreen or suntan lotion (depending on your sun tolerance). Nothing spoils the memory of a musical day in the sun faster than a painful sunburn to take home with you.

In addition to your sunblock, be sure to use insect repellant liberally, as well. It's tough to play a solid groove when your hands are busy scratching mosquito bites.

All of the above suggestions are just to take care of *you.* Don't forget about your drums! Setting up in an unshaded area plays havoc with drumhead tension and can result in drums that sound like soup kettles. Shells and plastic finishes can be damaged if left in direct sunlight too long. And don't forget that reflective chrome and bronze surfaces get hot enough to cause skin burns fairly quickly. I'll admit to having had a few fingers scorched on hot rims and cymbals.

Obviously, a drape of some sort to cover the set when you aren't playing would be a very good idea; a canopy that protected the set (and you as well) while you're playing would be even better. If you can find out beforehand what type of area your band will be playing in, it might be a worthwhile investment to go to a party-supply company and rent a lawn tent or similar awning to protect the entire band from the sun.

Of course, outdoor gigs don't just risk problems with the sun. Many such performances take place at night, when a whole new set of problems exists. Normally, summer nights are quite comfortable, which is the reason for outdoor evening shows in the first place. But summer nights can be fickle, so be prepared for the possibility of chilly air at some point. In some areas, summer evenings are accompanied by high humidity, dampness, and even fog. Depending on your proximity to a source of moisture (especially in the cases of beach or pool parties), you may find dampness settling on your kit. While this is generally not a tuning problem with plastic heads, it doesn't do the hardware or the drum finish any good, especially if you're near salt water. Again, a between-set cover is called for, and the kit should be wiped dry with an absorbent towel prior to being packed up.

Be aware that damp evening air can also create problems in your muscles, as well as your respiratory system. Nominal attention to the weather forecast for the evening of the gig (along with a little common-sense information-gathering about the playing location) should allow you to be dressed appropriately for an evening's performance under the stars.

An element of evening performance not related to weather, but with which you should be concerned, is darkness. If you're playing some sort of organized concert, it's likely that stage lighting—including backstage work light—will be provided. But if you're doing some sort of informal outdoor function, like a beach party, pool party, or promotional spot, you may find that you don't have any light to perform in, much less to set up or tear down by. I've run into situations where my band arrived ready to set up, only to discover that there was no electrical power whatever! Your only real insurance against this sort of problem is to make sure the employer knows your power requirements thoroughly beforehand, so that generators or extension cords can be provided. As for adequate lighting, if you can bring along a few portable floodlights, such as are used in patio ornamental lighting, you may find them very useful (if for no other reason than to give you work light by which to pack up your kit at the end of the night). At the very least, bring along a strong flashlight.

The two greatest problems that you're likely to face from the elements on an outdoor gig—day or night—are rain and wind. Rain generally dictates its own solution: You quit playing, pull the plug, and get yourself and your equipment under shelter as soon as possible. Luckily, in most cases your audience and/or employers will be doing the same, so nobody is going to blame you for doing it. However, wind is a different problem. While a fair breeze may cause no difficulty for the audience (and, in fact, none for your guitar player, either), it may be enough to tip cymbal and mic' stands, and to create wind howl in drum mic's. If you normally play on a drum riser and you can use bunji chords, turnbuckles, or other means of anchoring your stands to the riser's top, you should be in good shape. Otherwise, be prepared to weigh down your stands in some manner. In the past, I've used bricks, sandbags, tape, and several other methods—some very much on the spur of the moment. I heartily recommend advance preparation over on-the-spot creativity. Wind howl from microphones can usually be controlled by foam windscreens that either come with the mic's or can be purchased for them. In a pinch, a sock over the end of the mic' can serve, although the fidelity (not to mention the aesthetics) of the mic' will be reduced.

The Unexpected

There are a few unusual circumstances that can occur on outdoor gigs, some of which bear no real possibility for preparation. I've been caught in a sandstorm, had ashes from a forest fire twenty miles away settle on my kit, and once actually had to surrender the bandstand to a skunk. I don't have any real advice for situations like this; you'll have to improvise.

I don't mean to imply from all these "problem" stories that playing outdoor gigs is more trouble than it's worth. Quite the contrary—I've found them to be a great break from the normal routine and, generally, a lot of fun to do. I simply encourage you to take a moment to think about the special requirements to such gigs, and be prepared to meet them, so that you can spend your time on the gig enjoying the great outdoors!